Irish Drinking Songs Cigar Box Guitar Songbook

By Ben "Gitty" Baker

Here is a rousing collection of traditional drinking and work songs from Ireland, Scotland, England and beyond. Thirty five traditional classics perfect for pub sings, house sessions and Irish-themed parties. All of these timeless songs are arranged by Ben Gitty for 3-string "GDG" cigar box guitars.

Cover Photo: The photo on the cover of this book features three good friends of the author, from left to right: Dennis Duffy, Charlie Boyle and Tristan Duffy. The photo was taken at Charlie's Greenhouse in Dover, New Hampshire during one of the music sessions that take place there.

Copyright Notice

To the best of our knowledge, all of the songs contained in this book are public domain and not under active copyright in the United States or elsewhere. While we do not claim any copyright on the songs, the specific arrangements of the songs, as well as the design and layout of this songbook, are copyrighted 2019 by Hobo Music Works LLC.

Please do not reproduce this book, in whole or in part, without written permission from the author. Special permission for educational purposes may be available, please contact us at support@cbgitty.com to discuss options.

Table of Contents

About This Songbook	3
How to Read & Play Tablature	6
How to Read & Play Chord Forms	9
How to Play These Songs	11
3-String Open G GDG Chords	12
A Jug Of This	14
All For Me Grog	16
Auld Lang Syne	20
Beer, Beer, Beer	23
Black Velvet Band	26
The Bold Thady Quill	31
The Boys From the County Armagh	34
Carrickfergus	37
Donkey Riding	40
Finnegan's Wake	43
The Holy Ground	47
I'm A Man You Don't Meet Every Day (Jock Stewart)	51
The Irish Rover	54
The Jug Of Punch	59
The Juice Of the Barley	64
Landlord Fill the Flowing Bowl (Three Jolly Coachmen)	68
The Moonshiner	70
Nancy Whiskey	73
The Night That Paddy Murphy Died	75
Paddy Doyle's Boots	79
The Parting Glass	82
Poor Old Dicey Reilly	85
Rare Old Mountain Dew	88
Reilly's Daughter	92
The Rocky Road To Dublin	95
Rosin the Bow	99

Irish Drinking Songs Cigar Box Guitar Songbook · Copyright 2019 by Hobo Music Works · All Rights Reserved

Table of Contents

Rothsea-o	103
Seven Drunken Nights	106
South Australia	109
What Do We Do With A Drunken Sailor	112
Whiskey In the Jar	115
Whiskey You're the Devil	118
The Wild Colonial Boy	122
The Wild Rover	124
The Work Of the Weavers	127
More Resources	130
Educational Outreach	131

INTRODUCTION

About This Songbook

This is a collection of traditional Irish, Scottish and related drinking songs, arranged specifically for playing on a 3-string cigar box guitar tuned to Open G "GDG".

I have chosen these songs from amongst the older, well-known pieces that are assumed to be in the public domain... in other words, songs that have no active copyright.

For some songs where there have many versions and arrangements over the years, some newer arrangements may still be copyrighted, and in such cases I have made every effort to present the oldest, most traditional and un-copyrighted form.

Celtic music holds a very special place in my heart. From the rebel songs to the drinking songs, love songs and laments, this music is charged with so much passion and feeling that it cannot help but stir the spirit and soul. I am proud to be able to present this collection of my favorite traditional pieces to the Cigar Box Guitar world in easy-to-follow tablature, with full lyrics and chords, to help make sure this amazing music lives on.

I am indebted to my good friends in New Hampshire, from whom I have learned so much about traditional Irish tunes and songs: Patrick Boyle, Charlie Boyle, Tyler Foss, Kim Starling, Patricia O'Brien, Conor Makem, Frank Landford, Jack Krumm, Mark "Rocky" Rockwell, Dennis Duffy, Kevin McEneaney and others have all helped expand my repertoire and appreciation of this music - thank you all!

Ben "Gitty" Baker

February 25, 2019

INTRODUCTION

You'll Need a Cigar Box Guitar

To get started making music using this book, you will need a fretted 3-string cigar box guitar tuned to Open G "GDG". If you already have one, then you're good to go. If you don't have one yet, you have a few options.

Of course our recommendation is that you build your own! There are a host of free plans available over at **CigarBoxNation.com** and **CigarBoxGuitar.com**. If you want to skip the building and get right to playing, you'll need to buy one built by someone else.

The first place to check is the C. B. Gitty website, where you'll find a nice selection of hand-made-in-the-USA cigar box guitars. Here is the link to see the current selection: **www.CBGitty.com/cigar-box-guitars**

You can also look on eBay.com, Reverb.com, Etsy.com and elsewhere to find ready-made cigar box guitars. It can be tricky finding the best quality builders from all of the options out there. Be diligent, check reviews and feedback ratings, ask questions before buying... and make sure you get a fretted 3-string guitar.

"Nothin heavy, cuttah"
- Charlie Boyle

Keys and Arrangements

Almost all of the songs in this book are arranged in the keys of C or G (or sometimes both). These are the two most common keys for popular music, and also the easiest to play on a 3-string cigar box guitar tuned to GDG.

For many of the songs, multiple versions are presented, and you may wonder why this is. There are several reasons: vocal ranges, ease of playing, and playing skill practice.

- **Vocal Ranges** - different people are able to hit different ranges of notes when singing. A soprano can hit the highest notes, a bass singer can hit the low notes, and most of the rest of us fall somewhere in between. I have arranged some of the songs in two keys (usually C and G) because depending on the singer, one key may be easier than the other.
- **Ease of Playing** - you may find as you play your cigar box guitar more, that fingering the notes in one key is easier for you than another. In this case, having the same song tabbed out in multiple keys is handy, since you can pick the one that feels best to you.
- **Playing Skill Practice** - playing the same song in multiple keys is good practice to help you become more familiar with your cigar box guitar. This is true both for picking out the notes that make up the melody of a song, and for strumming the chords. In time, you might begin to notice patterns. For example, if you look at a song tabbed out in both the key of C and the key of G, you will notice that every C chord in the former is replaced by a G chord in the latter. Likewise, every F is replaced by a C, every G is replaced by a D. This is not coincidence, and you'll see it hold true every time. The specific notes that make up the song also change following the same pattern. This changing of a song from one key to another is called transposing, and follows specific rules. How to transpose songs from one key to another could be the subject of a separate book. The more you play and practice and study, the more you may begin to get a feel for it.

About Tunings

As mentioned above, the songs in this book are arranged for playing on a 3-string cigar box guitar tuned to Open G GDG. However, the same arrangements and chord forms will work on any 3-string instrument tuned to an open "power" chord (1-5-1): Open C (C G C), Open A (A E A), Open D (D A D), Open E (E B E), etc. The tab and chord forms will still work and sound good, you just won't be playing in the key indicated in the tab. The only time that will cause an issue is if you are trying to play with another musician who is reading the chord names from the tab. They will have to do some transposing on the fly.

The chart below shows what you're actually playing in with the alternate tunings, based on the source key shown in the tablature.

GDG Source Tab Key	AEA Effective Key	CGC Effective Key	DAD Effective Key	EBE Effective Key	FCF Effective Key
C	D	F	G	A	B^b
G	A	C	D	E	F
D	E	G	A	B	C

INSTRUCTIONAL

How to Read & Play Tablature

Tablature (tab) is a visual method for showing you how to play songs on a stringed instrument. It is made up of horizontal lines, which represent the strings on the instrument you're playing. On these lines are placed numbers, which tell you what string to pluck, and which fret to push down on with your finger, to sound a particular note. When played in order with the right cadence and rhythm, these notes make up a song.

Tab also often includes letters to represent chords for rhythm playing, and words of the song as well. See the sample line of tab below.

Tablature is very powerful in this way, as it allows pretty much anyone to easily play the notes of a song. There is one thing though—you have to know "how the song goes" beforehand, to get the cadence and rhythm right. You can't really learn a new song entirely from tablature, since the tab doesn't tell you anything about rhythm or how long to hold each note. But if you already know the song, you're good to go!

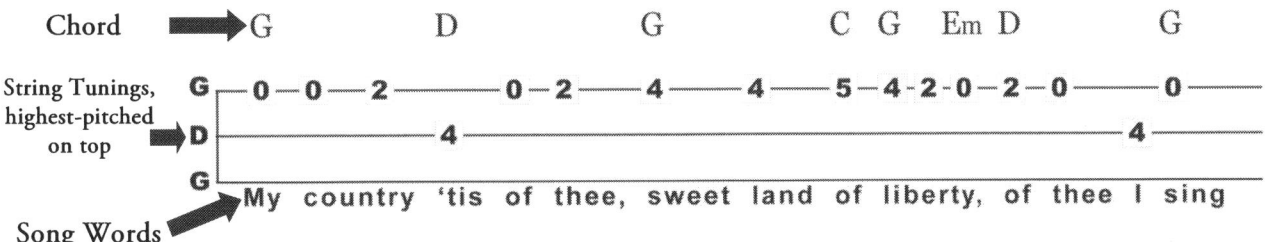

Take a look at the sample line of tab above. It is the first line from the old American patriotic song "My Country 'Tis of Thee".

The letters above the lines are chords that a rhythm guitar player can strum along with the song. Underneath the lines are the words of the song.

The three horizontal lines represent the strings of a 3-string cigar box guitar. The bold capital letters to the left of the lines show which string is which, and help you know what tuning the tablature is intended for.

It is important to realize that the top "G" line is the higher-pitched G on the guitar itself, which is actually on the bottom when you hold the guitar in playing position. Why is this? Well, the quick answer is that it's just how tab (and standard musical notation) has always been done. Higher pitch means higher up on the lines. Conventional 6-string guitar tab is the same way. It can seem confusing, but it's just something you have to get used to.

INSTRUCTIONAL

So to walk our way through playing the first few notes from the line of tab on the previous page, you would do the following:

1) Pluck the high G string (the one on the bottom when you are holding the guitar in playing position) open (unfretted), for "My".

2) Pluck the same open high G string again for the first part of "country".

3) Now hold your finger down on the second fret (by this we mean in the open space halfway in between the first and second frets), for the last part of "country". See the photo on the previous page.

4) Now fret the middle (D) string at the fourth fret (halfway in between frets 3 and 4) for "'tis". See the photo to the right.

5) Back to the open high G string for "of".

6) Now fret the high G string at the second fret (in between frets 1 and 2 again) for "thee".

7) And so forth through the rest of the line.

You may have noticed that tablature also doesn't tell you what finger to use for fretting. For that matter, regular sheet music notation doesn't either. A general rule of thumb is: use the first (index) finger for frets one and two; the middle finger for fret three; the third (ring) finger for frets four and sometimes five, and the little finger (pinky) for frets five and six. A lot of this comes down to what feels comfortable to you when playing—the only rules are the ones you set for yourself. The scale length of your instrument also determines what reaches are feasible.

Some songs require you to move on up the neck to hit the notes—almost always this is on the high G string, to reach higher notes. You can decide which fingers to use for these songs, whatever feels best to you.

More advanced tablature arrangements will show multiple strings being plucked/fretted at the same time. For the next set of instructions, refer to the tab sample on the next page.

So here, for the first note for the word "My", you actually strum all three strings open (unfretted) to get a nice "G" chord. Then it is the same as the previous example above until you get over to "thee". Here, the tablature is showing that you should fret the high G string on the second fret, leave the middle D string open, and fret the low G string on the second fret, and strum all three together.

I recommend using your middle finger for fretting the high G string and reach over with your index finger for the low G string. Be careful that neither finger touches that middle D, so that it can ring open and free!

INSTRUCTIONAL

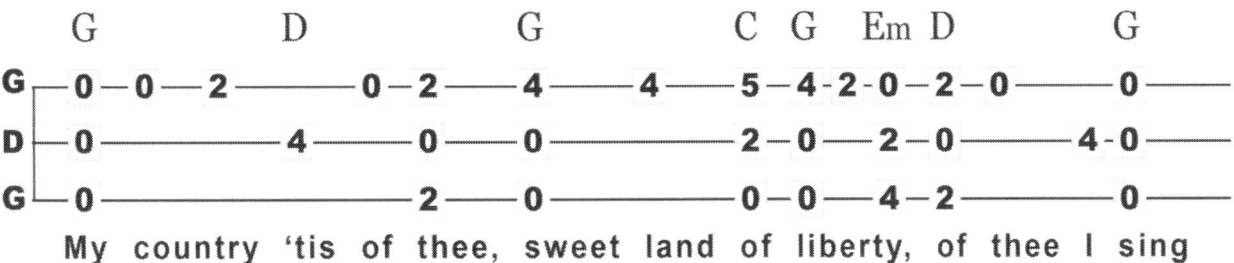

```
         G              D             G         C  G  Em  D         G
G ┌─0─0──2────────0─2────4──────4────5─4─2─0──2─0──────0──────
D │─0────────4──────0──────0──────────2─0──2─0──────4─0──────
G └─0──────────────2──────0──────────0─0───4─2──────0──────
```
My country 'tis of thee, sweet land of liberty, of thee I sing

It can be a little tricky to get used to these multi-finger forms (which are actually chord forms—you will see some of these same chord fingerings in the chord diagrams in the songs that follow).

The chord diagrams we include with the songs actually do recommend which finger you use for fretting each string, so with a little cross reference you will usually find at least a good starting point.

D

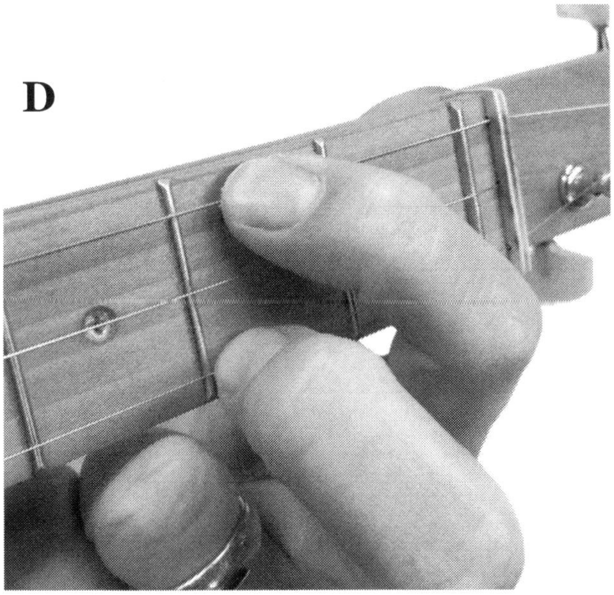

Em

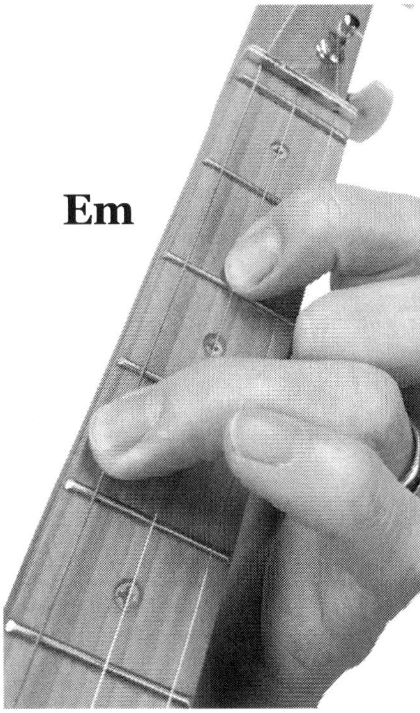

G

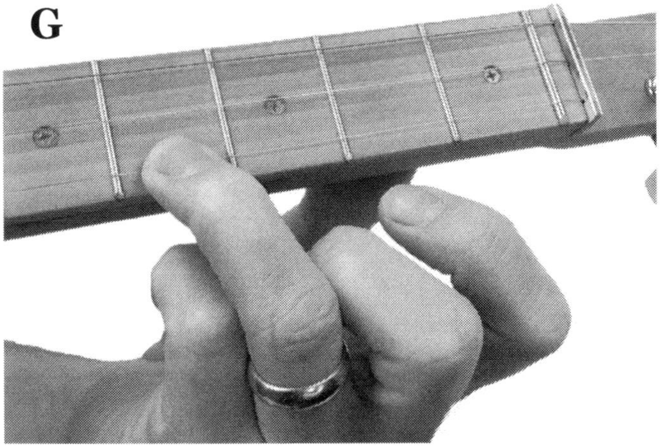

Irish Drinking Songs Cigar Box Guitar Songbook · Copyright 2019 by Hobo Music Works · All Rights Reserved

INSTRUCTIONAL
How to Read & Play Chord Forms

Chord forms can be intimidating. So many lines and letters and circles and numbers—what do they all mean? The next several pages will (hopefully) make it all clear. To start with, you need to know that a chord form is a vertical representation of a guitar neck. Check out the diagrams below to find each item as we identify them.

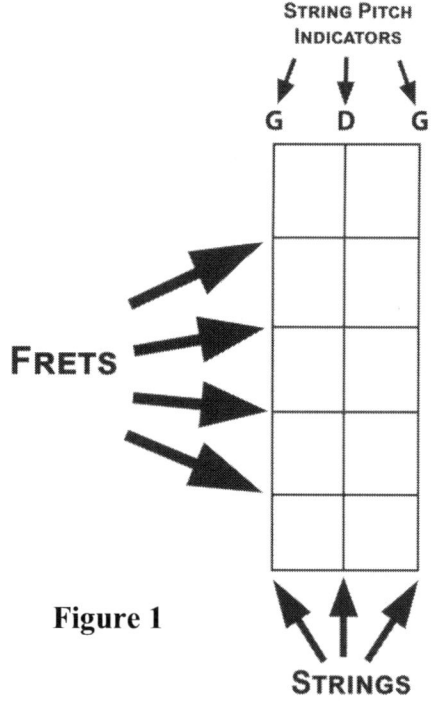

Figure 1

The **vertical lines represent the strings.** For a 3-string cigar box guitar, there will be 3 vertical lines, as shown in the images below. They are the same as if you hold a cigar box guitar neck in front of you vertically: the low G string is on the left and the high G string is on the right, with the middle D in between.

The **horizontal lines represent the frets**, same as you see on the front of your cigar box guitar neck. Above the top horizontal line will be 3 letters. These letters are **string pitch indicators**, and represent the notes that you are actually playing when fingering the chord. As shown in Figure 1, strumming all three strings open (unfretted) produces a G chord made up of the notes low G, D and high G. Unless otherwise indicated, the top horizontal line represents the nut of the guitar. See below for how you know when this is NOT the case.

OK, now check out **Figure 2** to the right. We've added a couple of additional components to this one. The big bold letter at the top is the **chord name**, in this case "F".

Note that the string pitch indicator letters have changed, showing that when strumming this chord different notes are being played.

Down on the lines of the diagram are some circles with numbers in them. These are the **finger placement indicators**, which tell you both what fret each string is being fingered on, and also suggests which finger you should use. So in the F chord diagram to the right, it is saying:

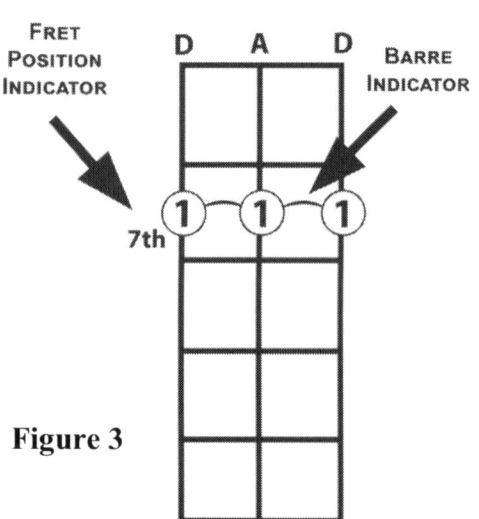

Figure 3

Irish Drinking Songs Cigar Box Guitar Songbook · Copyright 2019 by Hobo Music Works · All Rights Reserved

INSTRUCTIONAL

"put your first/index finger on the second fret of the low-pitch G string, your third/ring finger on the third fret of the middle D string, and your second/middle finger on the second fret of the high-pitch G string."

If a string does not have a finger placement indicator on it (no circle and number) that means it is to be left open/unfretted.

In Figure 3 on the previous page, a couple of "extras" are shown. First is the **Fret Position Indicator**. If you see a small "7th" or "5th" or "9th" or something there to the left of the low G string line, this indicates that this chord is fingered further up the neck. The fret position indicator will always be next to the fret it is indicating—so in Figure 3, you are fretting on the open space between the sixth and seventh frets, or just below the seventh fret.

Finally, the little curved lines between the finger placement circles are **"barre" indicators,** which tell you that you are using one finger and laying it across multiple strings—in this case, the first/index finger is being used to hold down all three strings at the seventh fret. The diagrams on this page show some of the most-used chords, with explanations.

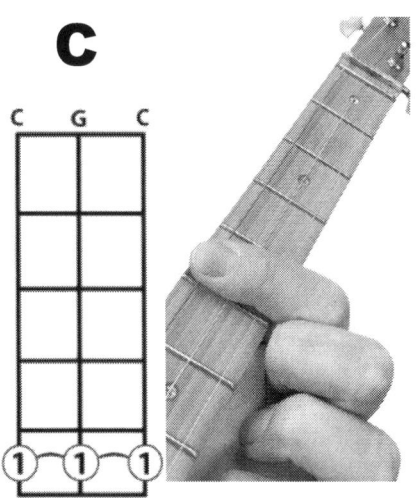

This form of "C" is a "barre" chord, where the index finger is used to cover all three strings at the fifth fret. The result is the C "151" power chord consisting of the notes C, G and C.

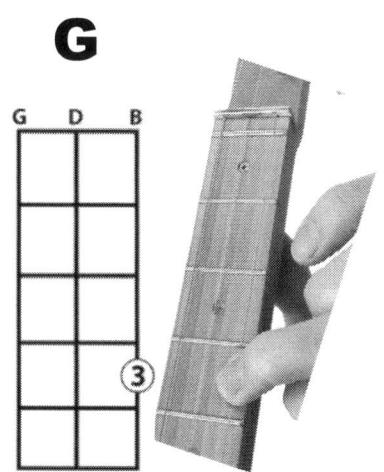

This form of the G chord is frequently used in this book, along with its "mirror" that frets the lower G string at the fourth fret. The G chord can also be played by strumming all three strings open, but fretting at the fourth fret can give it a fuller sound.

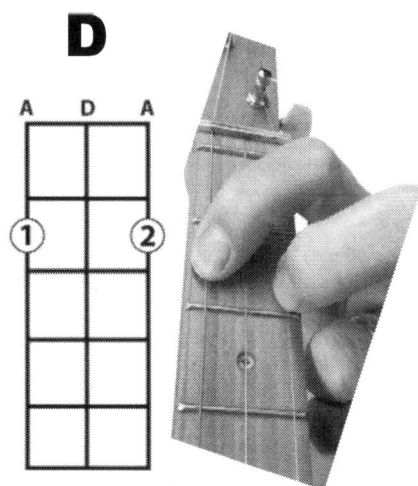

This is the most common D chord that I use when strumming songs. To play a full D major chord you have to go way up the fretboard and use all three fingers, so this one is a much easier option.

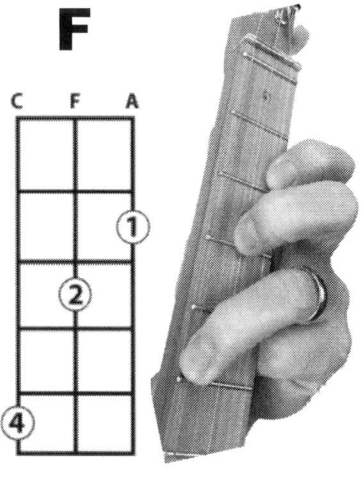

This version of the F chord requires three fingers, and gives a full "F major" sound. It can take some practice to get your fingers to make that stretch, especially on scale lengths over 23 inches. In the sample photo the ring finger is used for that low C, but you can use your pinky instead.

Irish Drinking Songs Cigar Box Guitar Songbook · Copyright 2019 by Hobo Music Works · All Rights Reserved

INSTRUCTIONAL
How to Play These Songs

Now that you have an idea of how to make sense of the tablature and chord forms, I want to talk a little bit about how to play the songs in this book.

First, as mentioned above, the tablature doesn't tell you anything about how the song is "supposed to go" - in other words, it doesn't tell you anything about the rhythm. For that, you have to either already know the song, or find somewhere to listen to it. Fortunately this is easier than it's ever been, if you have any sort of Internet access... YouTube should have multiple versions, historic and modern, of pretty much every song in this book.

So that brings us to my first piece of advice for playing these songs: listen to a version or two on YouTube first. Try to find the more traditional/older versions if you can, rather than more modern remakes.

Once you have a good idea of how the song is supposed to go, then it's time to start playing it. There are three basic ways these songs can be played: pick the basic melody, strum the chords, or a combination of picking and strumming.

- **Picking the Melody** - this involves plucking the individual notes that make up the melody of the song, one at a time and in the right order, with the timing/rhythm that you have in your head based on how the song is supposed to go. This is the most basic and straightforward way to play a song, and is a good way to start when learning a new tune.

- **Strumming the Chords** - a lot of guitar players don't really worry too much about picking the melody itself, and instead focus on strumming the chord accompaniment. If you ever go to a jam session or campfire singalong, you are unlikely to see any players plucking out the notes of the melody while people sing. Rather, you'll see and hear them strumming the chords. This is sometimes called "playing rhythm", and covering how to do it could be the topic of at least a chapter if not an entire book. Getting the hang of "strumming along" to a song is a great skill to have.

- **Combination of Picking and Strumming** - the "Melody & Chords" arrangements in this book are an attempt to get you started with this method. If you look closely at songs where I give both "Basic Melody" and "Melody & Chords" arrangements, you will notice the latter ones usually just have one or two extra strings/notes added under the basic melody line. Plucking these extra strings helps "fill out" the sound and makes for a more complete performance. This form of playing can be further expanded as you progress rhythmically, to create a sort of hybrid strum/note-picking method. This is what I usually use when playing my favorite songs on the Gitty Gang Show and elsewhere.

There is one important thing to remember as you dive into this: if you're having fun, you are doing it right. Getting good at playing takes time and practice, and you have to be patient with yourself. It doesn't have to be perfect... you don't have to sound like Elvis or Johnny Cash or Robert Johnson - you just need to sound like you. So take it easy, relax and have fun. Play the songs you know and like, and ignore the ones you don't. The only rules are the ones you set for yourself!

INSTRUCTIONAL

3-String Open G GDG Chords

The following chord forms are some of the most commonly used for the Open G GDG tuning. Multiple versions of some of the chords are given—when playing a song, some fingerings of chords just seem to fit better sound-wise than others. You are free to use whatever versions you want, based on what sounds best to you -- and what your fingers can reach. If you are having trouble making a transition between two chords, practice making the change over and over. You don't have to even strum, just practice getting your fingers to move back and forth between the two forms. This develops "muscle memory" and will make it much easier to learn and play songs. Feel free to substitute one chord form for another in any song, if it is easier for you to play.

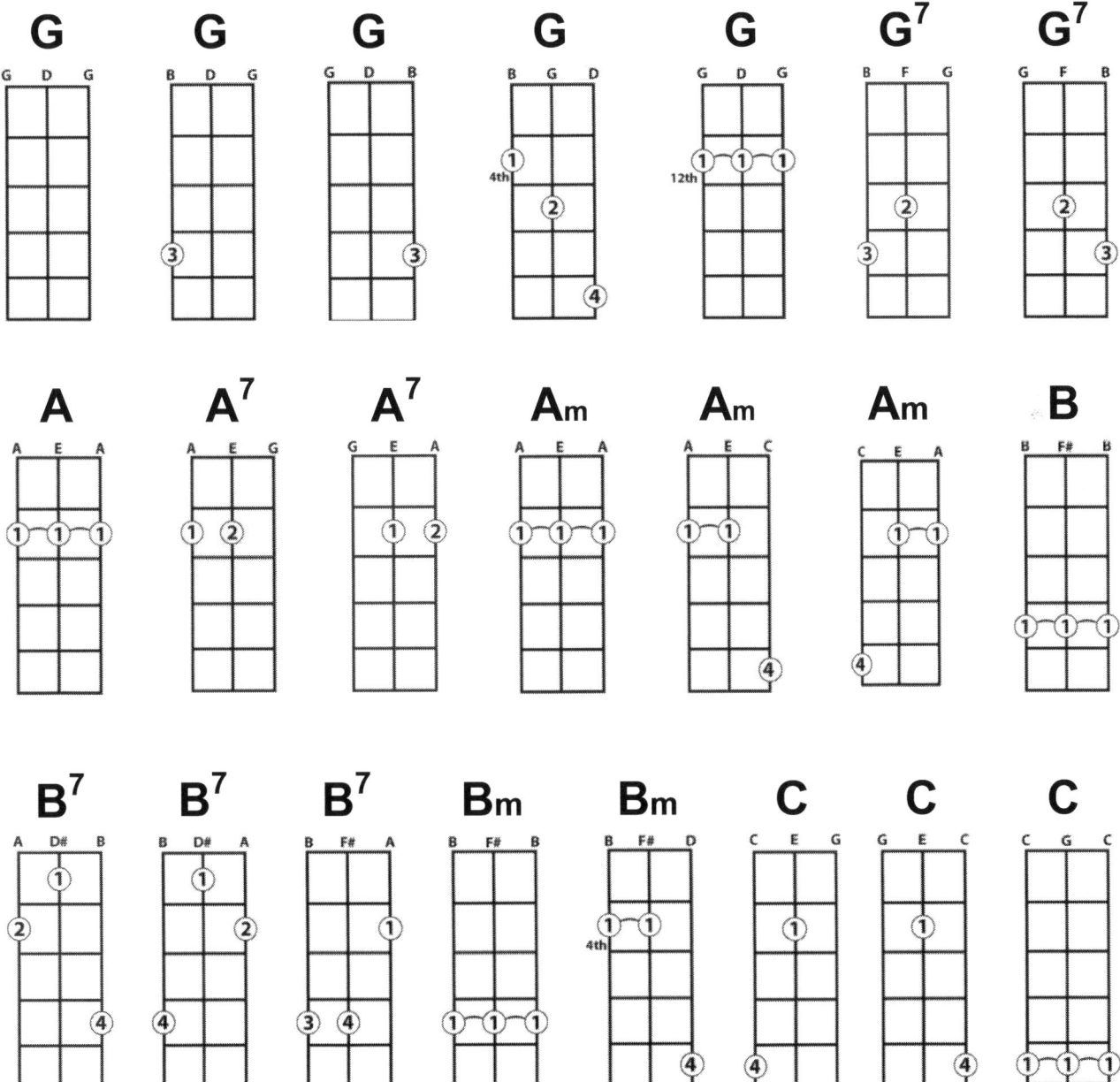

Irish Drinking Songs Cigar Box Guitar Songbook · Copyright 2019 by Hobo Music Works · All Rights Reserved

INSTRUCTIONAL

3-String Open G GDG Chords (continued)

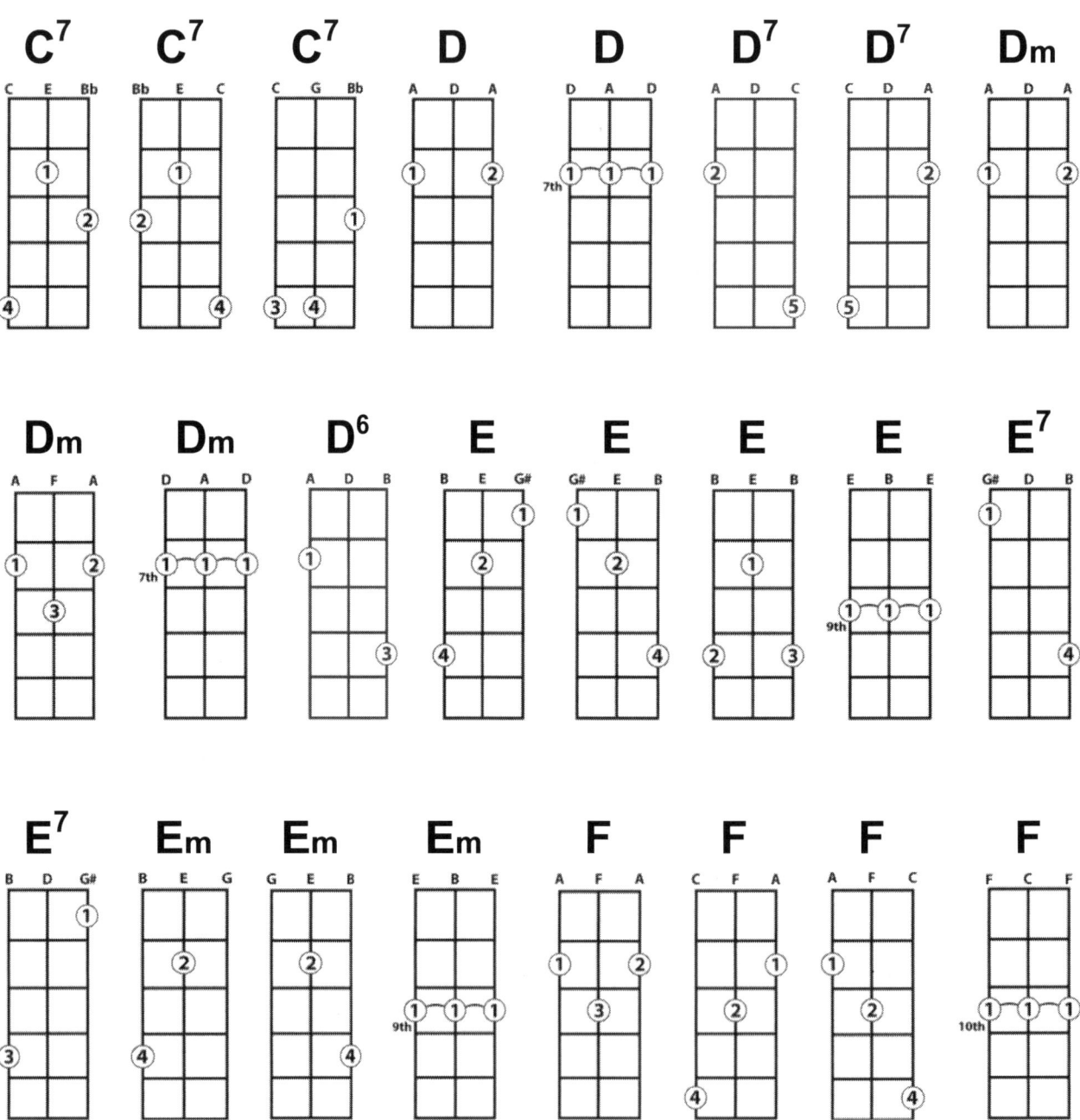

You may notice that the same chord form might appear more than once, with different names over it. This is because on a 3-string guitar sometimes the same fingering can sound different depending on the context of the song it is used in. For example, the "power chords" (where you barre all three strings across a single fret) can either sound like the major or minor version of the chord, depending on where they are used in the song. Using these power chords is the basis of the "one finger" method of rhythm playing taught by Glenn Watt and others.

DRINKING SONG

A Jug Of This

Basic Melody
Key of Em

Words and Music
Traditional

This is an old English folk song, thought to have come down from the oral tradition and first collected in 1907. Its alternate title is "Ye Mourners All" and has also been known by "Ye Mariners All". It is not often heard, but was recorded by The Clancy Brothers and Tommy Makem in 1962. There have been many variations to the lyrics over the years.

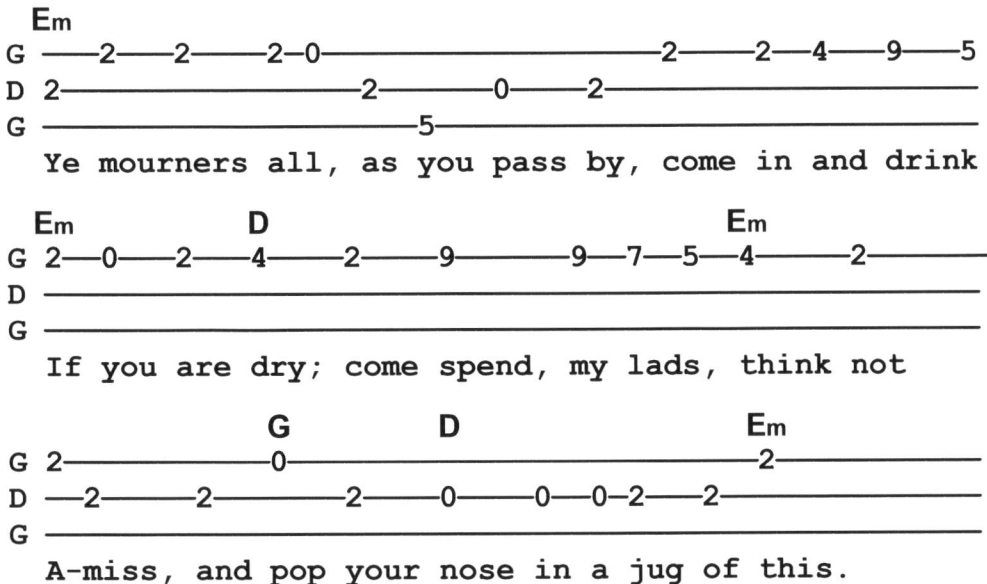

Additional Verses

Oh mourners all, if you've half a crown,
You're welcome all for to sit down.
Come spend, my lads, your money brisk,
And pop your nose in a jug of this.

Oh tipplers all, as you pass by,
Come in and drink if you are dry.
Call in and drink, think not amiss,
And pop your nose in a jug of this.

Oh now I'm old and can scarcely crawl,
I've an old grey beard and a head that's bald.
Crown my desire and fulfil my bliss,
A pretty young girl and a jug of this.

Oh when I'm in my grave and dead,
And all my sorrows are past and fled,
Transform me then into a fish,
And let me swim in a jug of this.

Chord Forms

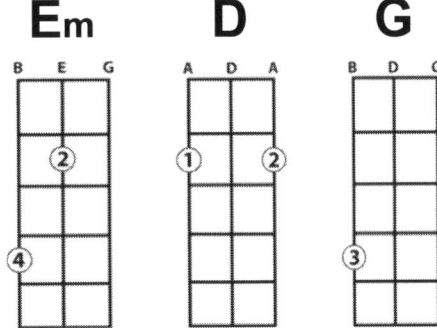

Playing Notes

For such a short and seemingly simple song, figuring out how to play this one can be rather tricky. That may explain why there are so few recordings of it.

The chords indicated above are my best approximation of what Liam Clancy was playing on the 1962 recording. I recommend listening carefully to that recording on YouTube to get an idea of their interpretation of how this song goes, where the chord changes are, etc.

A Jug Of This (continued)

DRINKING SONG

Two Versions
Key of Em and Am

Melody & Chords - Key of Em

```
      Em
   G ——2——2——2—0————————————2——2——4——9—5
   D 2—2——2——2—2—2——————0——2——2——2—2—9—5
   G 4—4——————4—4—4—5—0——4——4——4———9————
      Ye mourners all, as you pass by, come in and drink

      Em              D                       Em
   G 2—0——2——4——2——9——9—7—5—4————2
   D 2——2——2——0——0——9——9—7—7—2————2
   G 4————2——2——9——————————————4
      If you are dry; come spend, my lads, think not

                    G         D            Em
   G 2————————0——————————————————————2
   D 2—2——————2——0——2——0——0—0—2——2—2
   G ——4——————4——4——0——2——2—2—4——4—4
      A-miss, and pop your nose in a jug of this.
```

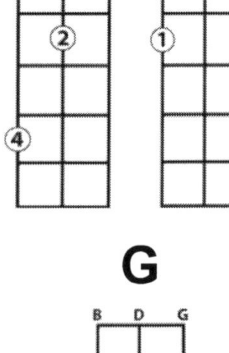
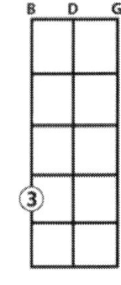

Basic Melody - Key of Am

```
      Am
   G ——————————————————————————————2——
   D ——0——0——0——————————0——0—2————3
   G 2————————5—2—2——0——2———————————
      Ye mourners all, as you pass by, come in and drink

      Am        G              Am
   G ——————————2——2—0——————————————
   D 0————0——2——0——————3—2———0
   G ——5——————————————————————————
      If you are dry; come spend, my lads, think not

                 C        G       Am
   G ——————————————————————————————
   D 0————————————————————————0————
   G ——2——2——5——2——0——0—0—2——2
      A-miss, and pop your nose in a jug of this.
```

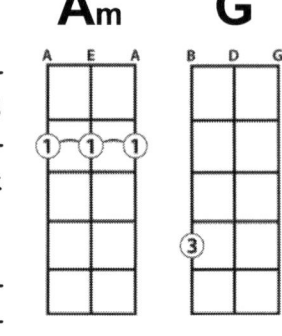
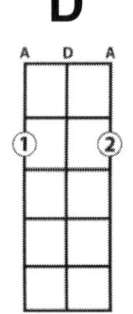

Irish Drinking Songs Cigar Box Guitar Songbook · Copyright 2019 by Hobo Music Works · All Rights Reserved

IRISH DRINKING SONG/SEA SHANTY

All For Me Grog

Basic Melody
Key of C

Words and Music
Traditional

This rollicking old drinking song tells the tale of a sailor who has sold all his possessions to buy booze. It has been recorded by most of the well-known Irish bands and singers over the years, including The Dubliners and The Clancy Brothers & Tommy Makem.

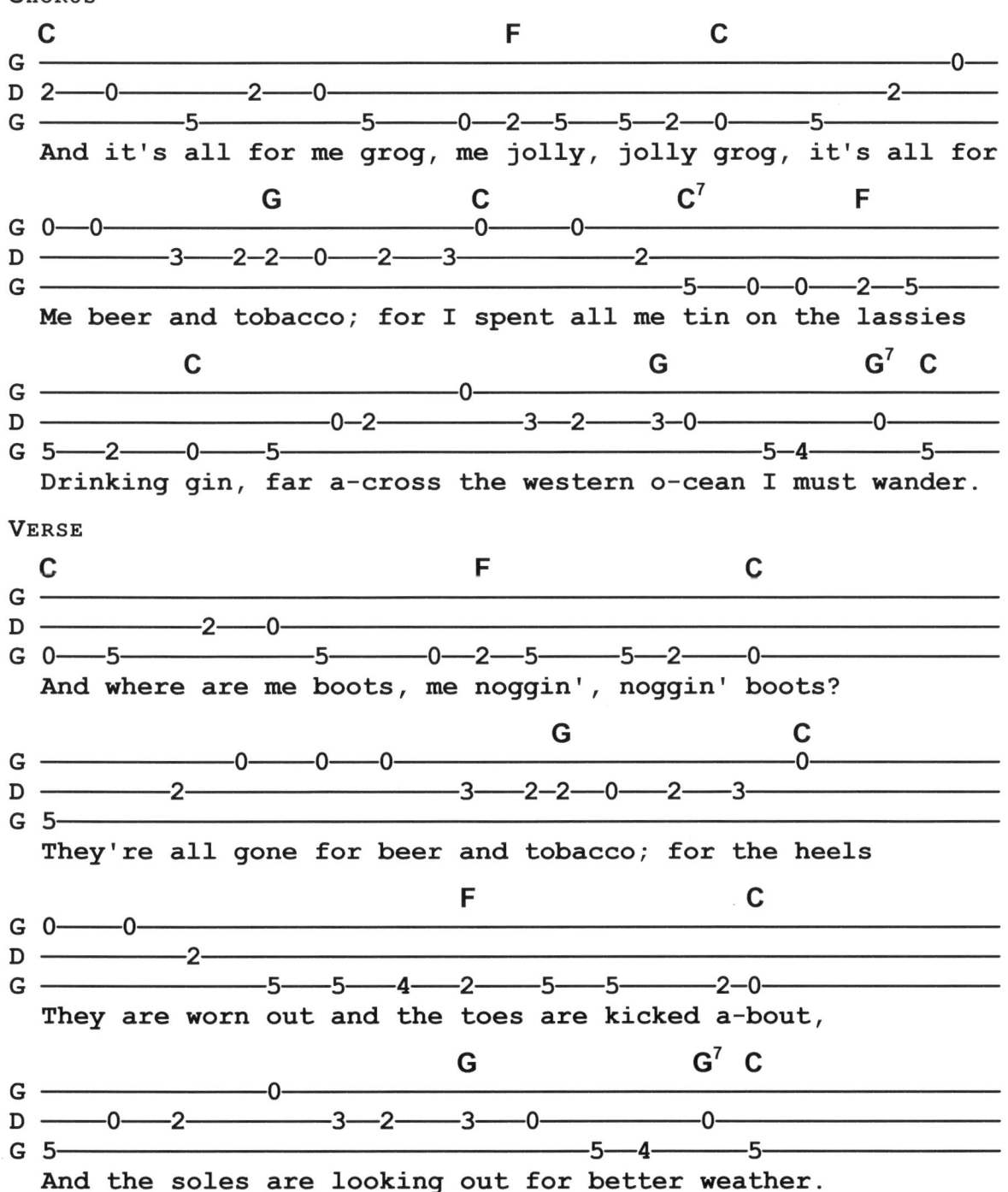

See Chord Forms and Additional Verses on Next Page.

Irish Drinking Songs Cigar Box Guitar Songbook · Copyright 2019 by Hobo Music Works · All Rights Reserved

IRISH DRINKING SONG/SEA SHANTY

All For Me Grog
(continued)

Chord Forms & Additional Verses — Key of C

Chord Forms

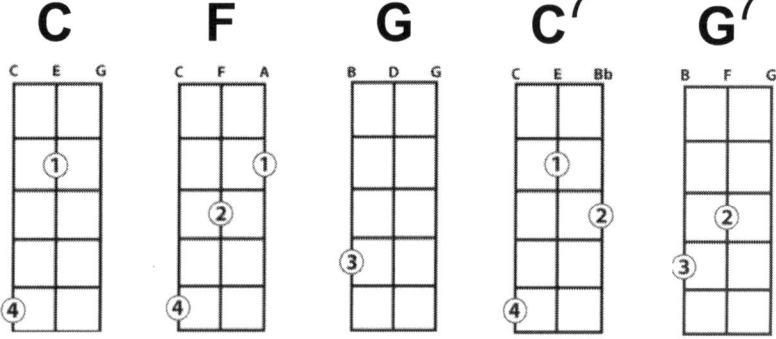

Additional Verses

Where is me shirt, me noggin', noggin' shirt?
It's all gone for beer and tobacco,
For the collar is all worn, and the sleeves they are all torn,
And the tail is looking out for better weather.

Now where is me bed, me noggin', noggin bed?
It's all gone for beer and tobacco,
For the sheets they were all worn,
And the mattress got all torn,
And the springs are lookin' out for better weather!

I'm sick in the head and I haven't been to bed,
Since I came ashore with me plunder.
I've seen centipedes and snakes,
And I'm full of pains and aches,
And I think I'll make a path for way out yonder.

> "My mother was from Scotland and my father was from Ireland. So I was born with the curse of the drink, but I'm too cheap to pay for it."
>
> **Patrick Boyle**

IRISH DRINKING SONG/SEA SHANTY

All For Me Grog
(continued)

Basic Melody
Key of G

CHORUS

```
        G                          C              G
G  4—2—0—4—2—0——————————0—0——————————0—4—7—
D  ——————————————0—2——————2—0——————————————
G  —————————————————————————————————————————
```
And it's all for me grog, me jolly, jolly grog, it's all for

```
                 D         G        G7        C
G  7—7—5—4—4—2—4—5—7———7—4—0—————————0—
D  ——————————————————————————0—0—2—————
G  ——————————————————————————————————————
```
Me beer and tobacco; for I spent all me tin on the lassies

```
        G                    D           D7  G
G  0—————0—2—4———7—5—4—5—2—0———2—0
D  ——2—0————————————————4——————————
G  ———————————————————————————————————
```
Drinking gin, far a-cross the western o-cean I must wander.

VERSE

```
        G              C         G
G  ——0—4—2——————0—0——————2—0
D  0————————0—2——————————————
G  ——————————————————————————
```
And where are me boots, me noggin', noggin' boots?

```
                           D         G
G  0—4—7—7—7—5—4—4—2—4—5—7—
D  —————————————————————————
G  —————————————————————————
```
They're all gone for beer and tobacco; for the heels

```
              C       G
G  7—7—4—0—0———0—0
D  ——————————4—2———2—0
G  ———————————————————
```
They are worn out and the toes are kicked a-bout,

```
                 D         D7  G
G  0—2—4—7—5—4—5—2—0———2—0
D  ——————————————4———————————
G  ———————————————————————————
```
And the soles are looking out for better weather.

G

C

D

G7

D7

Irish Drinking Songs Cigar Box Guitar Songbook · Copyright 2019 by Hobo Music Works · All Rights Reserved

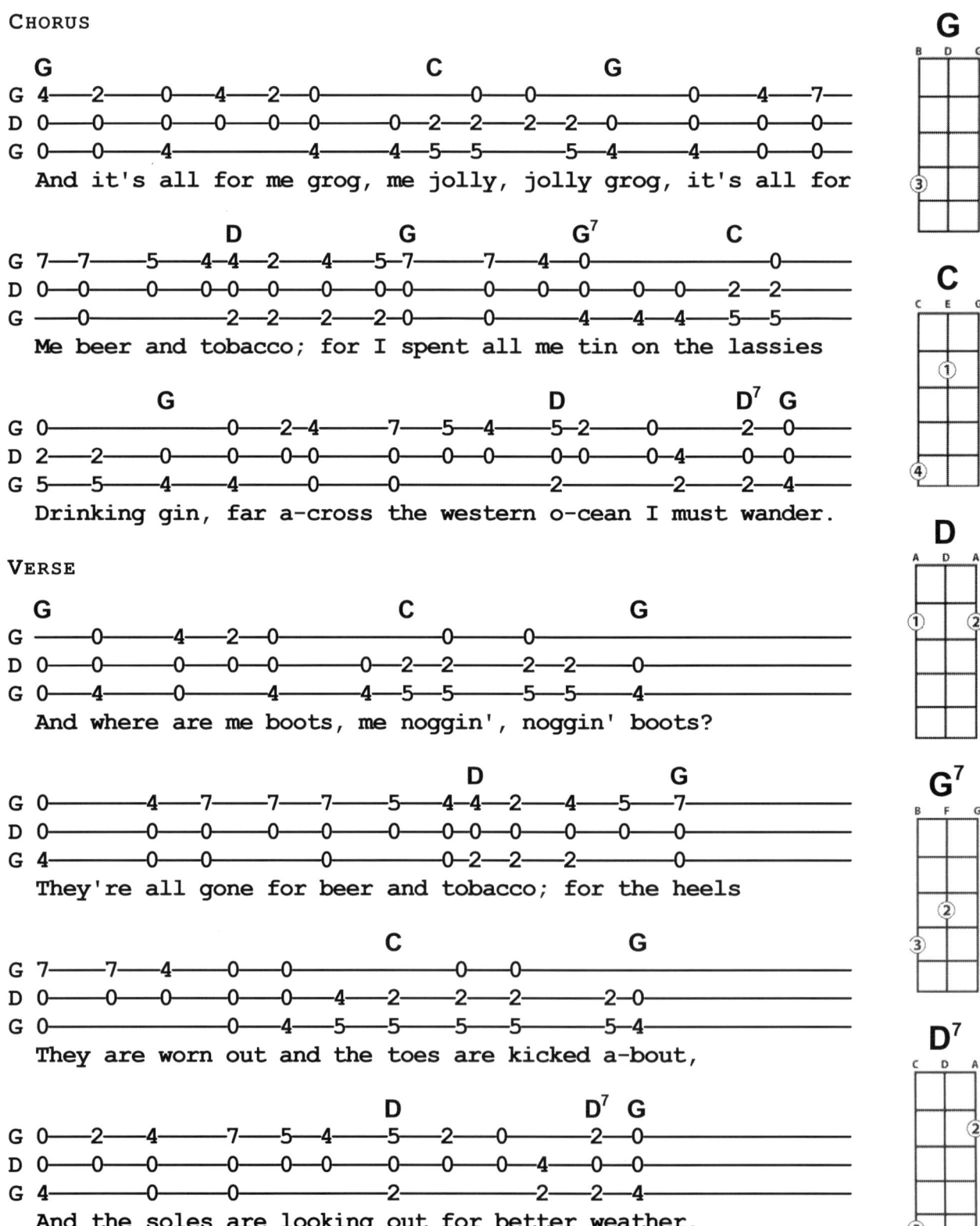

SCOTTISH BALLAD/DRINKING SONG

Auld Lang Syne

Basic Melody
Key of G

The words of this well-known song were originally written as a poem by Scots poet Robert Burns in 1788. The words were later set to music, and the tune began to be sung at the stroke of midnight on New Years' Eve to bid farewell to the old year.

Words by Robert Burns
Music Traditional

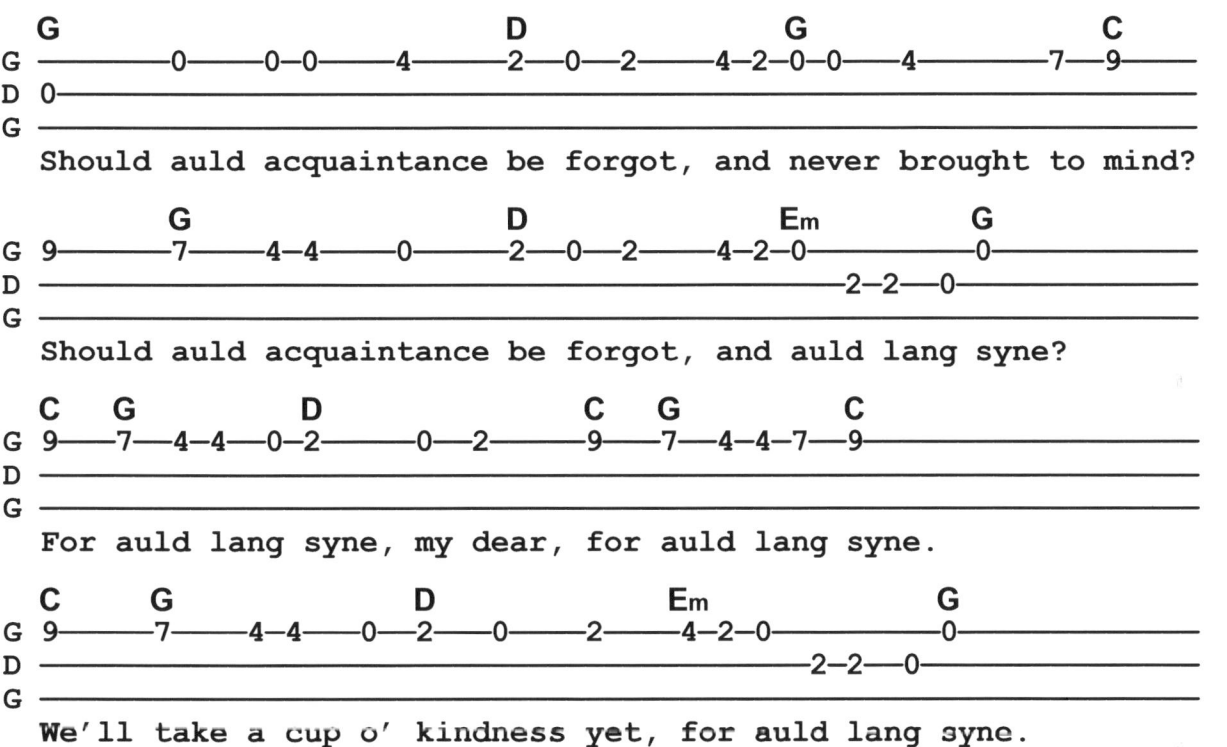

Chord Forms

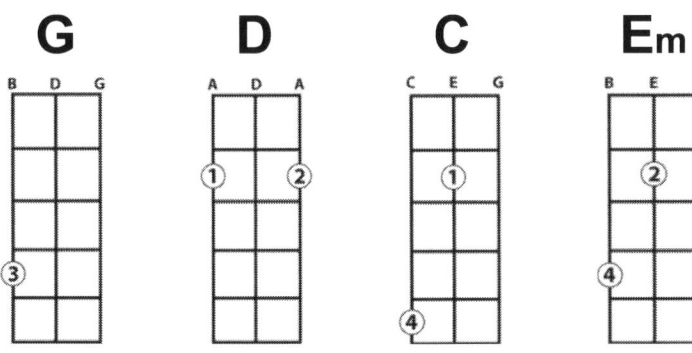

Additional Verses

And surely you'll buy your pint cup,
And surely I'll buy mine!
And we'll take a cup o' kindness yet,
For auld lang syne.

We two have run about the slopes,
And picked the daisies fine;

But we've wandered many a weary foot,
Since auld lang syne.

And there's a hand my trusty friend!
And give me a hand o' thine!
And we'll take a right good-will draught,
For auld lang syne.

Irish Drinking Songs Cigar Box Guitar Songbook · Copyright 2019 by Hobo Music Works · All Rights Reserved

SCOTTISH BALLAD/DRINKING SONG

Auld Lang Syne (continued)

Melody & Chords
Key of G

```
      G                          D              G              C
G ———————0———0-0———4———————2—0—2————4-2-0-0———4————————7—9—————
D 0———————0———0-0———0———————0-0-0————0-0-0-0———0————————0—10————
G 0———————0———0-0———0———————2———2————2—0-0-0———0————————9—————
```
Should auld acquaintance be forgot, and never brought to mind?

```
              G              D          Em           G
G 9————7———4-4———0————2—0—2————4-2-0—————————0—————
D 10———0———0-0———0————0-0-0————0-0-2—2-2—0-0—————
G 9————0———0-0———0————2———2————————4—4-4—4-0—————
```
Should auld acquaintance be forgot, and auld lang syne?

```
    C   G         D                 C   G         C
G 9——7——4-4—0-2————0—2———————9——7——4-4—7—9—————
D 10—0——0-0—0-0————0-0———————10—0——0-0-0—10————
G 9———0——0-0-2—————2—————————9——0——0-0—9————
```
For auld lang syne, my dear, for auld lang syne.

```
    C   G         D              Em               G
G 9——7——4-4—0-2————0—2————4-2-0———————0—————
D 10—0——0-0—0-0————0-0————2-2-2—2-2—0-0—————
G 9———0——0-0-2—————2——————0——4-4-4-4-0—————
```
We'll take a cup o' kindness yet, for auld lang syne.

Chord Forms

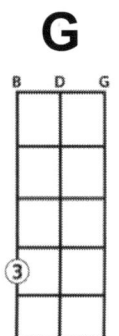 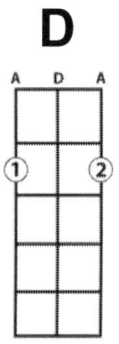 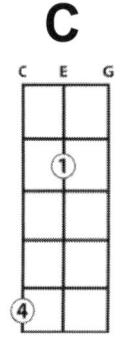 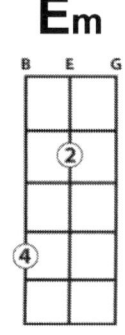

Robert Burns

SCOTTISH BALLAD/DRINKING SONG

Auld Lang Syne (continued)

Basic Melody
Key of C

```
        C                       G               C              F
G  ─────────────────────────────────────────────────────────0───2─
D  ─────────────────2───0───────0───2─0─────2──────────────────────
G  0──────5────5─5──────────5─────────────5─5─────────────────────
   Should auld acquaintance be forgot, and never brought to mind?

        C              G           Am          C
G  2────0──────────────────────────────────────────────────────────
D  ─────────2─2────0────────0────2─0───────────────────────────────
G  ───────────────5──────5────────────5─2─2─0─5────────────────────
   Should auld acquaintance be forgot, and auld lang syne?

   F  C           G       F  C           F
G  2──0────────────────────2──0──────0─2──────────────────────────
D  ─────2─2────0──────────0──────2─2────────────────────────────────
G  ──────5──────5──────────────────────────────────────────────────
   For auld lang syne, my dear, for auld lang syne.

   F  C           G           Am          C
G  2──0────────────────────────────────────────────────────────────
D  ─────2─2────0────────0────2─0────────────────────────────────────
G  ──────5──────5───────────────5─2─2─0─5──────────────────────────
   We'll take a cup o' kindness yet, for auld lang syne.
```

Chord Forms

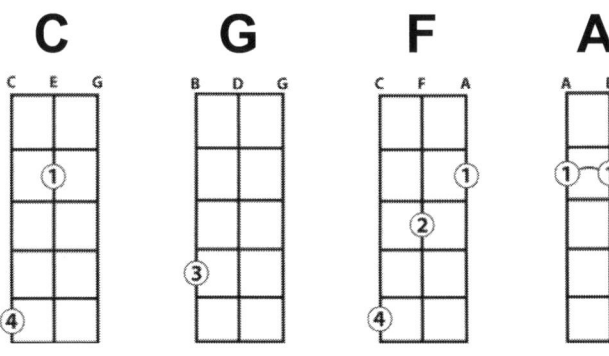

Irish Drinking Songs Cigar Box Guitar Songbook · Copyright 2019 by Hobo Music Works · All Rights Reserved

IRISH DRINKING SONG

Beer, Beer, Beer (Page 1)

Basic Melody
Key of C

This is one of the classic Irish drinking songs, which tells the fictional story of Charlie Mopps, the man who invented beer. Find the Clancy Brothers' version of this on YouTube for a definitive idea of how it should go.

Words and Music
Traditional

Intro/Bridge

```
      C    Em   Am            C    Em   Am
G  5———4————2————0——2—4———5————4————2————
D  ——————————————————————————————————————
G  ——————————————————————————————————————
```
Beer, beer, beer, tid-d-ly beer, beer, beer...

Verse

```
      C
G  0———————————————0———0———0——————————————
D  ——2———2———3———————————————3——2——0——————
G  ——————————————————————————5————————————
```
A long time a-go, way back in history,

```
      C                         F              G
G  0———5———5————5——5—5———0———2———0———————————————
D  ——————————————————————————————3———2————2———0——
G  ———————————————————————————————————————————————
```
When all there was to drink was nothin' but cups of tea...

```
      C                    F         C
G  0—5————5————5—5————0———0——2———0—5————2————0————
D  ————————————————————————————————————————————————
G  ————————————————————————————————————————————————
```
A-long came a man, by the name of Charlie Mopps,

```
                                                G    C
G  ————0——0—0—0———————0——0—0—0————————————0——————————————
D  2————————————2———————————————2———2————————0——2————————
G  ——————————————————————————————————————————————4———5———
```
And he invented a wonderful drink, and he made it out of hops.

Chord Forms

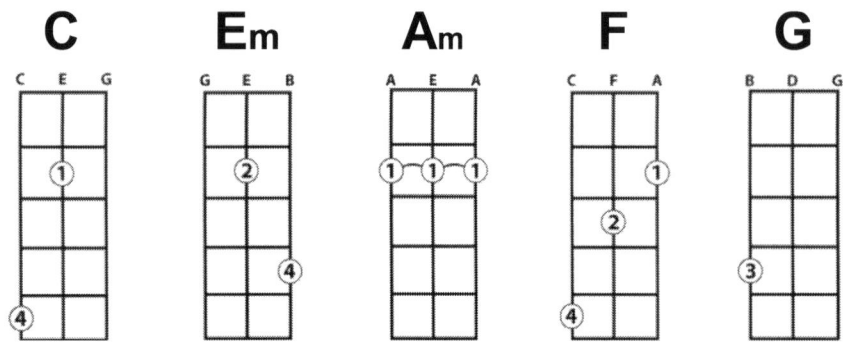

Irish Drinking Songs Cigar Box Guitar Songbook · Copyright 2019 by Hobo Music Works · All Rights Reserved

IRISH DRINKING SONG

Beer, Beer, Beer (Page 2)

Basic Melody
Key of C

CHORUS

```
      C
G  0——0—————————————————————————————————————————————
D  ————2———2—2—0—2-2-2————0-2—2———0———————————————
G  ——————————————————————————————————5-0————————
   Oh he ought to be  an  emperor, a sultan or a king;
      C            F          G
G  5——5—5—5——0———2-0—————————————————————
D  ——————————————3-2——0————————————————
G  ————————————————————————————————————
   And to his praises, we shall always sing.
      C                         F        C
G  0—5——5—5-5—5——0—0—0———2———0—5—2——0———
D  —————————————————————————————————————
G  —————————————————————————————————————
   Oh look what he has done for us, he's filled us up with cheer;
                                  G   C
G  0——0—0—0—0——0—0—0——0-2—4——5————
D  —————————————————————————————————
G  —————————————————————————————————
   God bless Charlie Mopps, the man who invented beer
      Em  Am        C   Em  Am
G  -4——2———0—2-4—5——4———2—————
D  ———————————————————————————
G  ———————————————————————————
   (beer, beer, tid-d-ly beer, beer, beer...)
```

Additional Verses

The Curtis Bar, the James' Pub, the hole-in-the-wall as well...
One thing ye can be sure of, it's Charlie's beer they sell.
So come on all ye lucky lads, at eleven o'clock we stop;
For five whole seconds, remember Charlie Mopps!
(One... Two... Three... Four... Five...)

A barrel of malt, a bushel of hops, stir it around with a stick,
The kind of lubrication, to make yer engine tick...
Forty pints of wallop a day will keep away the quacks,
It's only eight pence hapenny, and one and six in tax.

IRISH DRINKING SONG

Beer, Beer, Beer (continued)

Melody & Chords
Key of C

INTRO/BRIDGE

```
       C         Em       Am              C         Em       Am
G  5———————4————————2—————0———2—4——5————————4————————2———————————————————
D  2———————2————————2—————0———0—0——2————————2————————2———————————————————
G  0———————0————————2—————————————0————————0————————2———————————————————
   Beer, beer, beer, tid-d-ly beer, beer, beer...
```

VERSE

```
       C
G  0———————————————————0———0———0—————————————————————————————————————————
D  2—2———————2———3—2———2———2———3—2———0—————————————————————————————————
G  5—5———————5———5—5———5———5———5—5———0—5———————————————————————————————
   A long time a-go, way back in history,
       C                            F                G
G  0———5———5———————5———5—5—————0———2———0——————————————————————————————
D  2———2———2———————2———2—2—————2———3———3———————3———2———2———0——————————
G  5———0———0———————————0———————5———————5———5———5———4——————————————————
   When all there was to drink was nothin' but cups of tea...
       C                       F               C
G  0—5———5—————5—5———0———0———2———0—5———2———0——————————————————————————
D  0—2———2—————2—2———2———2———3———3—3———3———2——————————————————————————
G  4—0———0—————0—————————————5———————————5————————————————————————————
   A-long came a man, by the name of Charlie Mopps,
                                                        G       C
G  ———0—0—0—0———————0—0—0—0———0——————————0———————————————————————————
D  2—2—2—2—2———2—2—2—2—2—2———2——————————2———2———2———0———2—————————————
G  5———5—————————5—5—————5———5——————————5———5———5———0———0———4———5—————
   And he invented a wonderful drink, and he made it out of hops.
```

CHORUS

```
       C
G  0———0———————————————————————————————————————————————————————————————
D  2———2———2—————2———2———0———2—2—2—————0—2———2———0——————————————————————
G  5———————5—————5—5———5—5—5—5—————5—5—5———————0—5—0————————————————————
   Oh he ought to be an emperor, a sultan or a king;
       C               F           G
G  5———5—5———5—5———0———2—0————————————————————————————————————————————
D  2———2—2———2—2———2———3—3———3—2———0————————————————————————————————————
G  0———————————0———————5———5—5———4——————————————————————————————————————
   And to his praises, we shall always sing.
       C                            F                C
G  0———5———5———————5—5———5———0———0———0———2———————0—5———2———0————————————
D  0———2———2———————2—2———2———2———2———2———3———————3—3—3———3———2——————————
G  4———0———————————————0———————5———5———5—————————2———————5——————————————
   Oh look what he has done for us, he's filled us up with cheer;
                                                    G       C
G  0———0———0———0———0———0———0———0———0—2—4———5————————————————————————————
D  2———2———2———2———2———2———2———2———2—0—0———2————————————————————————————
G  5———5———5———5———5———5———————————5—0—0———5————————————————————————————
   God bless Charlie Mopps, the man who invented beer
       Em      Am              C       Em      Am
G  —4———————2—————0———2—4——5————4————————2——————————————————————————————
D  —2———————2—————2———2—2——2————2————————2——————————————————————————————
G  —0———————2—————————————0————————————2————————————————————————————————
   (beer, beer, tid-d-ly beer, beer, beer...)
```

Irish Drinking Songs Cigar Box Guitar Songbook · Copyright 2019 by Hobo Music Works · All Rights Reserved

Black Velvet Band

IRISH BALLAD
Basic Melody
Key of C

Words and Music
Traditional

The earliest known printed broadside versions of this song date from the late 1700's in England. Today it is usually considered to be an Irish song, with a recorded version by the Dubliners in 1967 being possibly the best known.

```
         C                                              G
G  0—0—0—0—0————————0———————————————————————————————————————
D  ————————————2—3—————3—2—0————0—2———————————————————————
G  ——————————————————————5————5—4—2—0———————————————————
    In a neat little town they call Belfast, apprentice to trade I was bound,

         C              Am           F        G         C
G  0———————————————————————————————————————————————————————
D  ——2-2-2———————————————0-2———2—0—2—3——————0————————————
G  ————————0—2—4—5——————————————————4—5—5—————————————
    And many the hours of sweet happiness I've spent in that neat little town.

                                                         G
G  0—0—0————0——————————————————————————————————————————
D  ————2—3————3—2—0————0—2——————————————————————————
G  ——————————————5————5—4—2—0——————————————————————
    Til sad misfortune o'ertook me, and caused me to stray from the land;

         C              Am           F        G         C
G  0———————————————————————————————————————————————————————
D  —3—2-2———2———————————0-2——2-0-2—3——————0—————————————
G  ——————0—2-4-5——————————————————4—5—5—————————————
    Far away from me friends and rela--tions, I followed the black velvet band.
```

Chorus

```
         C                                              G
G  0—0—0————0——————————————————————————————————————————
D  ————2—3————3—2—0————0—2——————————————————————————
G  ——————————————5————5—4—2—0——————————————————————
    Her eyes they shone like a diamond, you'd think she was queen of the land;

         C              Am           F        G         C
G  0———————————————————————————————————————————————————————
D  —3—2-2———2———————————0-2——2-0-2—3——————0—————————————
G  ——————0-2-4-5——————————————————4—5—5—————————————
    And her hair hung over her shoul-der, tied up with a black velvet band.
```

See Chord Forms and Additional Verses on Next Page.

Irish Drinking Songs Cigar Box Guitar Songbook · Copyright 2019 by Hobo Music Works · All Rights Reserved

IRISH BALLAD

Black Velvet Band
(continued)

Chord Forms & Additional Verses
Key of C

Chord Forms

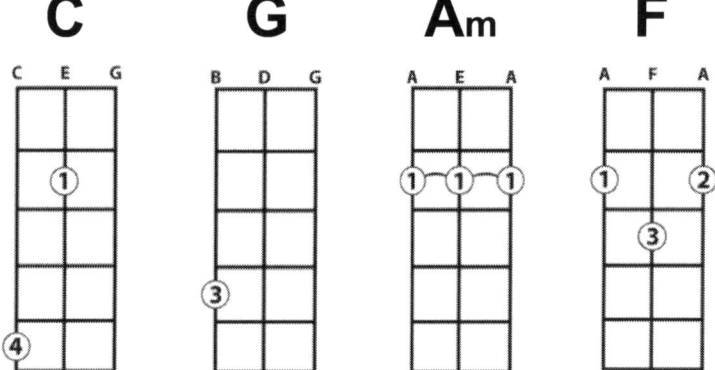

Additional Verses

As I went out strolling one evening,
Not meaning to go very far;
I met with a fickle young damsel,
A-sellin' her trade in the bar.
When a watch she took from a customer,
And slipped it right into my hand;
Then the law came and put me in prison,
Bad luck to her black velvet band!

Next morning before judge and jury,
For trial I had to appear;
Then the judge he says me young fellow,
The case against you is quite clear.
And seven long years is your sentence,
You're goin' to Van Dieman's land...
Far away from your friends and relations,
To follow the black velvet band.

So come all ye jolly young fellows,
I'll have you take warnin' by me;
And when ever you're into the liquor, me lads,
Beware of the pretty colleens.
For they'll fill you with whisky and porter,
'Til you are not able to stand...
And the very next thing that you know, me lads,
You've landed in Van Dieman's land.

Black Velvet Band
(continued)

IRISH BALLAD

Melody & Chords
Key of C

```
          C                                                           G
G  0—0—0—0—0———————————0————————————————————————————————————————
D  2—2—2—2—2—2—3——2—3—2—0———0—2————————0—0—0————————————————————
G  5———5——5—5—5—5—5—0-5—0——5—5————4-2—0—————————————————————————
   In a neat little town they call Belfast, apprentice to trade I was bound,
```

```
          C                 Am            F          G          C
G  0—————————————————————————————————————————————————————————————
D  2———2-2-2——0———0-0————2—0-2—2———0———2—3———0———0—0—2—————————
G  5—5-5-5———0———2-4———2—2-2-2——2——2-2———4———5—0—5——————————————
   And many the hours of sweet happiness I've spent in that neat little town.
```

```
                                                              G
G  0—0—0—0———————0—————————————————————————————————————————————
D  2—2—2—2—3—2—3—2—0————0—2—0———0—0—0—————————————————————————
G  5—5———5—5———5—5—0—5———0—0—5——4——2—0—————————————————————————
   Til sad misfortune o'ertook me, and caused me to stray from the land;
```

```
          C                 Am            F          G          C
G  0—————————————————————————————————————————————————————————————
D  0——3—2—2———2—0————0—0—0-2———2-0-2———3——0———0—0—2———————————
G  4—4—5-5———5—0————2—4-5-2-2———2-2-2———2—4———5—0—5——————————————
   Far away from me friends and rela--tions, I followed the black velvet band.
```

CHORUS

```
          C                                                           G
G  0—0—0———0———————0—————————————————————————————————————————————
D  2—2———2———2——3——2-3-2———0————————0—2—2———0—0—0————————————————
G  5-5———5———5—————5-5—0———5———0—0—5——4—2—0———————————————————————
   Her eyes they shone like a diamond, you'd think she was queen of the land;
```

```
          C                 Am            F          G          C
G  0———————————————————————————————————————————————————————————5
D  0——3—2—2———0-0-0—2—0-2———2———0-2—3-0———0-0—5—————————————————
G  4—4—5—5———0-2—4—5—2-2———2—2-2——2-4———5—0—5——————————————————
   And her hair hung over her shoul-der, tied up with a black velvet band.
```

IRISH BALLAD

Black Velvet Band (continued)

Basic Melody
Key of G

```
      G                                                  D
G  7—7—7—7—7—4—5—7—5—4—2—0—2—4—0—————————————————————
D  ———————————————————————————————————————4—2—0———————
G  ——————————————————————————————————————————————————
```
In a neat little town they call Belfast, apprentice to trade I was bound,

```
   G              Em            C       D        G
G  7—4—4—4—————————0—2—4—4—————2—4—5—————0—2—0—
D  ——————0—2—4—————————————————————4—————————————
G  ———————————————————————————————————————————————
```
And many the hours of sweet happiness I've spent in that neat little town.

```
                                                   D
G  7—7—7—4—5—7—5—4—2—0——2—4—0——————————————————
D  ————————————————————————————————4—2—0—————————
G  ————————————————————————————————————————————————
```
Til sad misfortune o'ertook me, and caused me to stray from the land;

```
   G                Em            C       D        G
G  7—5—4—4—4————————0—2—4——4—2—4—5—————0—2—0—
D  ——————0—2—4—————————————————————4—————————————
G  ———————————————————————————————————————————————
```
Far away from me friends and rela--tions, I followed the black velvet band.

CHORUS

```
   G                                              D
G  7—7—7—4—5—7—5—4—2—0—2—4—0————————————————————
D  ————————————————————————————————4—2—0—————————
G  ————————————————————————————————————————————————
```
Her eyes they shone like a diamond, you'd think she was queen of the land;

```
   G              Em            C       D        G
G  7—5—4—4————————0—2—4——4—2—4—5—————0—2—0—
D  ——————0—2—4—————————————————————4—————————————
G  ———————————————————————————————————————————————
```
And her hair hung over her shoul-der, tied up with a black velvet band.

Chord Forms

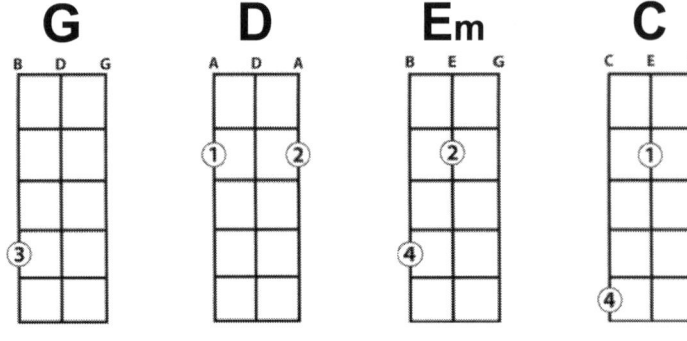

Irish Drinking Songs Cigar Box Guitar Songbook · Copyright 2019 by Hobo Music Works · All Rights Reserved

IRISH BALLAD

Black Velvet Band (continued)

Melody & Chords
Key of G

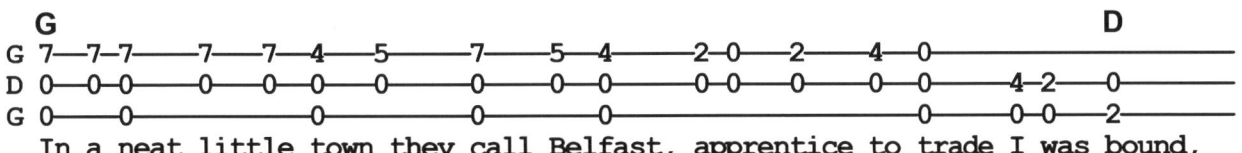
In a neat little town they call Belfast, apprentice to trade I was bound,

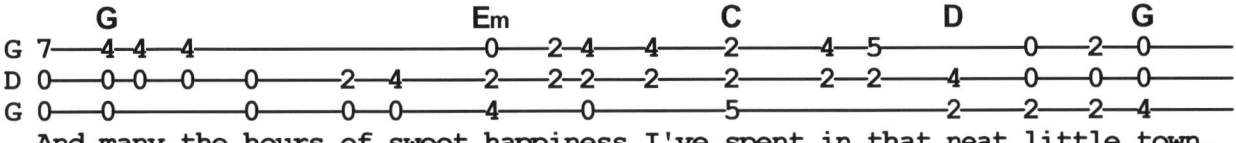
And many the hours of sweet happiness I've spent in that neat little town.

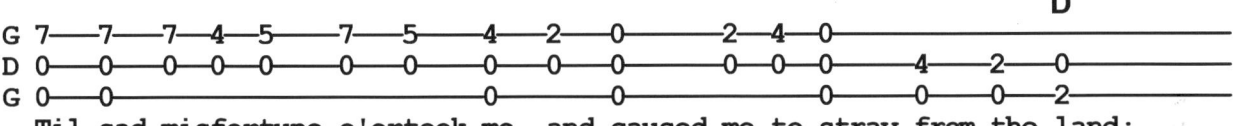
Til sad misfortune o'ertook me, and caused me to stray from the land;

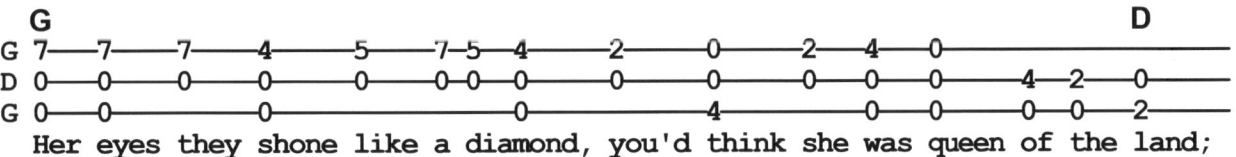
Far away from me friends and rela--tions, I followed the black velvet band.

CHORUS

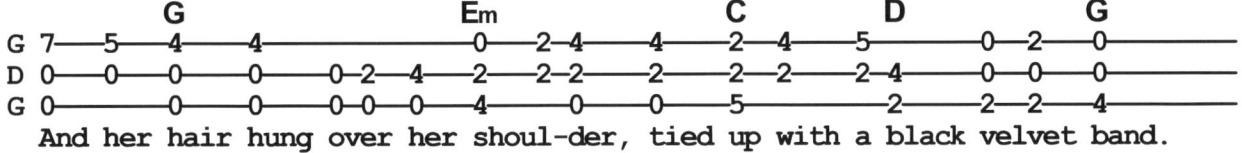
Her eyes they shone like a diamond, you'd think she was queen of the land;

And her hair hung over her shoul-der, tied up with a black velvet band.

Chord Forms

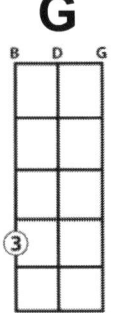
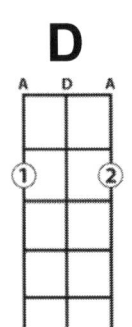
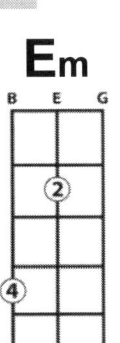
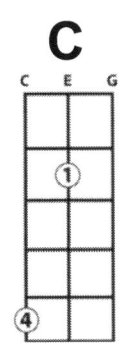

IRISH SONG

The Bold Thady Quill

Basic Melody
Key of C

It is said that this song was written by an Irish farmer, Johnny Tom Gleeson, around 1895 about one of his itinerant laborers. The Clancy Brothers and Tommy Makem helped revive the popularity of this old song.

Words by Johnny Tom Gleeson
Music Traditional

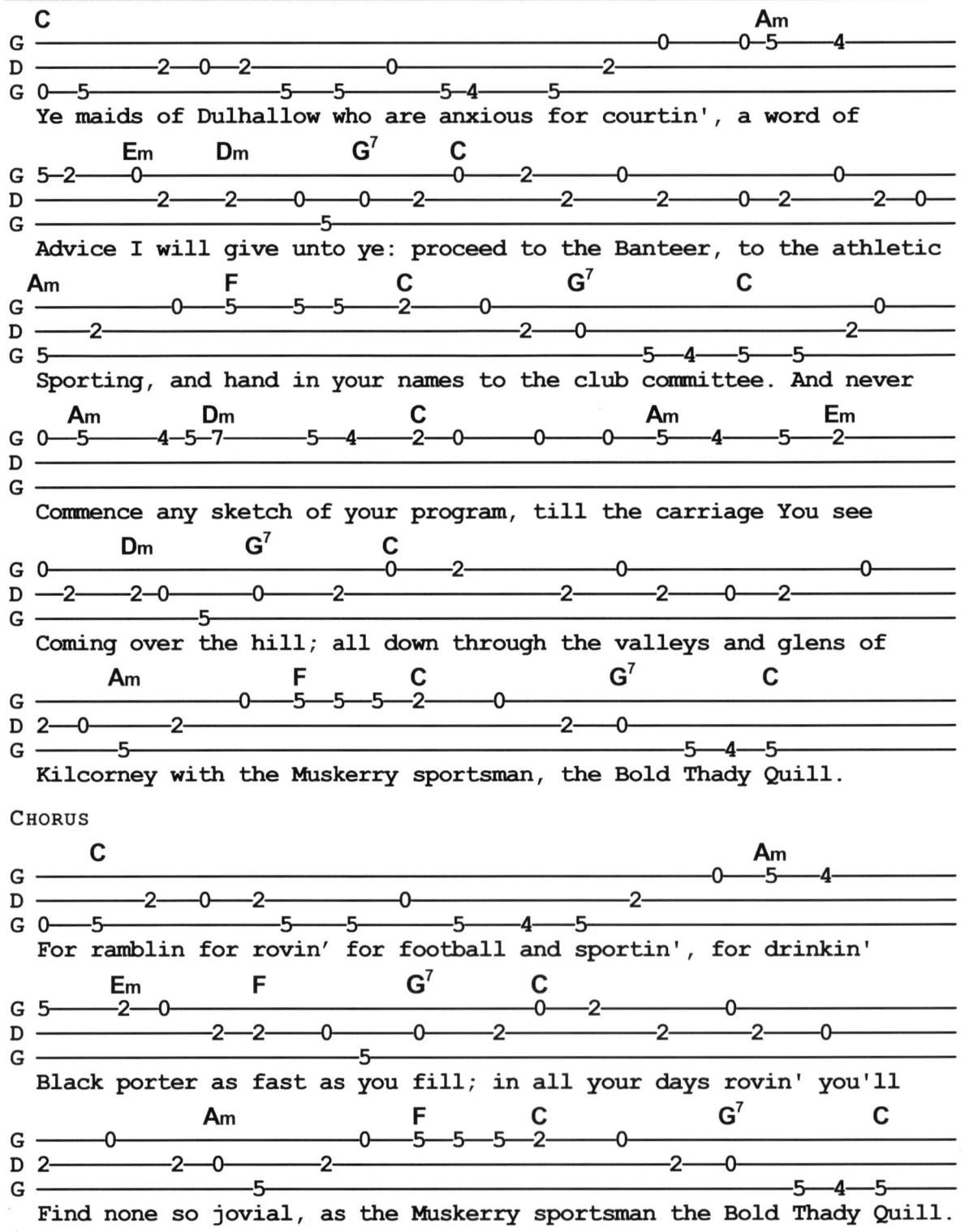

See Chord Forms and Additional Verses on Next Page.

The Bold Thady Quill
(continued)

IRISH SONG
Chord Forms and Additional Verses
Key of C

Chord Forms

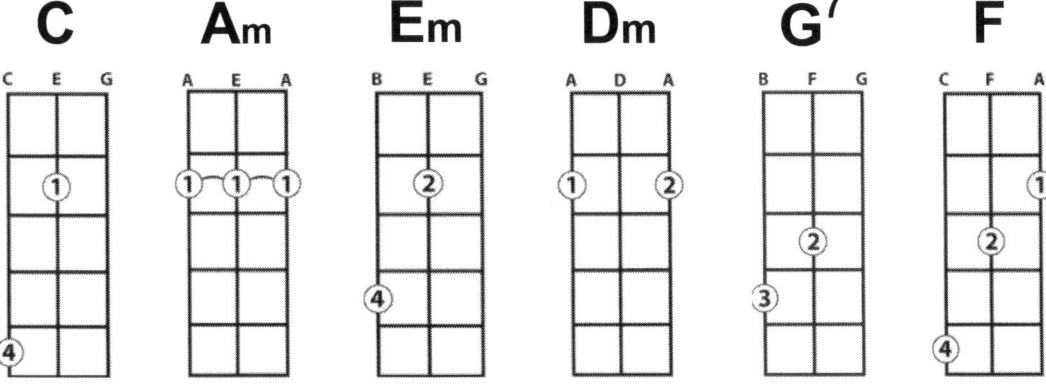

Additional Verses

Thady was famous in all sorts of places,
At the athletic meeting held out in Cloghroe;
He won the long jump without throwing off his braces,
Going fifty-four feet from the heel to the toe.
At the put of the shot was a Dublin man foremost,
But Thady out-reached and exceeded him still;
Around the whole field rang the wild ringing chorus,
'Here's luck to our hero, the bold Thady Quill'.

At the great hurling match between Cork and Tipperary,
That was held in the park on the banks of the Lee;
Our own darling boys were afraid of being beaten,
So they sent for Bold Thady in Ballinagree.
Well he hurled the ball left and right in their faces,
He showed those Tipperary boys daring and skill;
If they touched on his lines he would certainly brain them,
And the papers sang praises of the Bold Thaddy Quill.

In the year ninety-one before Parnell was taken,
Thady was outrageously breaking the peace;
He got a light sentence for causing commotion,
And six months hard labour for beatin' police.
But in spite of coercion, he's still agitating,
Each drop of his life's blood, he's willing to spill;
To gain for old Ireland complete liberation,
Till then, there's no rest for the bold Thady Quill.

At the Cork Exhibition there was a fair maiden,
Who's fortune exceeded one million or more;
But a poor constitution had ruined her completely,
And medical treatment had failed o're and o're.
Ah mother she says sure I know what will ease me,
And all the diseases most certainly kill;
Give over your potions and medical treatment,
I'd rather one squeeze from the Bold Thady Quill.

The inclusion of this song on the 1959 album "Come Fill Your Glass With Us" by The Clancy Brothers and Tommy Makem helped to re-introduce it to the folk music world.

The Bold Thady Quill
(continued)

IRISH SONG
Melody & Chords
Key of C

```
      C                                          Am
G ─────────────────────────────────0────0─5──4───
D ─────2─0─2─────────0──────────2──2────2─2──2───
G 0─5──5───5─0─5─5──5─0─5─4──5──5────5──5─2──────
  Ye maids of Dulhallow who are anxious for courtin', a word of

    Em    Dm      G⁷        C
G 5─2────0────────────0────2────────0──────────────
D 2─2───2─2────2──0──0─2───2─2──2─2─0─2───2─2──2─0
G ──2───4─4────2──2─5─4────4─5───5─────0─5─5─5──0
  Advice I will give unto ye: proceed to the Banteer, to the athletic

    Am       F        C          G⁷          C
G ──────0───5─5─5───2──0──────────────────────0────
D ──────2────2─3─3─3──2──────2─2──0──────────2─2──
G 5──2──────2─2─2────5─────5─4──5─4──5──5─5──5
  Sporting, and hand in your names to the club committee. And never

    Am     Dm                C            Am           Em
G 0─5────4─5─7─────5─4─────2─0────0───0─5──4────5─2───
D 2─2────2─2─0─────0─0─────2─2────2───2─2──2────2─2───
G ──2─────────────5─5──────2──────────2─────────4─────
  Commence any sketch of your program, till the carriage You see

        Dm       G⁷      C
G 0─────────────────0───2───────0────────────0────
D 2─2───2─0──0──────2───2───2──2─2──0──────2──2──
G 4─4───2─2──5──4──0─5──────5──5─5──0──────5─────
  Coming over the hill; all down through the valleys and glens of

     Am       F        C         G⁷           C
G ──────0───5─5─5───2──0──────────────────────────
D 2──0──2────2─3─3─3──2──────2─2──0──────────────
G 5──0─5────2─2─2────5─────5─4──5─4──5─────────
  Kilcorney with the Muskerry sportsman, the Bold Thady Quill.
```

CHORUS

```
      C                                          Am
G ─────────────────────────────────0────5──4──────
D ─────2─0─2─────────0──────────2──2────2──2──────
G 0─5──5───0─0─5──5─0──5─4──5──5────5──5─2──2─────
  For ramblin for rovin for football and sportin', for drinkin'

    Em    F      G⁷        C
G 5──2──0────────────0─2──────0──────────
D 2──2─2─2─2─2──0──0─2──2─2───2─2─2─0────
G 2────4────4─2──2─5──0──0─5──5────5──2──
  Black porter as fast as you fill; In all your days rovin' you'll

      Am          F        C         G⁷           C
G ────0───────5─5─5──2──0─────────────────────5──
D 2─2──2──0──2─2─3─3─3──2────2─2──0───────────5──
G 5──────0─2─5──2─2────5────5──4──5─4──5──────5──
  Find none so jovial, as the Muskerry sportsman the Bold Thady Quill.
```

See Chord Forms on Previous Page.

IRISH SONG

The Boys From the County Armagh

Basic Melody

Key of G

This song is the pride of people from the County Armagh in northern Ireland, including many of those whose ancestors emigrated to the Dover, New Hampshire area to work in the mills in the mid-to-late 1800's. The Dover Rovers often perform this in concert, with Tyler Foss leading. The third verse is a recent addition by the creator of this book, Ben "Gitty" Baker, who had always felt the song ended too soon.

Words by Thomas Keenan

Music Traditional

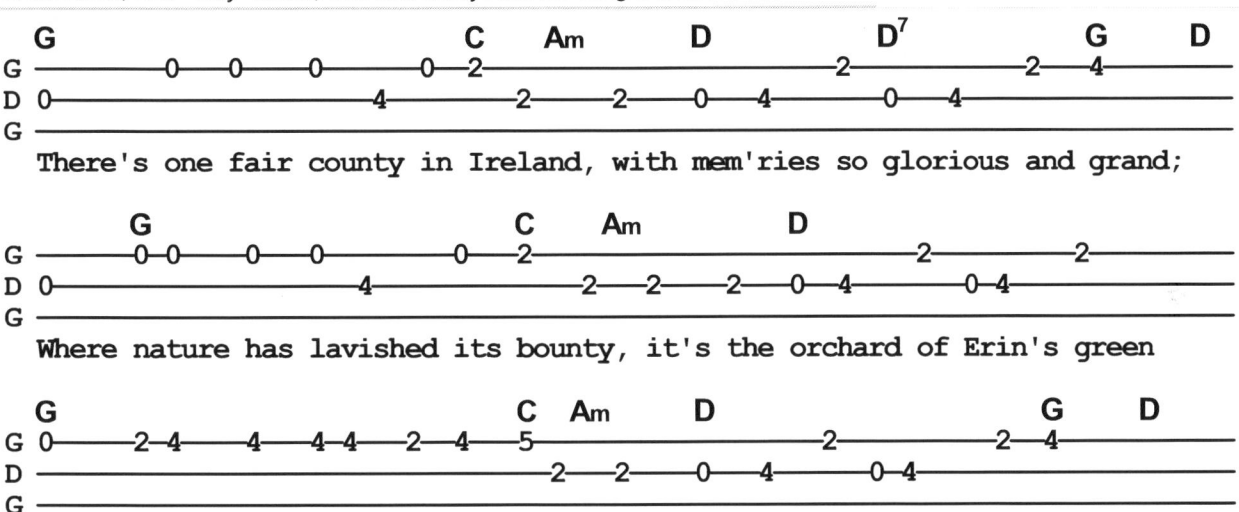

There's one fair county in Ireland, with mem'ries so glorious and grand;

Where nature has lavished its bounty, it's the orchard of Erin's green

Land. I love her cathe-der-al city, once founded by Patrick so true;

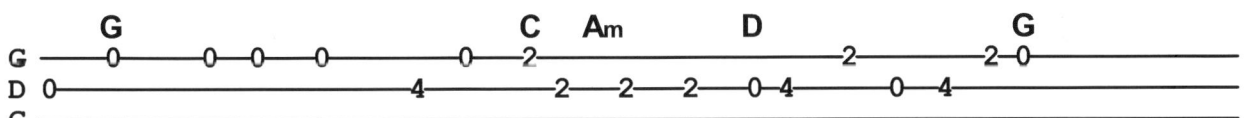

And there in the heart of its bosom lie the ashes of Brian Boru.

CHORUS

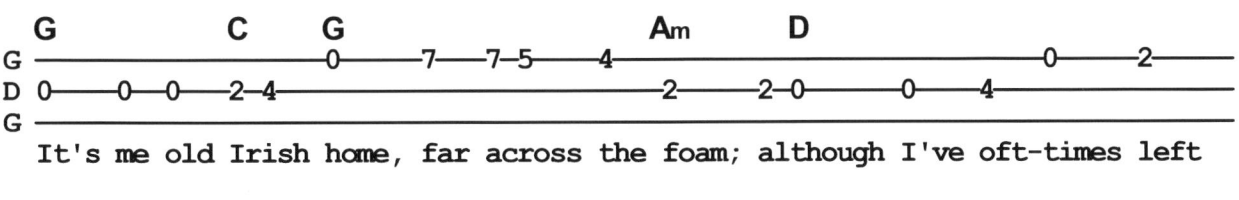

It's me old Irish home, far across the foam; although I've oft-times left

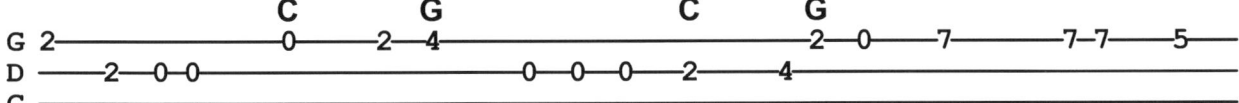

It, in foreign lands to roam. No matter where I wander, through cities near

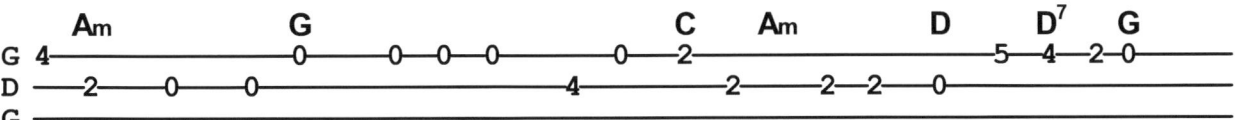

Or far; sure my heart is at home in old Ireland, in the County of Armagh!

See Chord Forms and Additional Verses on Next Page.

Irish Drinking Songs Cigar Box Guitar Songbook · Copyright 2019 by Hobo Music Works · All Rights Reserved

IRISH SONG

The Boys From the County Armagh (continued)

Chord Forms and Additional Verses
Key of G

Chord Forms

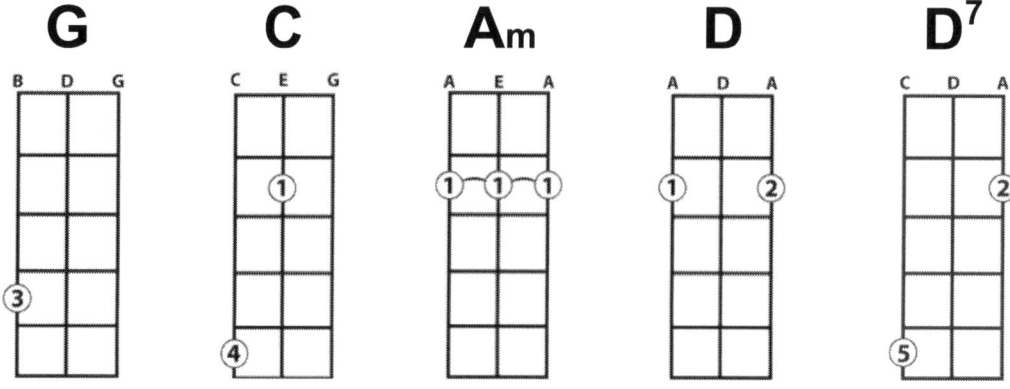

Additional Verses

I've traveled that part of the county,
Through New Town, Fork Hill, Crossmaglen;
Around by the gap of Mountnorris,
And down by Blackwater again.
Where the girls are so hale and so hearty,
None finer in Erin Go Bragh;
But where are the boys that can court them,
Like the boys from the County Armagh?

'Twas me grandparents first left Ireland,
To come to Amerikay.
They settled in Dover, New Hampshire...
And that's where you will find me today.
But my mind oft goes back to old Ireland,
To a place that is fairer by far...
'Tis up in the north you will find it,
And it goes by the name of Armagh!

A home scene from County Armagh, Ireland, 1903.

IRISH SONG

The Boys From the County Armagh (continued)

Melody & Chords

Key of G

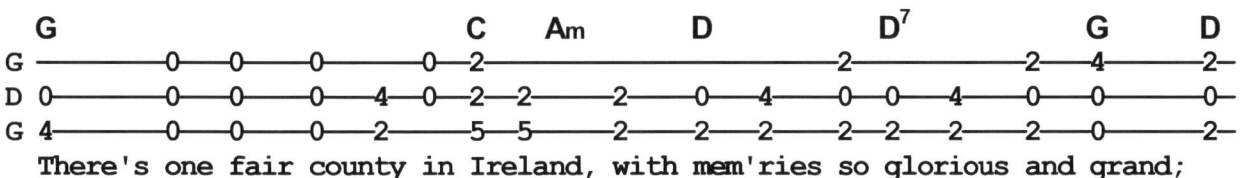
There's one fair county in Ireland, with mem'ries so glorious and grand;

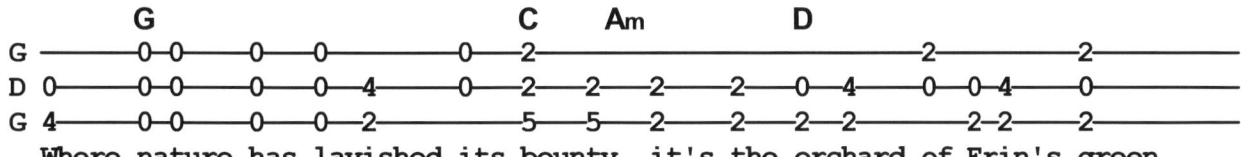
Where nature has lavished its bounty, it's the orchard of Erin's green

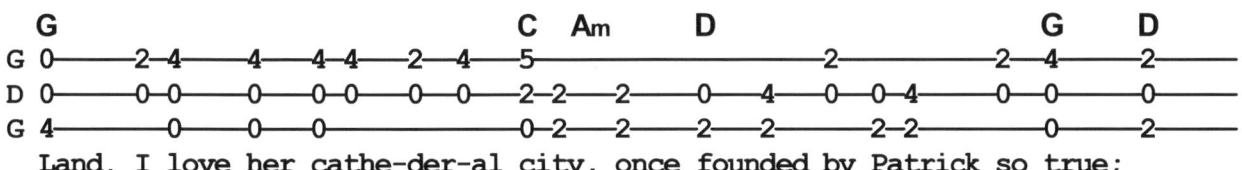
Land. I love her cathe-der-al city, once founded by Patrick so true;

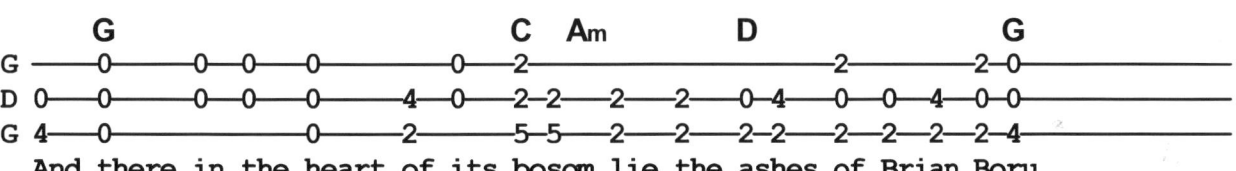
And there in the heart of its bosom lie the ashes of Brian Boru.

CHORUS

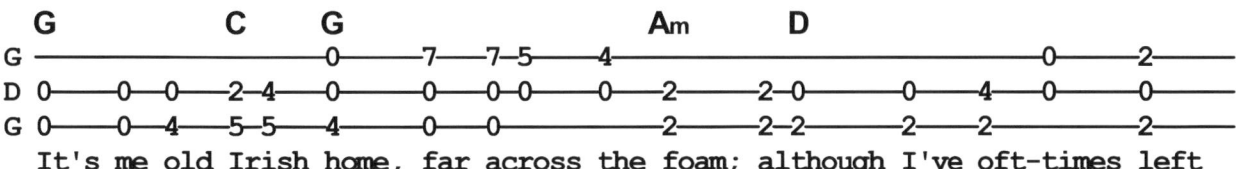
It's me old Irish home, far across the foam; although I've oft-times left

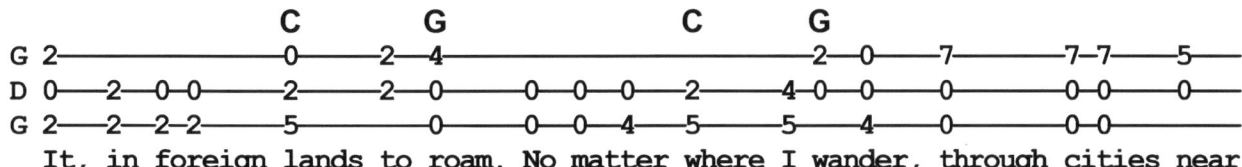
It, in foreign lands to roam. No matter where I wander, through cities near

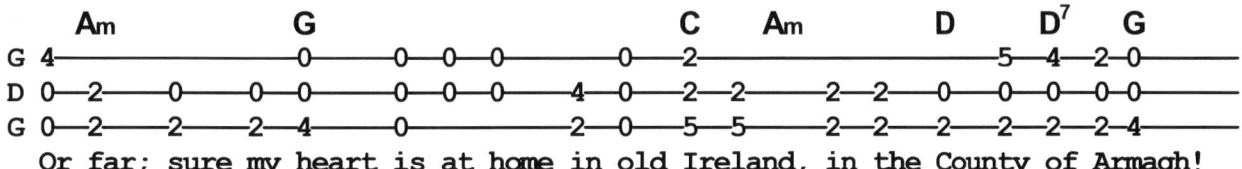
Or far; sure my heart is at home in old Ireland, in the County of Armagh!

See Chord Forms and Additional Verses on Previous Page.

Irish Drinking Songs Cigar Box Guitar Songbook · Copyright 2019 by Hobo Music Works · All Rights Reserved

IRISH SONG

The Boys From the County Armagh (continued)

Basic Melody

Key of C

```
      C                        F    Dm      G            G7              C   G
G ─────────────────────────────────────────────────────────────────────────────
D ─────────────────────────────────0──────────────0─────────────0─────────2────
G 0────5──5────5──4──5────2────2────────0──4──────────0──4──────────────────────
  There's one  fair  county in Ireland, with mem'ries so glorious and grand;

      C                        F    Dm      G
G ─────────────────────────────────────────────────────────────────
D ─────────────────────────────────0──────────────0──────────0─────
G 0────5──5────5──5──4────5────2────2──2──0──4──────0──4─────────────
  Where nature has lavished its bounty, it's the orchard of Erin's green

      C                        F    Dm      G                 C   G
G ─────────────────────────────────────────────────────────────────
D ─────0──2────2──2──2──0──2──3────────────────0──────────────0──2──
G 5─────────────────────────────2──2──0──4──────0──4─────────────────
  Land. I love her cathe-der-al city, once founded by Patrick so true;

      C                        F    Dm      G            C
G ─────────────────────────────────────────────────────────────────
D ─────────────────────────────────0──────────────0──────0──────────
G 0────5────5──5──5────4──5────2────2──2──0──4──────0──4──5──────────
  And there in the heart of its bosom lie the ashes of Brian Boru.
```

CHORUS
```
      C        F    C                 Dm      G
G ──────────────────0──0────────────────────────────────────────
D ──────────────3─────────2──────────────2──0──────────0────────
G 0────0──0──2──4──5─────────────2──────2──0──────0──4──5────────
  It's me old Irish home, far across the foam; although I've oft-times left

               F              C              F           C
G ─────────────────────────────────────────────0─────────0──0──
D 0────────────────0──2─────────────0──────────────────────3───
G ────2──0──0──5────────────0──0──2────4──5──────────────────────
  It, in foreign lands to roam. No matter where I wander, through cities near

      Dm            C                  F    Dm      G    G7    C
G ──────────────────────────────────────────────────────────────
D 2─────────────────────────────────────0──────────────3──2──0──
G ────2──0──0──5────5──5──5────4──5────2────2──2──0──────────5──
  Or far; sure my heart is at home in old Ireland, in the County of Armagh!
```

Chord Forms

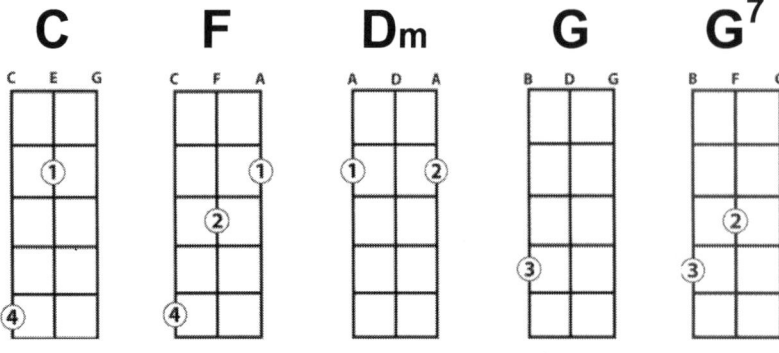

Irish Drinking Songs Cigar Box Guitar Songbook · Copyright 2019 by Hobo Music Works · All Rights Reserved

IRISH BALLAD

Carrickfergus

Basic Melody
Key of G

Carrickfergus is the name of a town in County Antrim in Northern Ireland. This song is based on an old Gaelic song "Do Bhi Bean Uasal", believed to have originated in the southwest of Ireland in County Limerick or County Clare.

Words and Music
Traditional

```
      G       Am   D        G        Em       Am      D
G  0—0—————————————————————————————————————————————————————
D  ————4—2————————0—————————————————————————————————————————
G  ————————2—4—5—————4—2—0———2—4—5———5—4—2—0—————————————————
   I wish I wa-s in Carrickfe-r-gus; only for ni-gh-ts in

           G           Am   D        G         Em
G  ——————————0—0————————————————————————————————————————————
D  ———————————————————4——————2—————0—————————————————————————
G  0———2—0———————————————2—4———5————4—2—0—————————————————————
   Ballygrand. I would swim over the deepest o-o-cean,

         Am     D      G
G  ————————————————————————————————
D  ————————————————————————————————
G  2—4—5———5—4—2——2—0—2—0——————————
   Only for ni-gh-ts in Ballygrand.

      G         Em                        D
G  —————————————0———0—2—4—2———0———2————————————————————
D  0——0———0———0————————————————————4—0——0———0———0———————
G  ———————————————————————————————————————————————————
   But the sea is wide and I cannot swim o-o-ver; and neither

   Em       C       D                Am      D
G  0—2—4———4—5————4—2———0—0———0—————————————————————————
D  —————————————————————————————4——————2—————————————0——
G  —————————————————————————————————————————2—4—5———————
   Ha-a-ve I wings to fly; I wish I could find me a handsome

      G       Em         Am    D              G
G  ——————————————————————————————————————————————————————
D  ——————————————————————————————————————————————————————
G  4—2—0———0—2—4—5———5—4—2———2—2—4——————2—0———————————————
   Boatsman; to ferry me o-o-ver to my love and die.
```

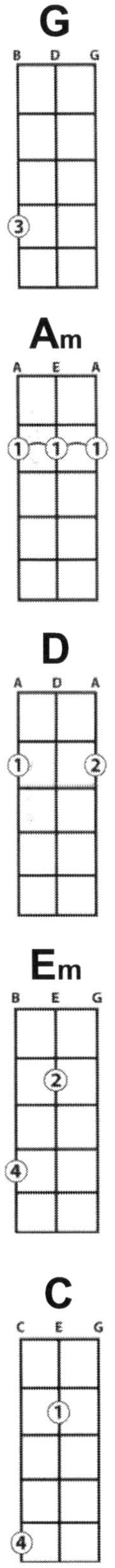

Additional Verses

Now in Kilkenny, it is reported,
They have marble stones there, as black as ink.
With gold and silver, I would support her;
But I'll sing no more now, till I get a drink.
I'm drunk today, and I'm seldom sober.
A handsome rover, from town to town.
Ah but I'm sick now, my days are numbered.
So come all you young men, and lay me down.

Playing Notes

There are several places in the song above where the chord change is indicated in between notes, or at/just past the end of words. This is part of the flowing nature of the song, where the chord change comes during the pause in between words.

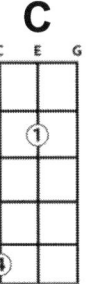

Carrickfergus (continued)

IRISH BALLAD
Basic Melody
Key of C

```
       C           Dm  G          C        Am         Dm          G
G  5—5———————4—2——————————————————————————————————————————————————————
D  ————————————0—2—3———2—0————————0—2—3————3—2—0——————————————————————
G  ——————————————————————5————————————————————————————5———————————————
   I  wish  I  wa-s  in  Carrickfe-r-gus;  only  for  ni-gh-ts  in

              C              Dm  G              C          Am
G  ——————————5—5——————4———2——————————————0——————————————————————————
D  ——0————————————————————0—2—3—————————2—0——————————————————————————
G  5————5——————————————————————————————————————————5—————————————————
   Ballygrand.  I  would  swim  over  the  deepest  o-o-cean,

             Dm           C
G  ———————————————————————————————————————————————————————————————
D  0—2—3———3—2—0—0————————————————————————————————————————————————
G  ——————————————————5—4—5—————————————————————————————————————————
   Only  for  ni-gh-ts  in  Ballygrand.

      C           Am              G
G  0———0———0———0—5———5———7—9—7———5———7—4—0———0———0———0
D  ———————————————————————————————————————————————————
G  ———————————————————————————————————————————————————
   But  the  sea  is  wide  and  I  cannot  swim  o-o-ver;  and  neither

   Am         F      G                  Dm          G
G  5—7—9———9—10——————9—7———5—5—————5—4——2——————————————0——
D  ———————————————————————————————————————————0———2—3—————
G  ———————————————————————————————————————————————————————
   Ha-a-ve  I  wings  to  fly;  I  wish  I  could  find  me  a  handsome

      C    Am             Dm         G              C
G  ——————————————————————————————————————————————————————
D  2—0—————————0—2—3———3—2—0———0—0————————0——————————————
G  ————5————5——————————————————————5————————5————————————
   Boatsman;  to  ferry  me  o-o-ver  to  my  love  and  die.
```

Chord Forms

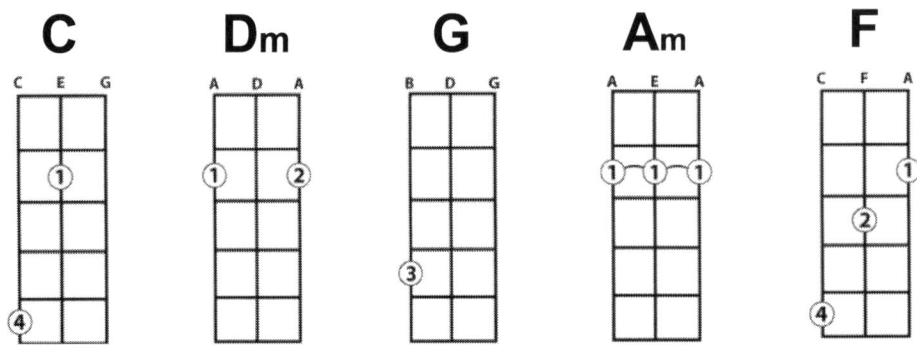

IRISH BALLAD

Carrickfergus (continued)

Melody & Chords
Key of C

```
       C        Dm    G                C         Am          Dm         G
G  5—5———4—2——————————0—————————————————————————————————————————————————
D  2—2——2—0—0—2—3—0——2—0———————0—2—3——3—2—0——————————————————————————
G  0—0——2—2—0—4—4——5—2—5————2—2—2———2—2—2—4———————————————————————————
   I  wish I wa-s in Carrickfe-r-gus;  only  for  ni-gh-ts in

              C            Dm   G                C         Am
G  ——————————5—5————4———2—————————0——————————————————————————
D  ——0———2—2————2———0—0—2—3—3————2—0———————————————————————
G  5—4—5————0—0———————2—2—2—2——————5—0—5——————————————————
   Ballygrand.  I  would  swim  over  the  deepest o-o-cean,

          Dm       G       C
G  ——————————————————————5———————————————————
D  0—2—3—3—2—0—0———0—5————————————————————————
G  2—2—2—2—2—2—4—5—4—5—————————————————————————
   Only for ni-gh-ts in Ballygrand.

       C           Am                    G
G  0———0———0———0—5———5———7—9—7———5———7—4—0———0———0———0—
D  2———2———2———2—2———2———7—7—7———2———0—0—0———0———0———0—
G  5———————5———2———————————————————0———0———4———4—
   But the sea is wide and I cannot swim o-o-ver; and neither

   Am          F         G                  Dm        G
G  5—7—9—9—10——9—7——5—5——5—4——2————————————0—
D  2—5—7—7—7——7—0——5—5——5—0——0——0—2—3——0—
G  2————————7——0——0——0—0——2——2—0—4—4—
   Ha-a-ve I wings to fly; I wish I could find me a handsome

       C       Am          Dm     G              C
G  —————————————————————————————————5—
D  2—0————0—2—3—3—2—0—0—0———0—5—
G  5—2—5——5—2—2—2—2—2—2—0—0—5——4—5—
   Boatsman; to ferry me o-o-ver to my love and die.
```

Chord Forms

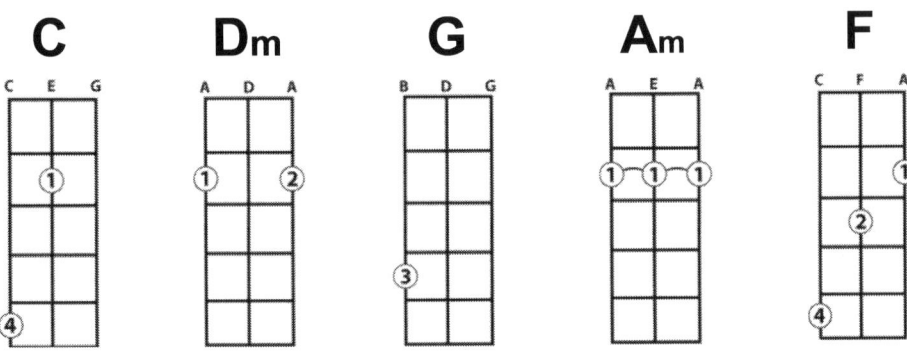

SEA SHANTY / WORK SONG

Donkey Riding

Basic Melody
Key of Em

Words and Music
Traditional

This old work song appeared in the mid 1800's, and is based on the older Scottish song "Bonnie Hieland Laddie." The "donkey" in the song is thought to be an old "steam donkey" steam-powered winch engine used for logging and other hard work, rather than the farm animal. This is a great song for belting out while downing a few pints of beer with friends.

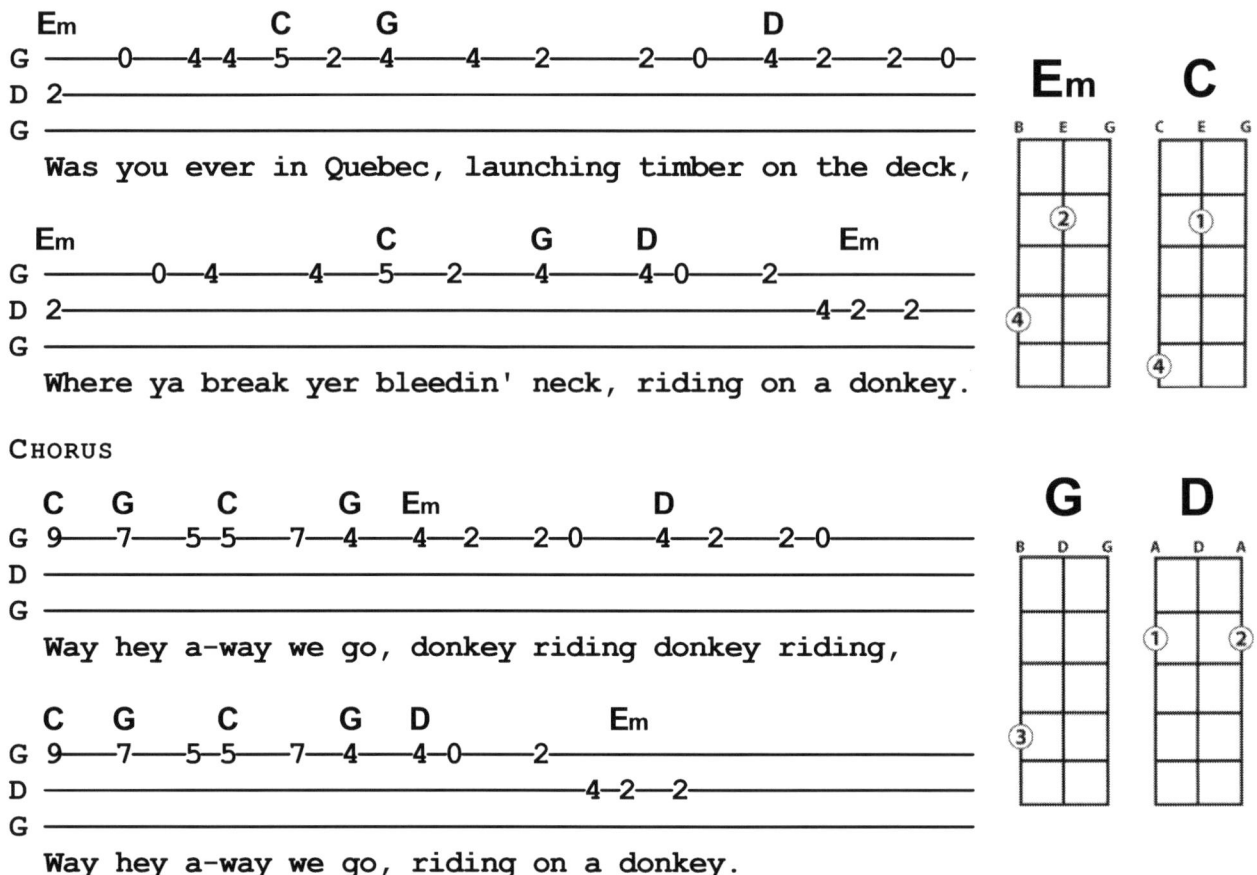

```
    Em          C   G                     D
G ——0—4-4—5—2—4——4—2——2—0—4—2—2-0—
D 2
G

    Was you ever in Quebec, launching timber on the deck,

    Em              C       G       D           Em
G ——0—4——4—5—2—4——4-0——2
D 2                                       4-2—2
G

    Where ya break yer bleedin' neck, riding on a donkey.
```

Chorus

```
    C   G   C   G   Em          D
G 9—7—5-5—7—4——4—2—2-0——4—2—2-0
D
G

    Way hey a-way we go, donkey riding donkey riding,

    C   G   C   G       D       Em
G 9—7—5-5—7—4——4-0——2
D                               4-2—2
G

    Way hey a-way we go, riding on a donkey.
```

Additional Verses

Was you ever round Cape Horn, where the weather's never warm,
Wish to God you'd never been born, riding on a donkey.

Was you ever in Miramichi, where they you tie up to a tree,
Have a girl sit on your knee, riding on a donkey.

Was you ever in Fortune Bay, hear the girls all shout hurray,
Here comes dad with last month's pay, riding on a donkey.

Was you ever in Fredericton, see the king he does come down,
See the king in his golden crown, riding on a donkey.

SEA SHANTY / WORK SONG

Donkey Riding (continued)

Melody & Chords
Key of Em

```
   Em              C    G                        D
G ——————0——4-4——5——2——4————4——2————2—0——4—2——2-0—
D 2——2————2-2——2——2——2————0——0————0—0——0—0——0-0—
G 4————————0————0——0——0————0——0————0——0——2-2—————
  Was you ever in Quebec, launching timber on the deck,

   Em              C         G    D         Em
G ————————0——4————4——5——2————4————4-0————2———————
D 2————————2-2————2——2——2————0————0-0————0-4-2——2
G 4——————————0————————0——0————0————2————0-2-4——4—
  Where ya break yer bleedin' neck, riding on a donkey.
```

CHORUS

```
  C    G    C    G    Em            D
G 9————7————5-5——7————4————4——2————2-0——4——2——2-0—
D 10———0————0-2——0————0————2——2————2-2——0——0——0-0—
G 9————0—————————0————0————————————4————2——————2-2
  Way hey a-way we go, donkey riding donkey riding,

  C    G    C    G    D         Em
G 9————7————5-5——7————4————4-0————2——————————————
D 10———0————0-2——0————0————0-0————0-4-2——2———————
G 9————0—————————0————0————2————————2-2-4——4—————
  Way hey a-way we go, riding on a donkey.
```

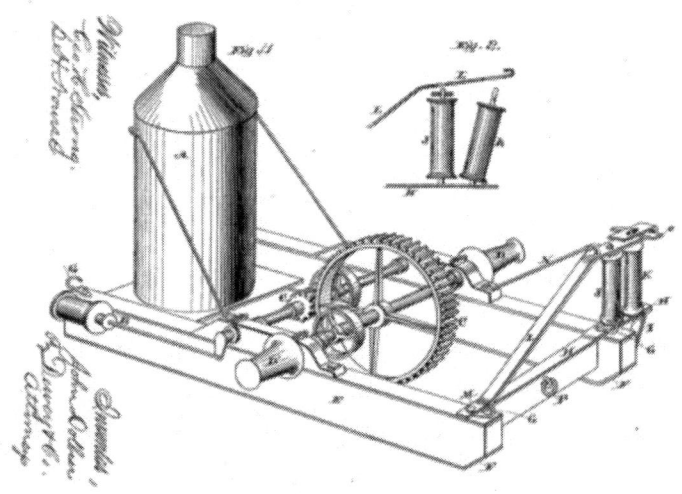

Diagram from an 1882 steam donkey patent.

SEA SHANTY/WORK SONG

Donkey Riding (continued)

Two Versions
Key of Am

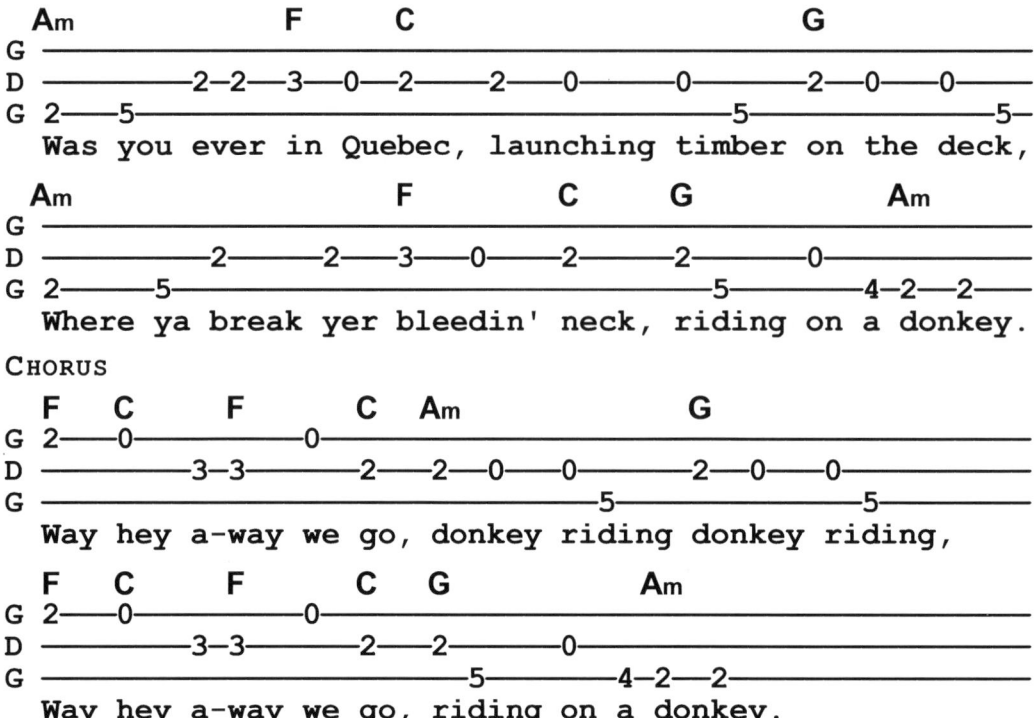

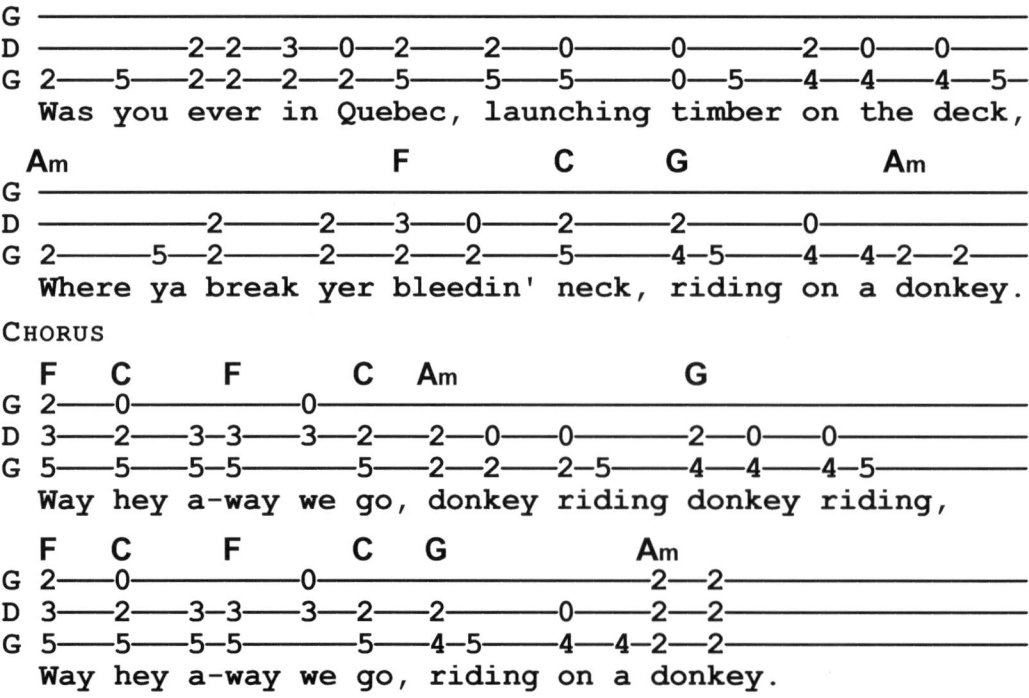

IRISH STREET BALLAD

Finnegan's Wake

Basic Melody
Key of C

This is one of the quintessential Irish drinking songs, covering all of the favorite Irish topics in one go: living, dying, drinking and fighting. It tells the tale of Tim Finnegan's revival in the middle of his own funeral. The song is said to have been the inspiration for James Joyce's novel of the same name. The version by the Dubliners is perhaps the best-known, and it has been recorded more recently by the Irish-American band Dropkick Murphys.

Words and Music Traditional

```
       C                    Am                  F              G
G   0---------------------2---2------------4-5--5--4--2-0-------------
D   ---2--2--2---2-----------0--2-------------------------2---0--0-----
G   -----------------------------------------------------------------
```
Tim Finnegan lived in Watling street, a gentleman Irish mighty odd;

```
                C                    Am                F
G   -----------------------2---2------2--4-5---4--4---2-
D   0----0-2--2--2---2--------0--2-----------------------
G   -----------------------------------------------------
```
He'd a beautiful brogue so rich and sweet, and to rise in the world

```
       G     C                              Am
G   0-2--2--4-5---0--5--5--5-5--7--7--5--4--2--0---0
D   --------------------------------------------------
G   --------------------------------------------------
```
He carried a hod. Well Tim had a bit of the tipplin' way, with a

```
    C                        Am               C                Am
G   5---5--5---5-5---7---5--4--2---0-5---5--5--7--5--4
D   ---------------------------------------------------
G   ---------------------------------------------------
```
Love of the liquor poor Tim was born. To help him on his way each

```
                   F              G    C
G   2---0--0---0-2---2--2--2--0---2--4--5
D   -------------------------------------
G   -------------------------------------
```
Day, he had a drop of the craythur every morn!

CHORUS

```
       C                          Am
G   ----------------------2---2--2--4
D   2-----2--2-2---0----0--2----------
G   ----------------------------------
```
Whack-fol-a-dol will ye dance with yer partners,

```
    F              G              C
G   5---4--2---0---------------------
D   ------------2--0---0---2--2-2--0
G   ---------------------------------
```
Round the floor yer trotters shake. Wasn't it the

```
    Am           F        G        C
G   ---2-2---4-5---4-2---0-2--2-4---5
D   2--------------------------------
G   ---------------------------------
```
Truth I told ya lots of fun at Finnegan's wake!

See Chords and Additional Verses on Next Page.

IRISH STREET BALLAD

Finnegan's Wake
(continued)

Chord Forms and Additional Verses

Key of C

Additional Verse

One mornin' Tim was rather full,
His head felt heavy, which made him shake.
He fell from the ladder and he broke his skull,
And they carried him home his corpse to wake.
They rolled him up in a nice clean sheet,
And laid him out upon the bed,
With a gallon of whiskey at his feet,
And a barrel of porter at his head.

His friends assembled at the wake,
And Mrs. Finnegan called for lunch.
First they brought in tea and cake,
Then pipes, tobacco and whiskey punch.
Biddy O'Brien began to cry,
"Such a nice clean corpse did you ever see?
Tim mavourneen why did you die?"
"Get ahold a your gob" said Biddy McGee.

Then Maggie O'Connor took up the job,
"O Biddy, " says she "you're wrong I'm sure."
Biddy gave her a belt on the gob,
And left her sprawling on the floor.
Then the war did soon engage,
It was woman to woman and man to man;
Shillelagh law was all the rage,
And a row and a ruction soon began.

Then Mickey Maloney raised his head
When a noggin of whiskey flew at him
It missed and landed on the bed,
And the liquor scattered over Tim;
Well be-God, see how he rises...
Timothy rising from the bed,
Sayin' "Fling your whiskey around like blazes,
Thundering Jesus, do you think I'm dead?"

Chord Forms

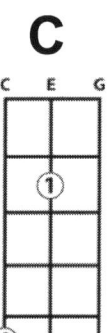
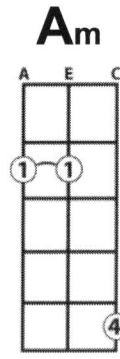
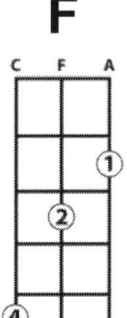

Irish Drinking Songs Cigar Box Guitar Songbook · Copyright 2019 by Hobo Music Works · All Rights Reserved

IRISH STREET BALLAD

Finnegan's Wake
(continued)

Melody and Chords

Key of C

```
     C                    Am                    F              G
G  0———————————————————————2———2———————4—5——5——4———2—0—————————————
D  2———2—2—2———2———————0—2———2———2———2—3——3——3———3—3———2———0—0—————
G  5———5—5—5———5———————2—2———2———2———2————————————————2———2—4—————
   Tim Finnegan lived in Watling street, a gentleman Irish mighty odd;

        C                    Am                F
G  —————————————————————————2———2———————2—4—5——4—4———2—————————————
D  0———0—2———2—2———2——————0—2———2———2———2—3——————3—3—3—————————————
G  0———0—5———5—5———5——————2—2———2———2———2——————————————————————————
   He'd a beautiful brogue so rich and sweet, and to rise in the world

     G    C                             Am
G  0—2—2——4—5———0———5—5——5—5———7—7——5———4———2———0———0—————————————
D  0—0—0——0—2———2———2———2—2———0—0——2———2———2———2———2—————————————
G  —————————0———————0—————0——————————2———2—————————————————————
   He carried a hod. Well Tim had a bit of the tipplin' way, with a

     C                    Am              C                Am
G  5——5—5——5—5——7——5——4——2————0—5——5—5——7——5——4—————————————
D  2——2—2——2—2——0——2——2——2————2—2——2—2——0——2——2—————————————
G  0————————2——————2———————5—0————————0——————2—————————————
   Love of the liquor poor Tim was born. To help him on his way each

                     F             G    C
G  2———0—0———0—2———2—2———2———0———2—4——5—————————————————————————
D  2———2—2———2—3———3—3———3———0———0—0——2—————————————————————————
G  2—————————5—————————————0—————0—0——0—————————————————————————
   Day, he had a drop of the craythur every morn!

CHORUS

     C                    Am
G  —————————————————————2———2———2———4—————————————————————————
D  2———2—2—2———0———0—2——2———2———2———2—————————————————————————
G  5———5—5—5———2———2—2——————————————2—————————————————————————
   Whack-fol-a-dol will ye dance with yer partners,

     F           G           C
G  5———4———2———0—————————————————————————————————————————————
D  3———3—3———3—2———0———0———2———2—2—0—————————————————————————
G  2———————5———0———0———4———5———5—5—2—————————————————————————
   Round the floor yer trotters shake. Wasn't it the

     Am            F           G       C
G  —————2—2——4—5——4—2——0—2——2—4———5—————————————————————————
D  2———2—2———2—3——3—3——0—0——0—0———2—————————————————————————
G  2———————2————2——————————0———0——5—————————————————————————
   Truth I told ya lots of fun at Finnegan's wake!
```

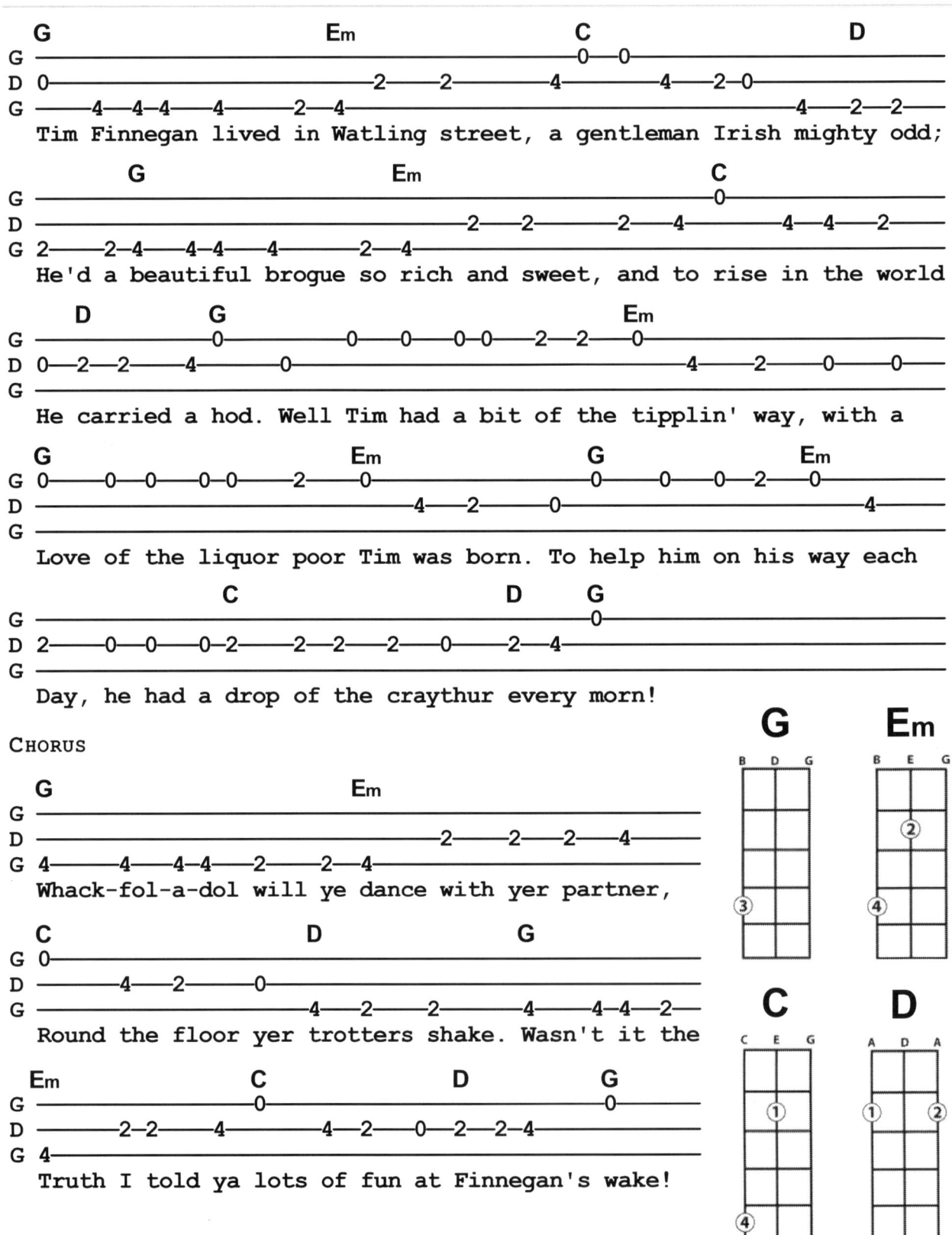

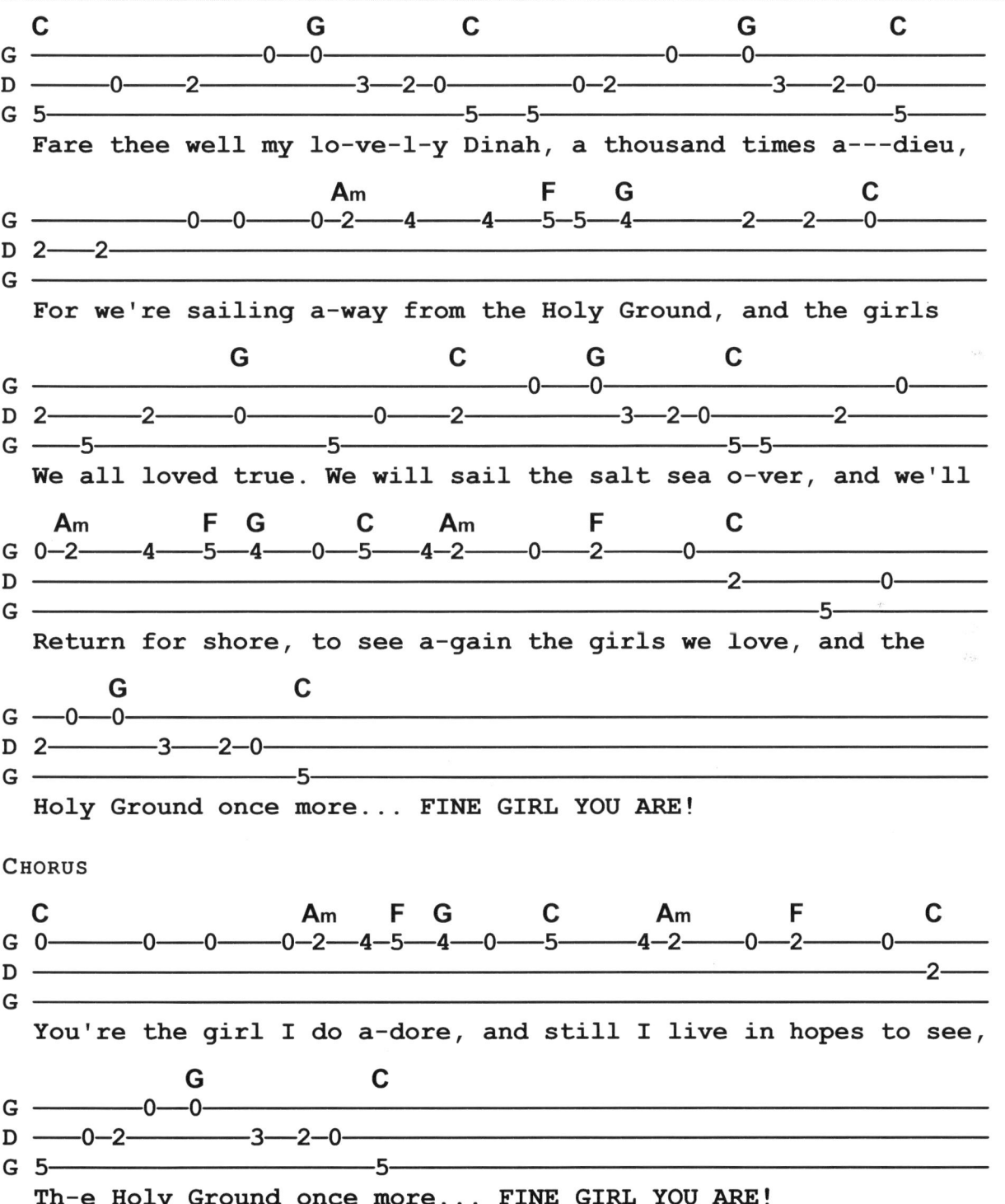

The Holy Ground
(continued)

IRISH SEA SONG

Additional Verses and Chord Forms

Key of C

Additional Verses

And now the storm is raging,
And we are far from shore;
And the good old ship is tossing about,
And the rigging is all torn.
And the secrets of my life, my love,
You're the girl I do adore!
And still I live in hopes to see
The Holy Ground once more...
FINE GIRL YOU ARE!

And now the storm is over,
And we are safe and well.
We will go into a public house,
And we'll sit and drink black ale!
We will drink strong ale and porter,
And we'll make the rafters roar,
And when our money is all spent
We'll go to sea once more...
FINE GIRL YOU ARE!

Chord Forms

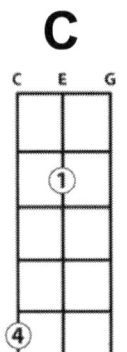
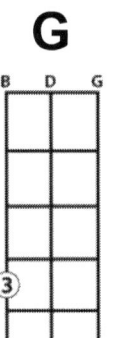
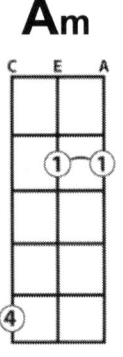
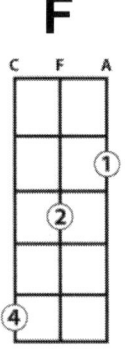

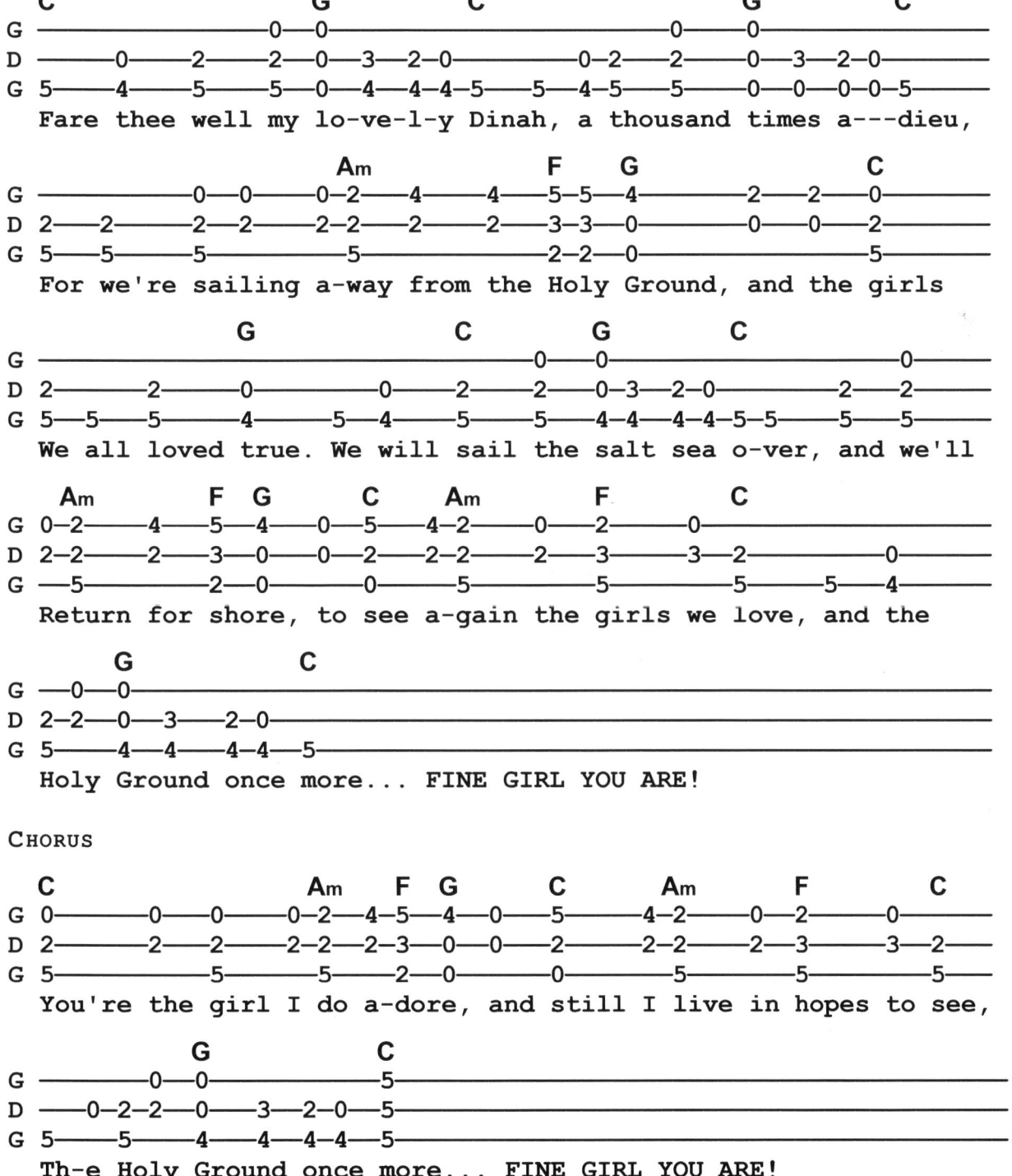

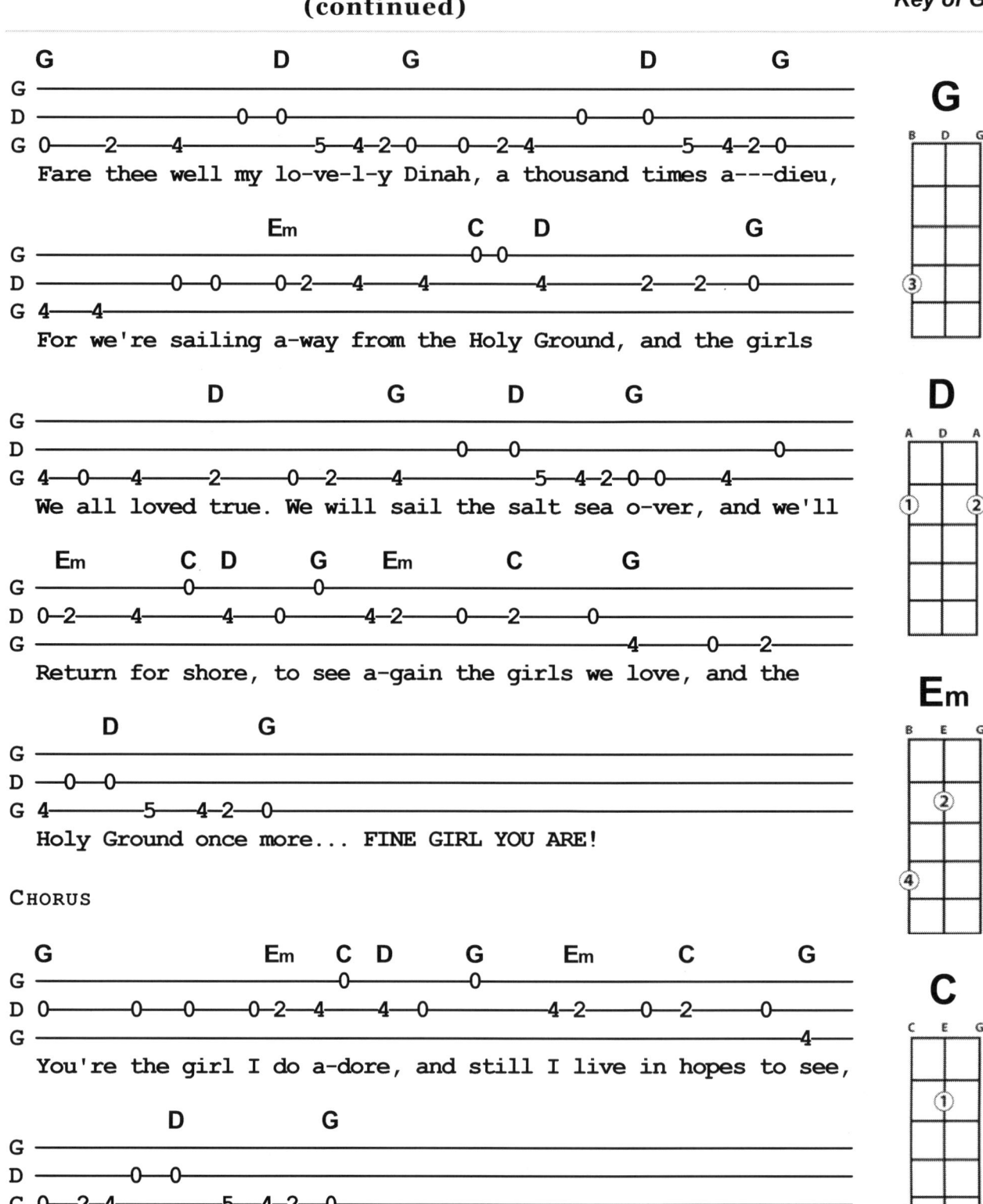

SCOTTISH-IRISH BALLAD

I'm A Man You Don't Meet Every Day (Jock Stewart)

Basic Melody

Key of C

This old folk song is of either Scottish or Irish origin, and is written from the point of view of a wealthy landowner buying rounds of drinks in a pub. This is one of the gentler of the traditional drinking songs, but very beautiful in its own right.

Words and Music

Traditional

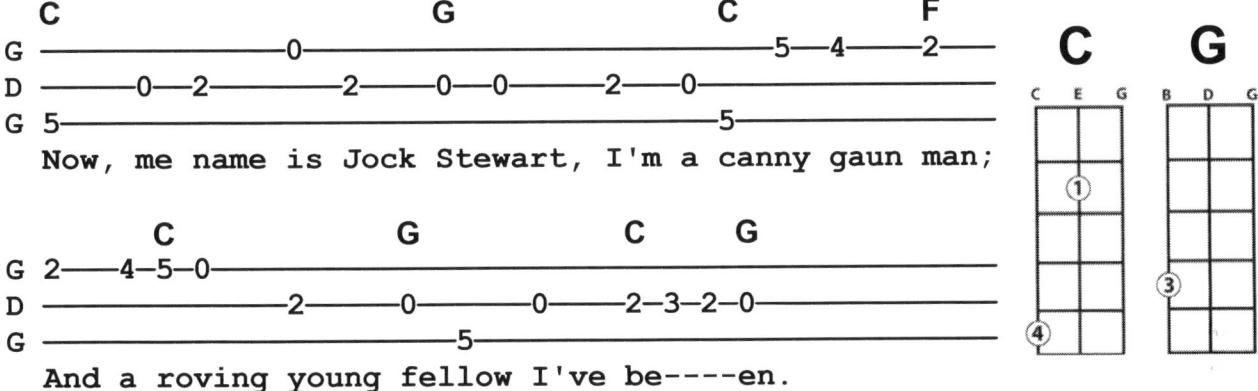

```
      C                  G                 C           F
G ———————————0————————————————————————5—4——2——
D ——0—2———————2——0—0———2—0————————————
G 5——————————————————5——————————————
  Now, me name is Jock Stewart, I'm a canny gaun man;

        C              G         C     G
G 2——4—5—0——————————————————————————
D ——————————2———0———0——2-3-2-0—————
G ——————————5—————————————————————
  And a roving young fellow I've be————en.
```

CHORUS

```
    G   C            G                 Am       F
G ————————0——————————————————————5——4——2——
D ——0—2———————2——0———2—0———————————————
G 5————————————————————5————————————————
  So be easy and free, when you're drinkin' with me;

        C              G     C
G 2——4—5—0———————————————————
D ——————————2———0———0—————————
G ——————————————5———5—————————
  I'm a man you don't meet every day.
```

Additional Verses

I have acres of land, and men at command;
And I've always a shilling to spare...

I'm a piper by trade, I'm a roving young blade;
And it's many the tunes I do play...

Let us catch well the hours, and the minutes that fly;
And we'll share them together this day...

I go out with my dogs, and my gun for to shoot;
All down by the River Kildare...

So come fill up your glass, with whiskey or wine;
And whatever the cost, I will pay...

Irish Drinking Songs Cigar Box Guitar Songbook · Copyright 2019 by Hobo Music Works · All Rights Reserved

SCOTTISH-IRISH BALLAD

I'm A Man You Don't Meet Every Day (Jock Stewart)
(continued)

Melody & Chords

Key of C

```
      C              G              C         F
G ————————0———————————————————————5—4———2—
D ———0—2———2—2———0—0———2—0———2—2———3—
G 5———0—5———5—5———4—4———4———4—5—0—0———2—
    Now, me name is Jock Stewart, I'm a canny gaun man;
```

```
         C           G         C     G
G 2——4—5—0—————————————————————————————————
D 3——3—2—2———2———0—————0———2—3—2—0—————————
G ————————0———5———4—5———4———5—5—5—4—————————
    And a roving young fellow I've be————en.
```

Chorus

```
    G    C         G              Am        F
G —————————0——————————————————————5———4———2—
D ———0—2—2———2———0———2———0————————2———2———3—
G 5—4—5—5—5———4———4———4——————————5———2———2———5—
    So be easy and free, when you're drinkin' with me;
```

```
         C           G         C
G 2——4—5—0———————————————————5—————————————
D 3——3—2—2———2———2———0————0—5—————————————
G 5———0———5———4———5—4—5—————————————————————
    I'm a man you don't meet every day.
```

Notable recordings:
- Archie Fisher, 1976
- The Tannahill Weavers, 1979
- Dougie MacLean, 1979
- The Pogues, 1985
- The Dubliners, 1992
- Schooner Fare, 1995

The Schooner Fare version is on YouTube, and highly recommended.

SCOTTISH-IRISH BALLAD

I'm A Man You Don't Meet Every Day (Jock Stewart)

Basic Melody

Key of G

(continued)

```
    G              D          G        C
G ----------------------------------0---------
D ------------0--------------------4----2-----
G 0----2---4----4---2---2----4---2-0----------
    Now, me name is Jock Stewart, I'm a canny gaun man;

           G        D       G    D
G ------0-------------------------------------
D 2--4----0-----------------------------------
G ------------4---2--0--2---4-5-4-2-----------
    And a roving young fellow I've be----en.
```

CHORUS

```
    D   G      D                   Em     C
G ----------------------------------0---------
D ------0--------------------------4----2-----
G 0--2----4---4---2---4---2----0---------------
    So be easy and free, when you're drinkin' with me;

          G        D      G
G ------0-------------------------------------
D 2--4----0-----------------------------------
G ------------4-----2----0--2--0---------------
    I'm a man you don't meet every day.
```

Chord Forms

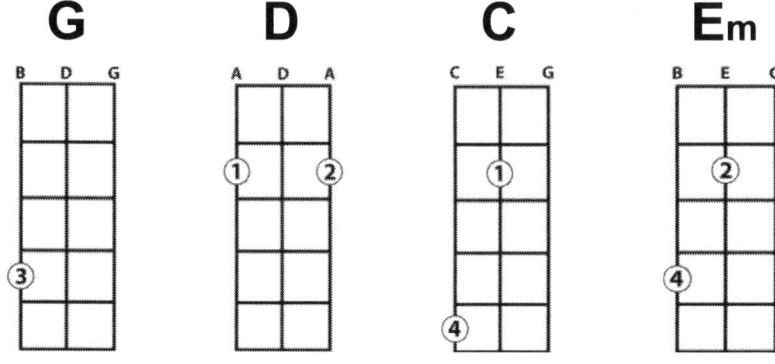

Irish Drinking Songs Cigar Box Guitar Songbook · Copyright 2019 by Hobo Music Works · All Rights Reserved

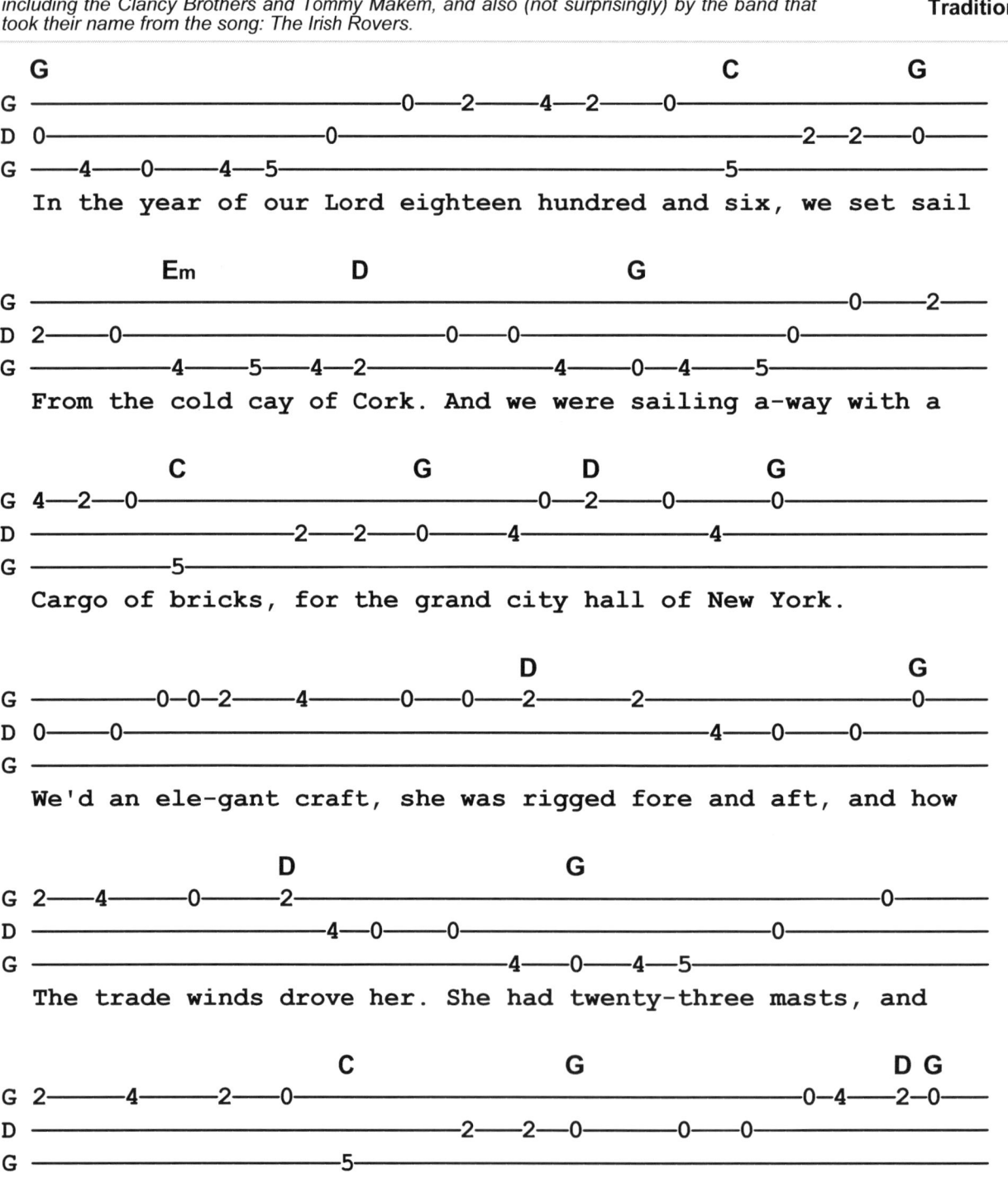

IRISH SEAFARING SONG

The Irish Rover
(continued)

Additional Verses and Chord Forms

Key of G

Additional Verses

We had one million bags of the best Sligo rags,
We had two million barrels of stone.
We had three million sides of old blind horses' hides,
We had four million barrels of bone.
We had five million hogs, and six million dogs,
And seven million barrels of porter.
And we had eight million bales of old nanny goats' tails
In the hold of the Irish Rover!

And there was Barney McGee from the banks of the Lee,
There was Hogan from County Tyrone,
And there was Johnny McGirk, who was scared stiff of work,
And a chap from Westmeath named Malone.
There was Slugger O'Toole who was drunk as a rule,
And fightin' Charlie Boyle from Dover,
And yer man Mick McGann, from the banks of the Ban,
Was the skipper of the Irish Rover.

We had sailed seven years when the measles broke out,
And the ship lost her way in a fog (GREAT FOG!)
And the whole of the crew was reduced unto two,
Just meself and the captain's old dog.
And then the ship struck a rock, oh Lord what a shock,
I nearly tumbled over... turned nine times around,
And the poor old dog was drowned...
I'm the last of the Irish Rover!

Chord Forms

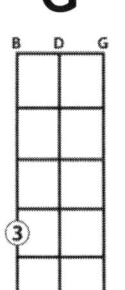

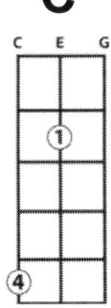
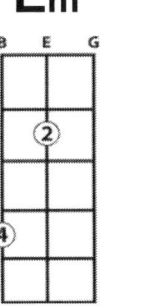

The Irish Rover
(continued)

IRISH SEAFARING SONG

Melody & Chords

Key of G

```
      G                                              C         G
G ————————————————0—2—4—2———0—0——————————
D 0—————————0——————0—0—0—0——0—2——2—2—0—
G 4—4—0——4—5—4——4—————0——0—5——5—5—4——
  In the year of our Lord eighteen hundred and six, we set sail
```

```
        Em        D            G
G ————————————————————————————————————0——2—
D 2——0—2—————0————0—0—————————0——0——0—
G 0——4—4—5—4—2——4——4—4———0—4——5-4—4——
  From the cold cay of Cork. And we were sailing a-way with a
```

```
        C         G          D        G
G 4—2—0—————————————————0—2——0——0———————
D 0—0—0—2——————2—2——0—4-0—0——0—4—0———
G 0—————5——5—5——0————2——2———2—4————
  Cargo of bricks, for the grand city hall of New York.
```

```
                              D                      G
G ————0-0-2——4————0——0—2——2——————————0——
D 0——0-0-0-0——0——0—0—0——0——4—0——0—0—
G 4——4—4———0——4——2——————2—2——2—4—
  We'd an ele-gant craft, she was rigged fore and aft, and how
```

```
              D            G
G 2——4——0——2——————————————————0———
D 0——0——0——0—4—0—0————————0——0——
G ——0————2—2—2—2—4—0—4—5——4——4——
  The trade winds drove her. She had twenty-three masts, and
```

```
            C          G              D G
G 2——4——2—0——————————————————0-4——2-0—
D 0——0——0—0—2——2—2—0——0—0—0-0—0-0—
G ——0————5——5—5—4——4—4—4-0——2-4—
  She'd stood several blasts, and we called her the Irish Rover.
```

IRISH SEAFARING SONG

The Irish Rover
(continued)

Basic Melody
Key of C

```
        C                                              F            C
G   0—————————————0——5——7——9——7——5————————2——2——0—
D   ——2—————2——3————————————————————3—————————————
G   ————5———————————————————————————————————————————
    In the year of our Lord eighteen hundred and six, we set sail

           Am      G                    C
G   2——0—————————————0——0—————————————0——5——7—
D   ——————2——3——2——0—————————2——2——3———————————
G   ————————————————————————5————————————————————
    From the cold cay of Cork. And we were sailing a-way with a

            F           C        G        C
G   9——7——5————2——2——0——4—5——7——5——4——5—
D   ——————3———————————————————————————————
G   ——————————————————————————————————————
    Cargo of bricks, for the grand city hall of New York.

                             G                 C
G   ————5—5——7——9——5——5——7——7—————————5—
D   5——5————————————————————————9——5——5———
G   ———————————————————————————————————————
    We'd an ele-gant craft, she was rigged fore and aft, and how

                       G          C
G   7——9——5——7————0——————————0——5—
D   ————————9——5——2————2——3—————————
G   ————————————5————————————————————
    The trade winds drove her. She had twenty-three masts, and

                    F         C            G C
G   7——9——7——5————2——2——0——0——0——5—9——7—5
D   ——————————3——————————————————————————
G   ——————————————————————————————————————
    She'd stood several blasts, and we called her the Irish Rover.
```

Chord Forms

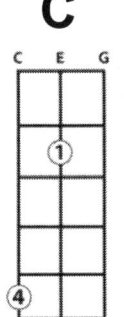
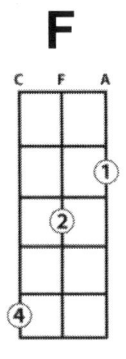
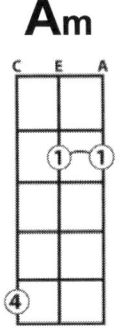
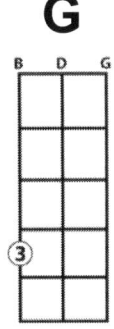

IRISH SEAFARING SONG

The Irish Rover
(continued)

Melody & Chords

Key of C

```
     C                                                      F         C
G  0——————————————0——5——7——9——7——5——————————2——2——0——
D  2——2——————————2——3——2——2——0——10-0——2——3——3——3——2——
G  5——5——5——5——5——5——0——————9——————5——5——5——5——5——
   In the year of our Lord eighteen hundred and six, we set sail
```

```
           Am          G                 C                
G  2——0——————————————0——0——————————————0——5——7——
D  2——2——2——2——3——2——0——0——0——2——————2——3-2——2——0——
G  ——————2——2——2——4——4——4——4——5——5——5-5——————
   From the cold cay of Cork. And we were sailing a-way with a
```

```
         F              C          G          C
G  9——7——5——————2——2——0——4-5——7——5——4——5——————
D  10-0——2——3——3——3——2——0-2——0——0——0——2——————
G  9——————5——————5——————5——————0——0——————0——————
   Cargo of bricks, for the grand city hall of New York.
```

```
                                     G                    C
G  ——————5-5——7——9——5——5——7——7——————————5——
D  5——5-5-5-5——5——5——5——0——0——9——5——5——5——
G  5——5——————5——————0——0——7——7——7——5——
   We'd an ele-gant craft, she was rigged fore and aft, and how
```

```
                         G          C
G  7——9——5——7——0——————————————0——————5——
D  5——5——5——0-9-5——0——2——2——3——2——5——
G  ——5——5——0——7-7——0——0——5——5——5——5——5——
   The trade winds drove her. She had twenty-three masts, and
```

```
             F                       C              G C
G  7——————9——7——5——————2——2——0——0——0——5-9——7-5——
D  5——————10——5——5——3——3——3——2——2——2——5-5——0-5——
G  ——————9——————5——————5——————5——————————0-5——
   She'd stood several blasts, and we called her the Irish Rover.
```

Chord Forms

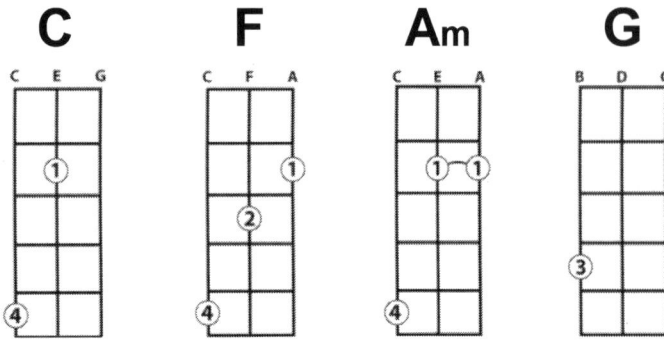

Irish Drinking Songs Cigar Box Guitar Songbook · Copyright 2019 by Hobo Music Works · All Rights Reserved

IRISH DRINKING SONG

Jug of Punch

Basic Melody
Key of C

This old song was one of the staples of the Clancy Brothers' live shows, with Patrick Clancy beautifully performing it. As he would say, the course of the song follows the same timeline of a good night of drinking: starting off softly and gently and progressively deteriorating. The lines starting with "Toora loora lo" are technically the chorus, but note the last line changes each time through to reflect the verse.

Words and Music

Traditional

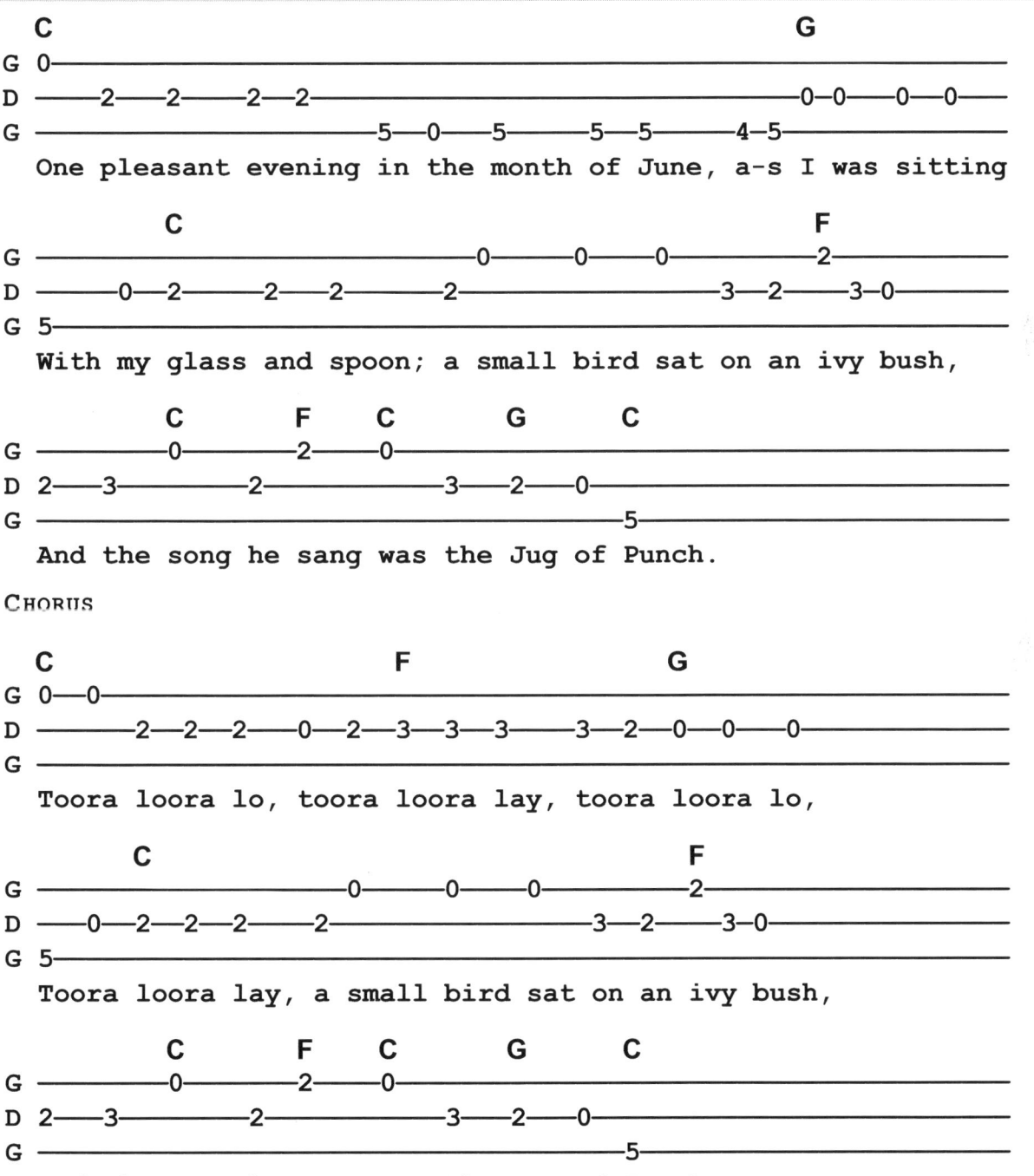

```
        C                                           G
G 0—————————————————————————————————————————————————————————————————
D ———2——2——2——2————————————————————————————————0—0————0———0——
G ————————————————5——0——5——————5—5—————4—5—————————————————
  One pleasant evening in the month of June, a-s I was sitting

         C                                    F
G ————————————————————0——————0——————0——————————————2————————
D ———0——2——2——2——————2————————————————3——2———————3—0————
G 5———————————————————————————————————————————————————————————
  With my glass and spoon; a small bird sat on an ivy bush,

        C    F    C       G    C
G ————————0——————2——0—————————————————————————————————————————
D 2——3————————2———————————3——2————0————————————————————
G ——————————————————————————————————————5—————————————————
  And the song he sang was the Jug of Punch.
```

CHORUS

```
        C                       F              G
G 0——0————————————————————————————————————————————————————————————
D ——————2—2—2——0—2—3—3—3——————3—2—0—0—0—————
G ————————————————————————————————————————————————————————————————
  Toora loora lo, toora loora lay, toora loora lo,

         C                                    F
G ————————————————————0——————0——————0——————————————2————————
D ———0——2——2——2——————2————————————————3——2———————3—0————
G 5———————————————————————————————————————————————————————————
  Toora loora lay, a small bird sat on an ivy bush,

        C    F    C       G    C
G ————————0——————2——0—————————————————————————————————————————
D 2——3————————2———————————3——2————0————————————————————
G ——————————————————————————————————————5—————————————————
  And the song he sang was the Jug of Punch.
```

See Chords and Additional Verses on Next Page.

Irish Drinking Songs Cigar Box Guitar Songbook · Copyright 2019 by Hobo Music Works · All Rights Reserved

IRISH DRINKING SONG

Jug of Punch
(continued)

Additional Verses and Chord Forms

Key of C

Additional Verses

What more diversion can a man desire,
Than to sit him down by an alehouse fire;
Upon his knee a pretty wench,
And on the table a jug of punch.
And toora loora lo, toora loora lay,
Toora loora lo, toora loora lay;
Upon his knee a pretty wench,
And on the table a jug of punch.

Let the doctors come with all their art,
They'll make no impression on my heart.
Even the cripple forgets his crutch,
When he's got outside of a jug of punch!
And toora loora lo, toora loora lay,
Toora loora lo, toora loora lay;
Even the cripple forgets his crutch,
When he's got outside of a jug of punch.

And if I get drunk, well me money's me own,
And them don't like me they can leave me 'lone;
I'll tune me fiddle and I'll rosin me bow,
And I'll be welcome where're I go!
And toora loora lo, toora loora lay,
Toora loora lo, toora loora lay,
I'll tune me fiddle and I'll rosin me bow,
And I'll be welcome wherever I go!

And when I'm dead and in my grave,
No costly tombstone will I have;
Just lay me down in my native peat,
With a jug of punch at my head and feet!
And toora loora lo, toora loora lay,
Toora loora lo, toora loora lay,
Just lay me down in my native peat...
With a jug of punch at my head and feet!

Chord Forms

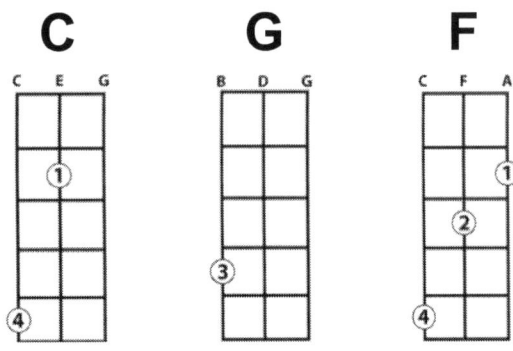

Irish Drinking Songs Cigar Box Guitar Songbook · Copyright 2019 by Hobo Music Works · All Rights Reserved

IRISH DRINKING SONG

Jug of Punch
(continued)

Melody & Chords
Key of C

```
       C                                              G
G  0————————————————————————————————————————————————————————
D  2——2——2——2——2—————————2——2——2——————2—2—0—0———0—0——
G  5——5——5——5—5——5—0——5——5—5————4-5-4-4——4—4——
   One pleasant evening in the month of June, a-s I was sitting
```

```
              C                                          F
G  ————————————————————————0——0——0—————2——
D  ——0——2——2——2————2-2——2——2——3—2—3-3—0——
G  5——4——5——5——5——5-5————5——5——5—5—5-5-2——
   With my glass and spoon; a small bird sat on an ivy bush,
```

```
           C    F    C         G    C
G  ————————0——————2—————0——————————————
D  2——3——2————2——3——2——3——2——0——2——
G  5——5——5——5—5——5——5——5——4——4——5——
   And the song he sang was the Jug of Punch.
```

CHORUS

```
       C                    F              G
G  0—0———————————————————————————————————————————
D  2——2——2——2——2——0——2——3——3——3——3——2——0——0——0——
G  5———5——5——5——4——5——5——5——5——5—5—5——4——4——4——
   Toora loora lo, toora loora lay, toora loora lo,
```

```
           C                                      F
G  ——————————————————0——0——0—————2——
D  ——0——2——2——2————2-2——2——2——3—2—3-3—0——
G  5——4——5——5——5——5-5————5——5——5—5—5-5-2————
   Toora loora lay, a small bird sat on an ivy bush,
```

```
           C    F    C         G    C
G  ————————0——————2—————0——————————————5——
D  2——3——2————2——3——2——3——2——0——2——
G  5——5——5——5—5——5——5——5——4——5——
   And the song he sang was the Jug of Punch.
```

Jug of Punch
(continued)

IRISH DRINKING SONG

Basic Melody
Key of G

```
       G                                              D
G  7—4—4—4—4—0——————0——————0—0——————0-2-2—2—2—
D  ——————————————————0——————————————4—————————
G  ———————————————————————————————————————————
```
One pleasant evening in the month of June, a-s I was sitting

```
          G                                           C
G  0——2—4——4—4———4-7——————7——————7—5—4—9-5-2—
D  ———————————————————————————————————————————
G  ———————————————————————————————————————————
```
With my glass and spoon; a small bird sat on an ivy bush,

```
        G     C    G      D    G
G  4——5—7——4—9——7—5——4—2—0
D  ———————————————————————
G  ———————————————————————
```
And the song he sang was the Jug of Punch.

Chorus

```
       G              C              D
G  7—7—4—4—4——2—4—5—5—5——————5—4—2—2—2—
D  —————————————————————————————————————
G  —————————————————————————————————————
```
Toora loora lo, toora loora lay, toora loora lo,

```
          G                                           C
G  0——2—4——4—4———4-7——————7——————7—5—4—9-5-2—
D  ———————————————————————————————————————————
G  ———————————————————————————————————————————
```
Toora loora lay, a small bird sat on an ivy bush,

```
        G     C    G      D    G
G  4——5—7——4—9——7—5——4—2—0
D  ———————————————————————
G  ———————————————————————
```
And the song he sang was the Jug of Punch.

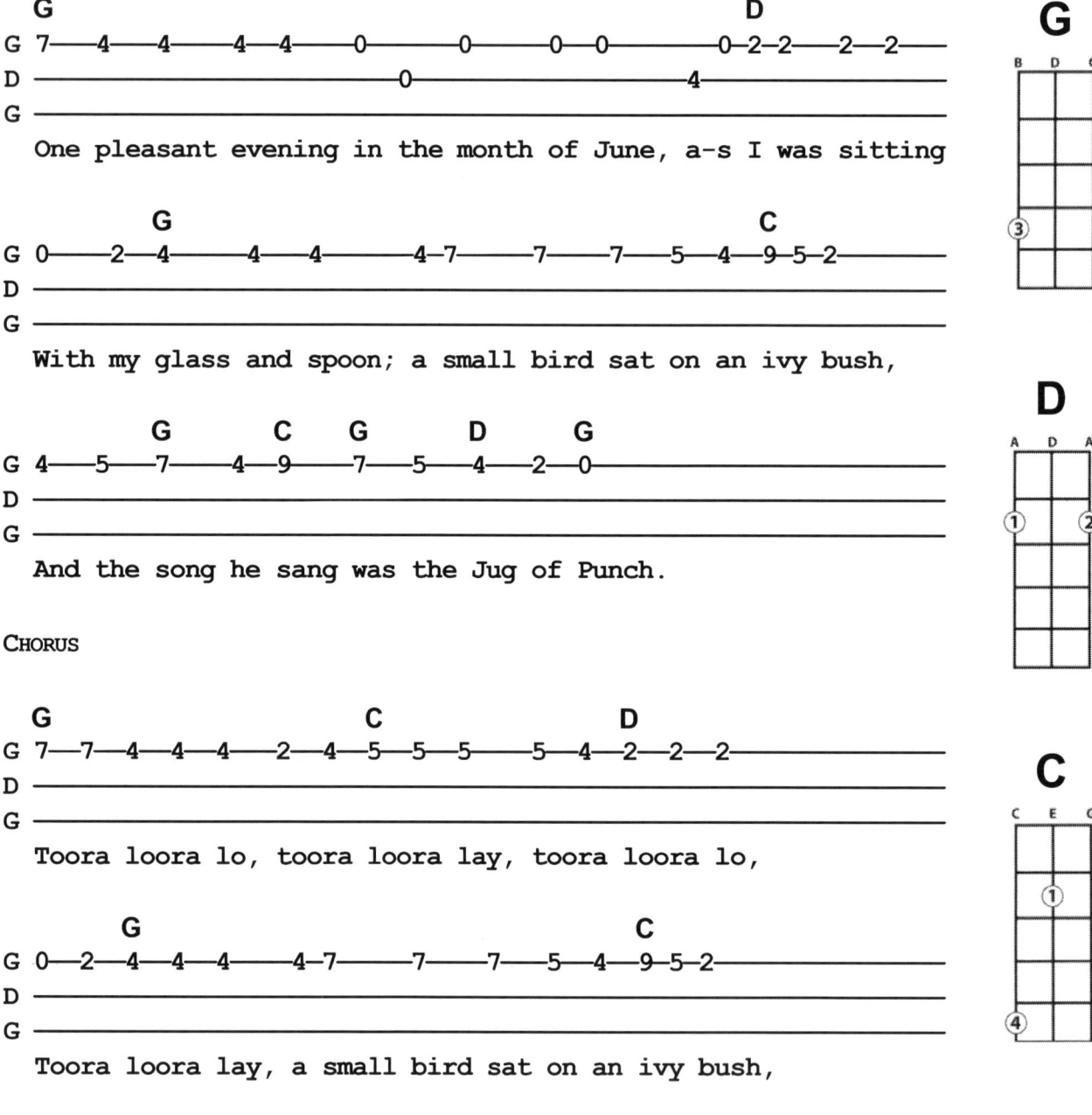

Irish Drinking Songs Cigar Box Guitar Songbook · Copyright 2019 by Hobo Music Works · All Rights Reserved

IRISH DRINKING SONG

Jug of Punch
(continued)

Melody & Chords
Key of G

```
         G                                                    D
G  7—4—4—4—4—0——0——0—0——0-2-2——2—2—
D  0——0—0—0—0—0——0——0—0——4-0-0-0——0—0—
G  0——0————0—0—4——4—4——2—2——2——
   One pleasant evening in the month of June, a-s I was sitting
```

```
            G                                    C
G  0——2—4—4—4—4-7——7——7—5—4—9————
D  0——0—0—0—0—0-0——0——0—0—0—10-10-7————
G  ———0——0——0-0——0————0——9—9—5————
   With my glass and spoon; a small bird sat on an iv-y  bush,
```

```
            G    C   G         D    G
G  4——5—7——4—9——7—5——4—2—0————
D  0——0—0——0—10—0——0—0—0—0————
G  0————0——9—0——2—2—4————
   And the song he sang was the Jug of Punch.
```

Chorus

```
         G                C                D
G  7—7—4—4—4——2—4—5—5—5——5—4—2—2—2————
D  0—0—0—0—0——0—0—2—2—2——2—2—0—0—0————
G  0——0——0————0——0—0——2——2————
   Toora loora lo, toora loora lay, toora loora lo,
```

```
            G                                    C
G  0——2—4—4—4—4-7——7——7—5—4—9————
D  0——0—0—0—0—0-0——0——0—0—0—10-10-7————
G  ———0——0——0-0——0————0——9—9—5————
   Toora loora lay, a small bird sat on an iv-y  bush,
```

```
            G    C   G         D    G
G  4——5—7——4—9——7—5——4—2—0————
D  0——0—0——0—10—0——0—0—0—0————
G  0————0——9—0——2—2—4————
   And the song he sang was the Jug of Punch.
```

IRISH DRINKING SONG

The Juice Of the Barley

Basic Melody
Key of C

The first line of the chorus of this song is a phonetic rendering of an Irish Gaelic line which goes "bainne na mbó ar na gamhna." Translated, it means "the cow's milk is alright for the calf." The next line points out that while milk might be alright for calves, it's the juice of the barley (in other words, beer) that's best for me. The Clancy Brother and Tommy Makem's version of this on YouTube, sung by Liam Clancy, is definitive.

Words and Music
Traditional

```
       C                                    F         C
G   0———————————————————————————————————2———4———5————
D   ———3———2———0———2———————2———2———3——————————————————
G   ———————————————————5————————————————————————————————
    In the sweet county Lim'rick, one cold winter's night;

       C                                    F         G
G   0———————————————————————————0———0—————————————————
D   ———3———2———0———2———————2———————————3———2———3———0——
G   ———————————————————5————————————————————————————————
    All the turf fires were burning when I first saw the light.

    G   C                                F         C
G   0———————————————————————————————2———4———5—————————
D   ———3———2———0———2———————2———2———3——————————————————
G   ———————————————————5————————————————————————————————
    And a drunken old midwife went tipsy with joy;

       C                                          F         G
G   5———7———9———————7———5———2———0—————————————————————
D   ———————————————————————————————2———3———2———3—0———
G   ————————————————————————————————————————————————————
    As she danced round the floor with her slip of a boy.
```

CHORUS

```
       G   C                    
G   0———————————————0———5———0—————————————————————————
D   ———3———2———0———2———————2——————————————————————————
G   ———————————————————5————————————————————————————————
    Singing ban-ya-na mo if an-gawn-ya,

       C                G⁷        C
G   0———————————————————————————————————————————————————
D   ———3———2———————0———2———3———0——————————————————————
G   ——————————————————————————————4———5—————————————————
    And the juice of the barley for me.
```

See Chords and Additional Verses on Next Page.

Irish Drinking Songs Cigar Box Guitar Songbook · Copyright 2019 by Hobo Music Works · All Rights Reserved

The Juice Of the Barley
(continued)

IRISH DRINKING SONG

Additional Verses and Chord Forms

Key of C

Additional Verses

Well when I was a gossoon of eight years old or so,
With me turf and me primer to school I did go;
To a dusty old school house without any door,
Where lay the school master blind drunk on the floor...

At the learning I wasn't such a genius I'm thinking,
But I soon beat the master entirely at drinking;
Not a wake or a wedding for five miles around,
But meself in the corner was sure to be found.

One Sunday the priest thread me out from the altar,
Saying you'll end up your days with your neck in a halter;
And you'll dance a fine jig between heaven and hell,
And his words they did frighten me the truth for to tell.

So the very next morning as the dawn it did break,
I went down to the vestry the pledge for to take;
And there in that room sat the priests in a bunch,
Round a big roaring fire drinking tumblers of punch.

Well from that day to this I have wandered alone,
I'm a jack of all trades and a master of none;
With the sky for me roof and the earth for me floor,
And I'll dance out my days drinking whiskey galore.

Chord Forms

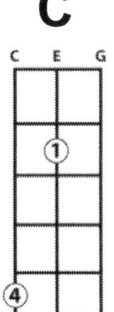
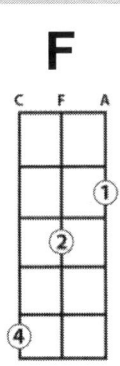
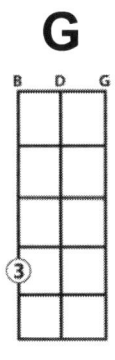

The Juice Of the Barley
(continued)

IRISH DRINKING SONG

Melody & Chords
Key of C

```
      C                              F         C
G  0————————————————————————————————————2———4———5———————
D  2———3———2———0———2———————2———2———3———3———3———2———————
G  5———5———5———5———5-5———5———5———5———5———2———0———————
   In the sweet county Lim'rick, one cold winter's night;

      C                              F         G
G  0————————————————————————0———0———————————————————————
D  2———3———2———0———2———2———2———2-3———2———3———0———————
G  5———5———5———5———5———5-5———5———5———2———2———4———————
   All the turf fires were burning when I first saw the light.

      G   C                          F         C
G  0————————————————————————————————————2———4———5———————
D  0———3———2———0———2———————2———2———3———3———3———2———————
G  4———4———5———5———5———5-5———5———5———5———2———0———————
   And a drunken old midwife went tipsy with joy;

      C                              F         G
G  5———7———9———————7———5———2———0——————————————————————
D  2———0———10——————0———2———2———2———2———3———2———3-0———
G  0———————9———————————————————5———5———5———2———2-4———
   As she danced round the floor with her slip of a boy.
```

CHORUS

```
      G   C
G  0————————————————————0———5———0———————
D  0———3———2———0———2———2———2———2———2———
G  4———4———5———5———5———5———5———0———5———
   Singing ban-ya-na mo if an-gawn-ya,

      C                  G⁷        C
G  0————————————————————————————5———————
D  2———3———2———0———2———3———0———5———————
G  5———5———5———5———5———4———4———4———5———
   And the juice of the barley for me.
```

Here's to the land of the shamrock so green,
Here's to each lad and his darlin' colleen,
Here's to the ones we love dearest and most,
May God bless old Ireland, that's this Irishman's toast!

The Juice Of the Barley
(continued)

IRISH DRINKING SONG

Basic Melody
Key of G

```
     G                              C           G
G ─────────────────────────────────────────────0───────
D 0─────────────────────────────────────2───4──────────
G ─────5───4───2───4───0───4───4───5────────────────────
  In the sweet county Lim'rick, one cold winter's night;

     G                              C           D
G ──────────────────────────────────────────────────────
D 0──────────────────────────0───0──────────────────────
G ─────5───4───2───4───0───4────────5───4───5───2───────
  All the turf fires were burning when I first saw the light.

   D  G                           C           G
G ─────────────────────────────────────────────0───────
D 0─────────────────────────────────────2───4──────────
G ─────5───4───2───4───0───4───4───5────────────────────
  And a drunken old midwife went tipsy with joy;

     G                              C           D
G 0───2───4───2───0─────────────────────────────────────
D ─────────────────────2───0────────────────────────────
G ──────────────────────────────4───5───4───5─2─────────
  As she danced round the floor with her slip of a boy.
```

CHORUS
```
     D    G                      
G ─────────────0───────────────────
D 0─────────────────0───0──────────
G ─────5───4───2───4───0───4────────
  Singing ban-ya-na mo if an-gawn-ya,

     G              D⁷          G
G ─────────────────────────────0───
D 0───────────────────4─────────────
G ─────5───4───2───4───5───2────────
  And the juice of the barley for me.
```

Chord Forms

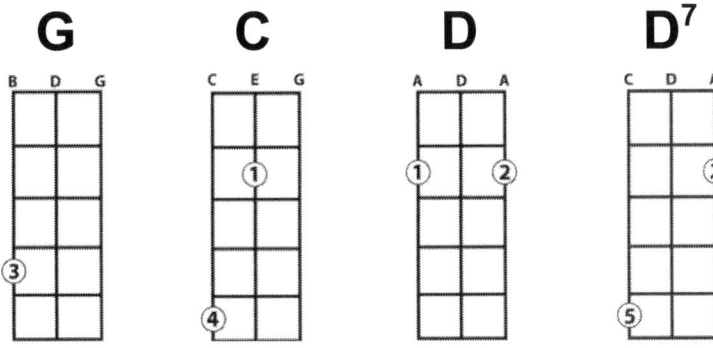

Irish Drinking Songs Cigar Box Guitar Songbook · Copyright 2019 by Hobo Music Works · All Rights Reserved

ENGLISH DRINKING SONG

Landlord Fill the Flowing Bowl (Three Jolly Coachmen)

Basic Melody

Key of G

Words and Music

Traditional

This old convivial drinking song has been around for hundreds of years, and is believed to be of English origin. It has also been known as "Three Jolly Coachmen", "For Tonight We'll Merry Merry Be", amongst other titles. There are plenty of versions on YouTube you can listen to for a reminder of how the song is supposed to go.

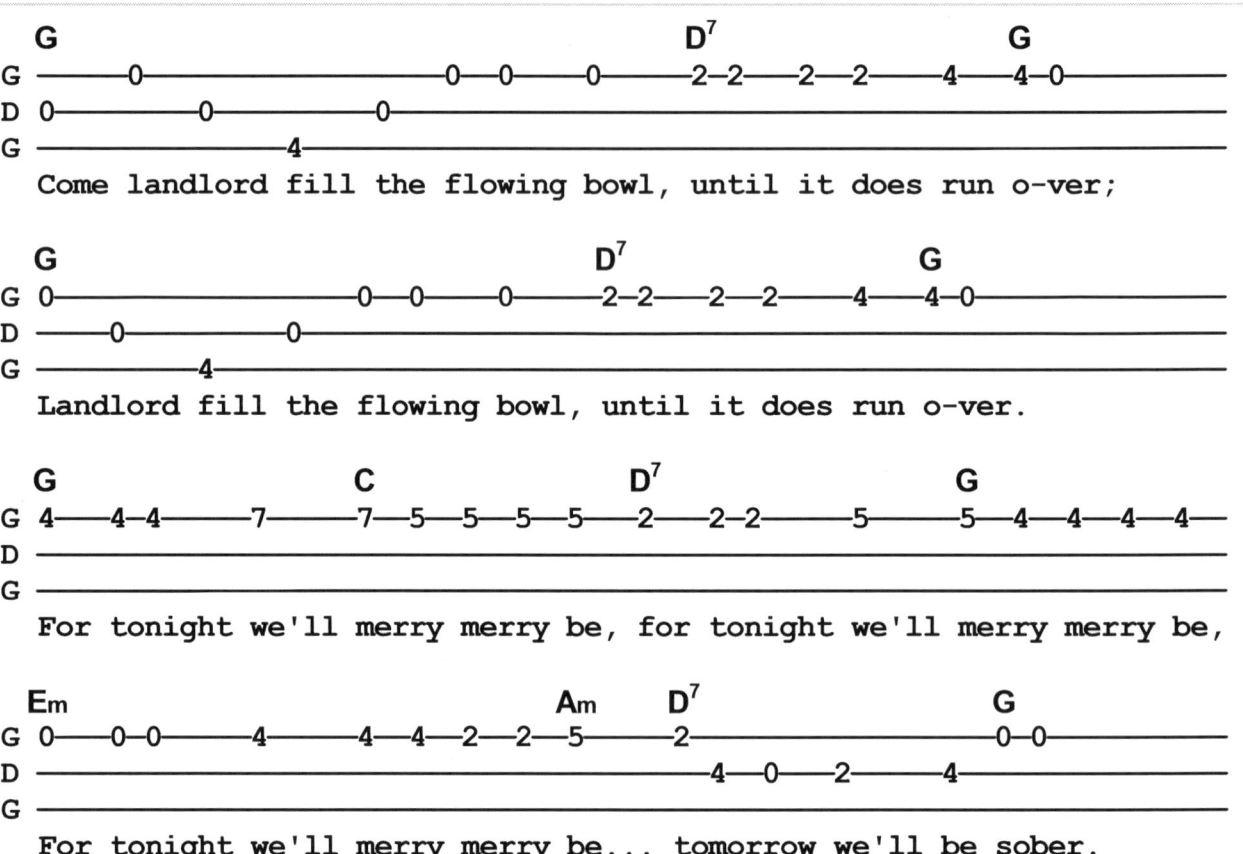

```
      G                                    D7            G
G ——0———————————0—0—0———2—2—2—2———4——4—0
D 0—————0———————0———————————————————————
G —————————4—————————————————————————————
  Come landlord fill the flowing bowl, until it does run o-ver;

      G                                    D7            G
G 0———————————0—0—0———2—2—2—2———4——4—0
D ———0———————0———————————————————————
G ———————4—————————————————————————————
  Landlord fill the flowing bowl, until it does run o-ver.

      G           C           D7            G
G 4——4—4————7——7—5—5—5—5——2—2—2————5——5—4—4—4—4——
D ——————————————————————————————————————————————
G ——————————————————————————————————————————————
  For tonight we'll merry merry be, for tonight we'll merry merry be,

      Em              Am    D7             G
G 0———0—0———4——4—4—2—2—5———2————————————0—0—
D ——————————————————————————4—0—2————4—————
G ——————————————————————————————————————————
  For tonight we'll merry merry be... tomorrow we'll be sober.
```

Chord Forms

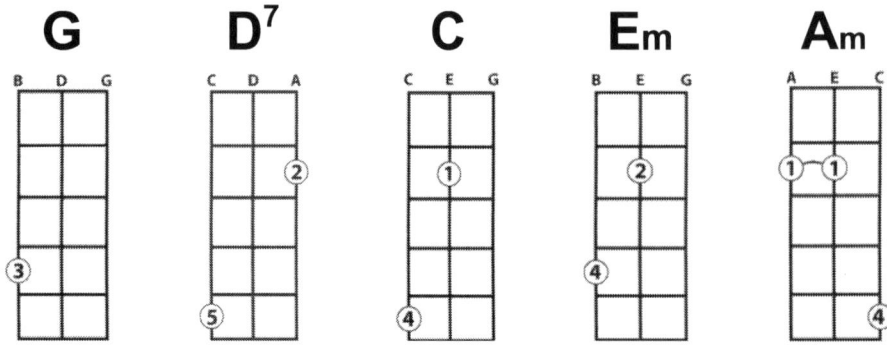

G D7 C Em Am

See Additional Verses on Next Page.

ENGLISH DRINKING SONG

Landlord Fill the Flowing Bowl
(Three Jolly Coachmen) (continued)

Melody & Chords
Key of G

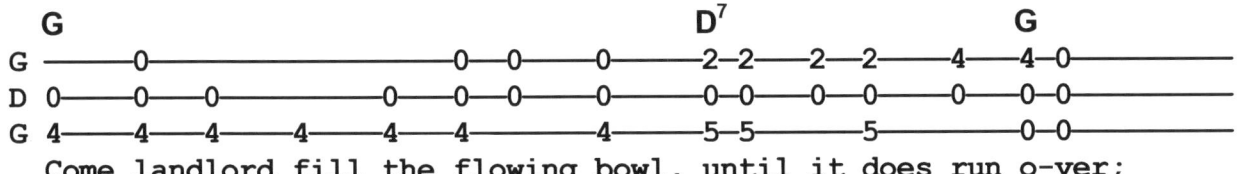
Come landlord fill the flowing bowl, until it does run o-ver;

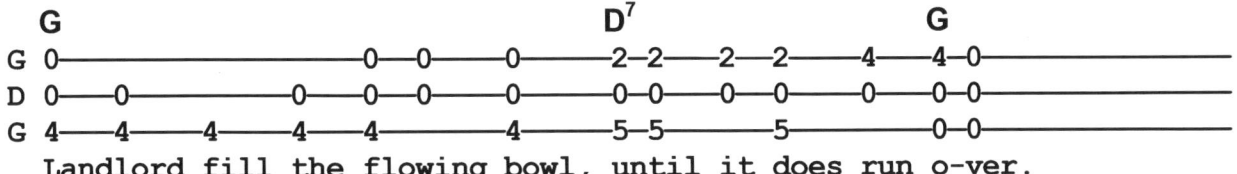
Landlord fill the flowing bowl, until it does run o-ver.

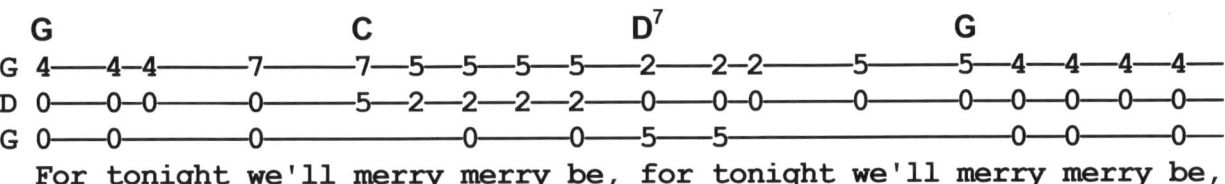
For tonight we'll merry merry be, for tonight we'll merry merry be,

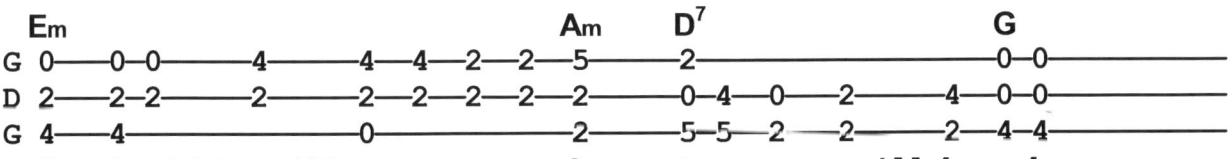
For tonight we'll merry merry be... tomorrow we'll be sober.

Additional Verses

For each verse, repeat the first two lines twice each time through, then repeat the third line three times, as spelled out in the first verse below.

Three jolly coachmen sat in an English tavern
Three jolly coachmen sat in an English tavern,
And they decided,
And they decided,
And they decided...
To have another flagon!

Here's to the man who drinks weak ale,
And goes to bed quite sober; (2X)
He fades as the leaves do fade (3X)
That drop off in October.

Here's to the man who drinks strong beer,
And goes to bed right mellow; (2X)
He lives as he ought to live (3X)
And dies a jolly good fellow.

Here's to the maid who steals a kiss,
And runs to tell her mother; (2X)
She's a foolish foolish thing (3X)
She'll never get another!

Here's to the girl who steals a kiss,
And comes to steal another; (2X)
She's a boon to all mankind (3X)
Soon she'll be a mother!

Here's to the one who drinks our ale,
And never does repay us; (2X)
Soon he will drink alone (3X)
And learn to be more generous!

Irish Drinking Songs Cigar Box Guitar Songbook · Copyright 2019 by Hobo Music Works · All Rights Reserved

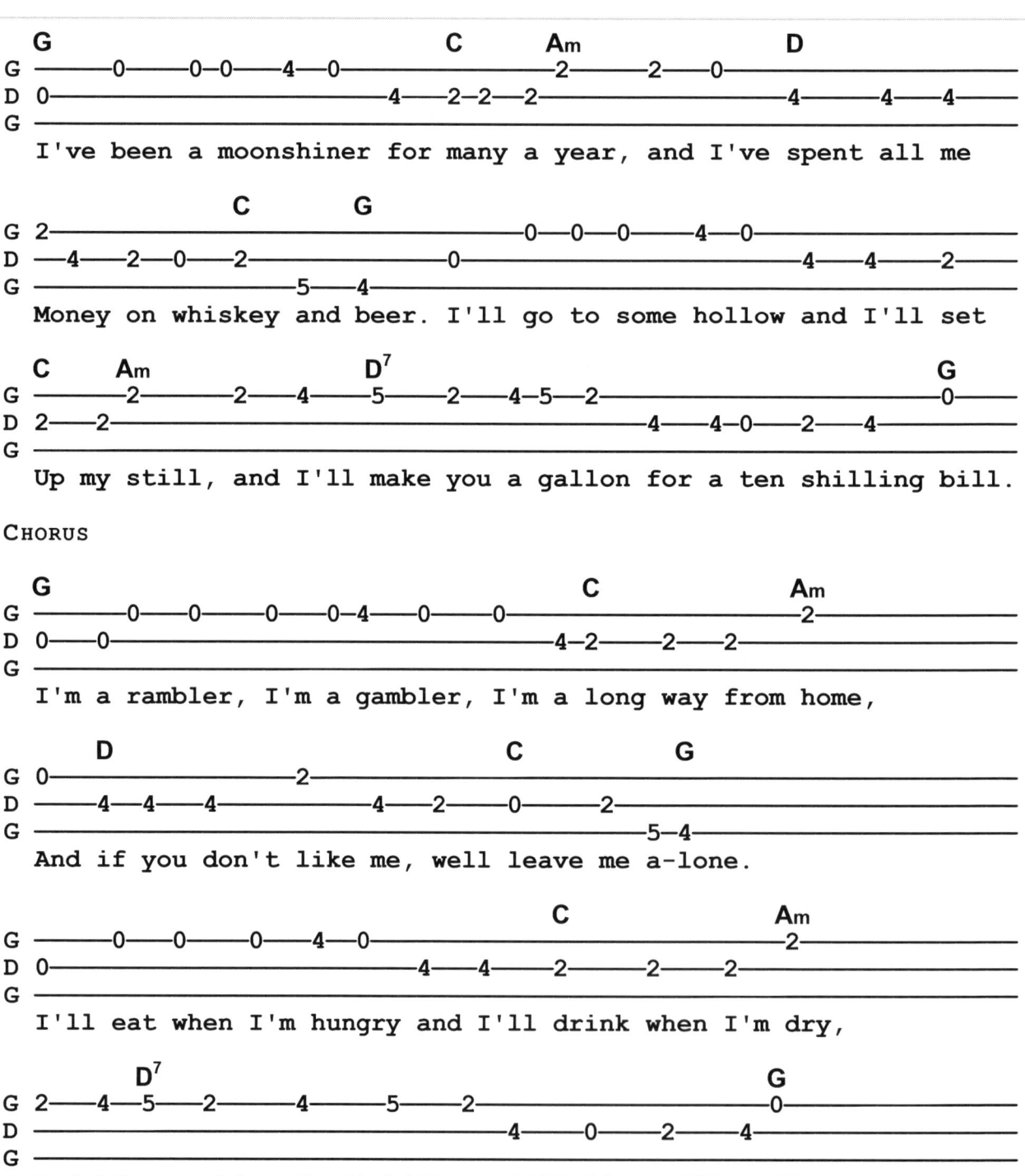

IRISH DRINKING SONG

The Moonshiner (continued)

Chord Forms and Additional Verses
Key of G

Chord Forms

G   **C**   **Am**   **D**

Additional Verses

I'll go to some hollow in this counterie,
Ten gallons of wash I can go on a spree;
No women to follow, the world is all mine,
I love none so well as I love the moonshine.

Oh, moonshine, dear moonshine, oh, how I love thee,
You killed me old father, but dare you try me;
Now bless all moonshiners and bless all moonshine,
Their breath smells as sweet as the dew on the vine.

IRISH/CELTIC

The Moonshiner (continued)

Melody & Chords
Key of G

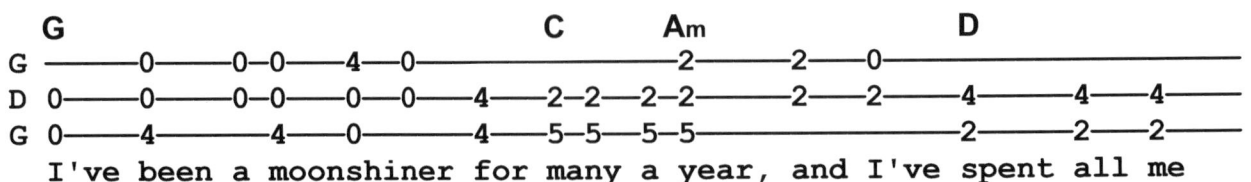
I've been a moonshiner for many a year, and I've spent all me

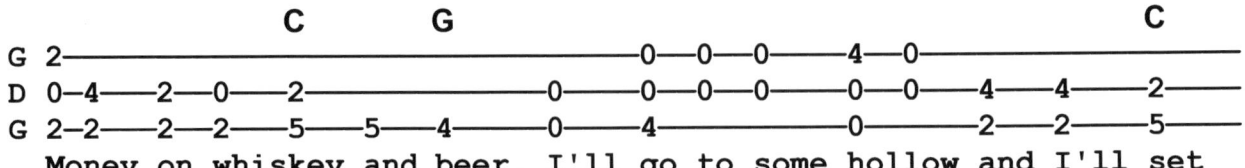
Money on whiskey and beer. I'll go to some hollow and I'll set

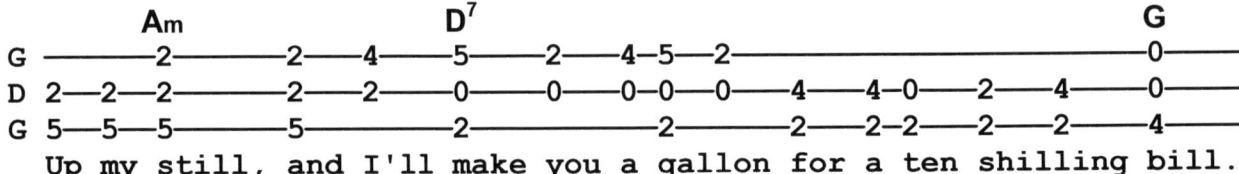
Up my still, and I'll make you a gallon for a ten shilling bill.

CHORUS

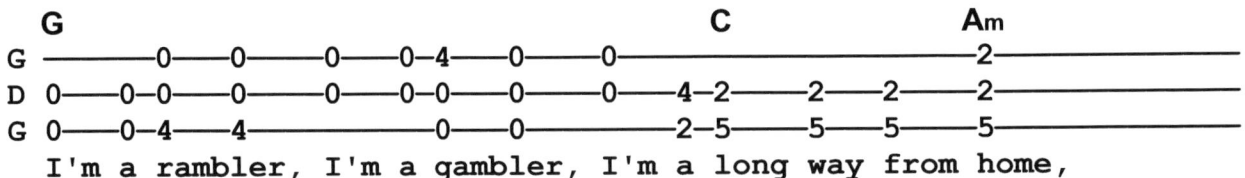
I'm a rambler, I'm a gambler, I'm a long way from home,

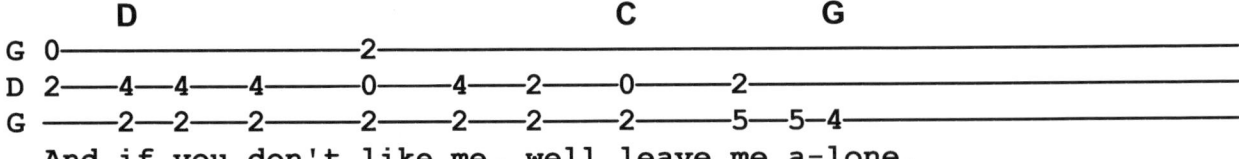
And if you don't like me, well leave me a-lone.

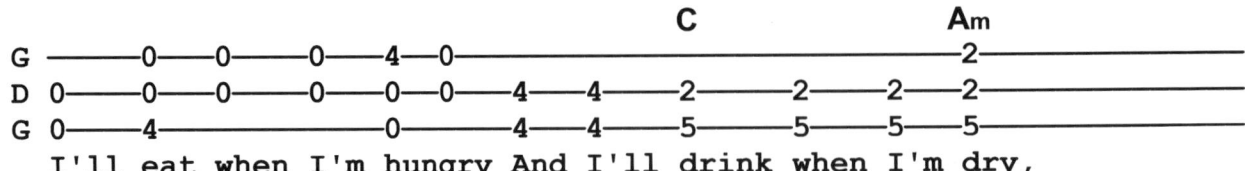
I'll eat when I'm hungry And I'll drink when I'm dry,

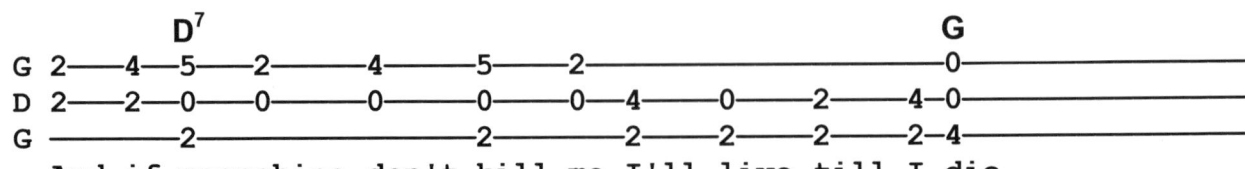
And if moonshine don't kill me I'll live till I die.

See Chord Forms and Additional Verses on Previous Page

SCOTTISH-IRISH DRINKING SONG

Nancy Whiskey

Basic Melody
Key of G

Words and Music
Traditional

There have been many different versions of this song over the years, and it has gone by a number of names. It has long been a part of both the Irish and the Scottish folk traditions. It tells the tale of a weaver from Carlton in Scotland (a small town long ago absorbed by Glasgow) who lets his love of whiskey get the better of him.

```
    G    Em      C     D       G    Em      C     D
G   0——2—4——4——0—2——0————————0——2—4——7——7—9—9————7—
D   ——————————————————2——0—————————————————————————
G   ————————————————————————————————————————————————
```
I'm a weaver a Carlton weaver, I'm a rash and a rovin' blade.

```
    G    Em     C     D       G    Em      C     D
G   9—7——4——0——2——0————————0——0—4—4——0——2—0—————————
D   ——————————————2——0———————————————————————2——0——
G   ————————————————————————————————————————————————
```
I have silver in my pockets, and I follow the rovin' tra-de.

CHORUS

```
    G    Em     C     D       G    Em     D     G
G   0——2——4——4——2——0————————0——2——4——7——4—2—0——————
D   ——————————————2——0——————————————————————————————
G   ————————————————————————————————————————————————
```
Whiskey whiskey, Nancy Whiskey; whiskey, whiskey Nancy-o.

Additional Verses

As I walked out in Glasgow City,
Nancy Whiskey I chanced to smell;
I went in, sat down beside her.
Seven long years, I loved her well.

The more I kissed her, the more I loved her.
The more I kissed her, the more she smiled;
I forgot my mother's teaching,
Nancy soon had me beguiled.

When I rose early in the morning,
To quench my thirst it was my need.
I tried to rise but was not able,
Nancy had me by the knees.

Well I'll go back to the Carlton weaving,
I'll surely make those shuttles fly;
For I'll make more at the Carlton weaving
Than every I did in the roving way.

So come all you weavers, you Carlton weavers;
Come all you weavers where ere you be;
Beware of whiskey, Nancy Whiskey,
She'll ruin you as she ruined me.

Chord Forms

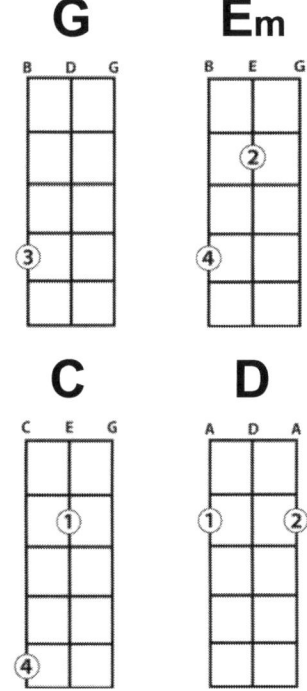

Irish Drinking Songs Cigar Box Guitar Songbook · Copyright 2019 by Hobo Music Works · All Rights Reserved

SCOTTISH-IRISH DRINKING SONG

Nancy Whiskey (continued)

Two Versions
Keys of G & C

Melody & Chords - Key of G

```
     G     Em         C         D         G     Em         C         D
G  0——2—4——4———0—2———0——————————0——2—4——7———7—9—9——————7————
D  0——————0—2——2———0—2———2———2—0———0——0—2——0———0—5—5——————7————
G  4——————0—0——0—5——5———5—2———4———0——0—0——5—5——————7————

     G     Em         C         D         G     Em         C         D
G  9—7————4——0———2—0——————————0——0—4—4———0——2—0————————————
D  9—0————0—2——2———2—2———2—0———0——0—2—2———2——2—2———2——0————
G  ——————0——5—5——5—2———4———0———0———5—5————5——2————

     G     Em         C         D         G     Em         D     G
G  0——2—4——4———2—0——————————0——2——4——7———4—2—0————
D  0——————0—2——2———2—2———2—0———0——0—2——0———0—0—0————
G  4——————0—0——5—5——5—2———4———0———2—2—4————
```

I'm a weaver a Carlton weaver, I'm a rash and a rovin' blade.
I have silver in my pockets, and I follow the rovin' tra-de.
Whiskey whiskey, Nancy Whiskey; whiskey, whiskey Nancy-o.

Basic Melody - Key of C

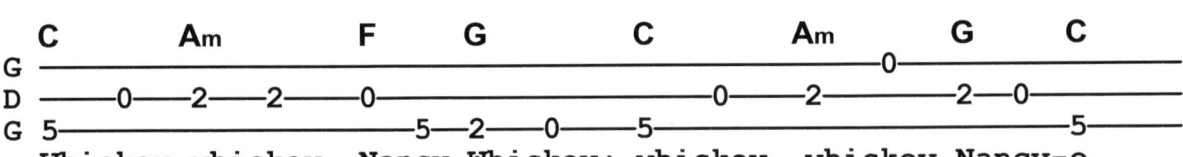

I'm a weaver a Carlton weaver, I'm a rash and a rovin' blade.
I have silver in my pockets, and I follow the rovin' tra-de.
Whiskey whiskey, Nancy Whiskey; whiskey, whiskey Nancy-o.

Chord Forms (Key of C)

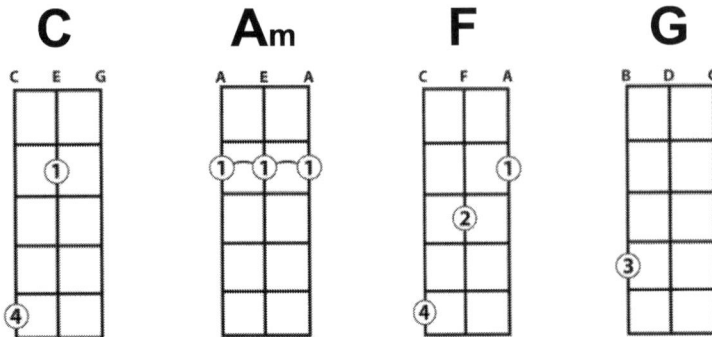

Irish Drinking Songs Cigar Box Guitar Songbook · Copyright 2019 by Hobo Music Works · All Rights Reserved

IRISH DRINKING SONG

The Night That Paddy Murphy Died

Basic Melody

Key of G

Words and Music

Traditional

This great old traditional song is thought to have originated among Irish immigrants in Newfoundland in the late 1800's. It tells the tale of a raucous group of Irish folks holding a wake for their deceased friend Paddy Murphy. The band Great Big Sea's recording of this classic has helped revive its popularity.

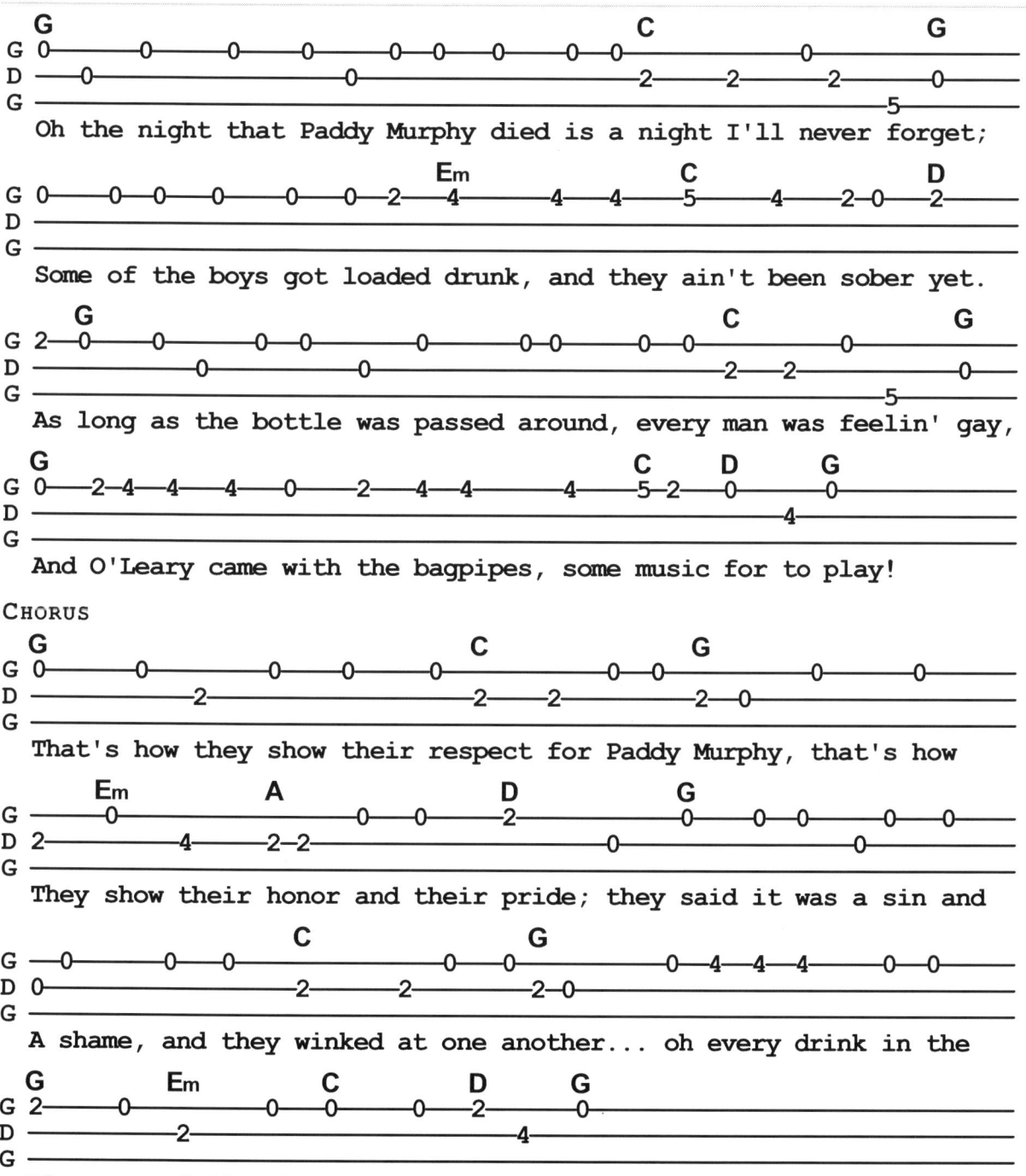

See Chord Forms and Additional Verses on Next Page

Irish Drinking Songs Cigar Box Guitar Songbook · Copyright 2019 by Hobo Music Works · All Rights Reserved

IRISH DRINKING SONG

The Night That Paddy Murphy Died (continued)

Chord Forms and Additional Verses

Key of G

Chord Forms

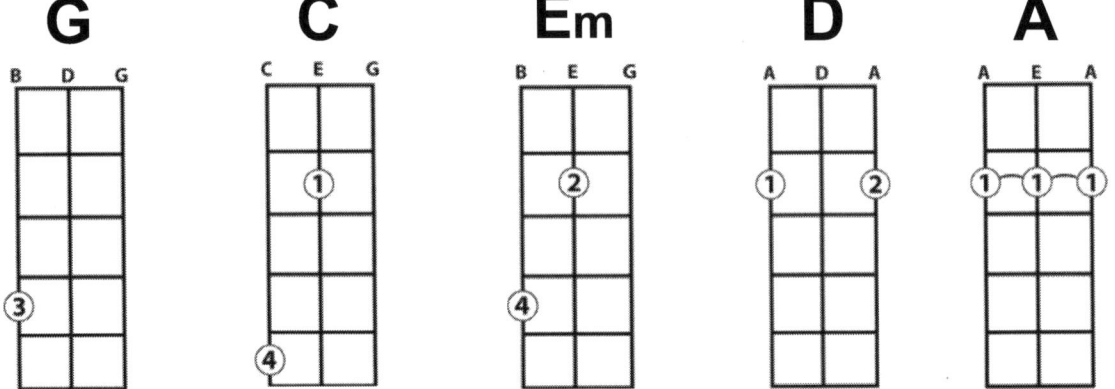

Additional Verses

As Mrs. Murphy sat in the corner, pourin' out her grief;
Kelly and his gang came tearing down the street.
They went into an empty room, and a bottle of whiskey stole;
They put the bottle with the corpse, to keep the whiskey cold!

At two o'clock in the morning, after emptyin' the jug;
Doyle lifts up the icebox lid, to see poor Paddy's mug.
They stopped the clock so Mrs. Murphy couldn't tell the time,
And at quarter after two they argued it was nine!

Well they emptied out the jugs, but still they had a thirst;
The next thing they had done, well you'll think it was the worst;
And Mrs. Murphy fainted when the news fell on her ears,
They scraped the ice right off the corpse, and put it in their beers!

Well we stopped the hearse on George's Street, outside some damn saloon;
We all went in and half-past eight, and staggered out at noon.
We went down to the graveyard, so holy and sublime...
Found out when we got there, we'd left the corpse behind!

IRISH DRINKING SONG

The Night That Paddy Murphy Died (continued)

Melody & Chords

Key of G

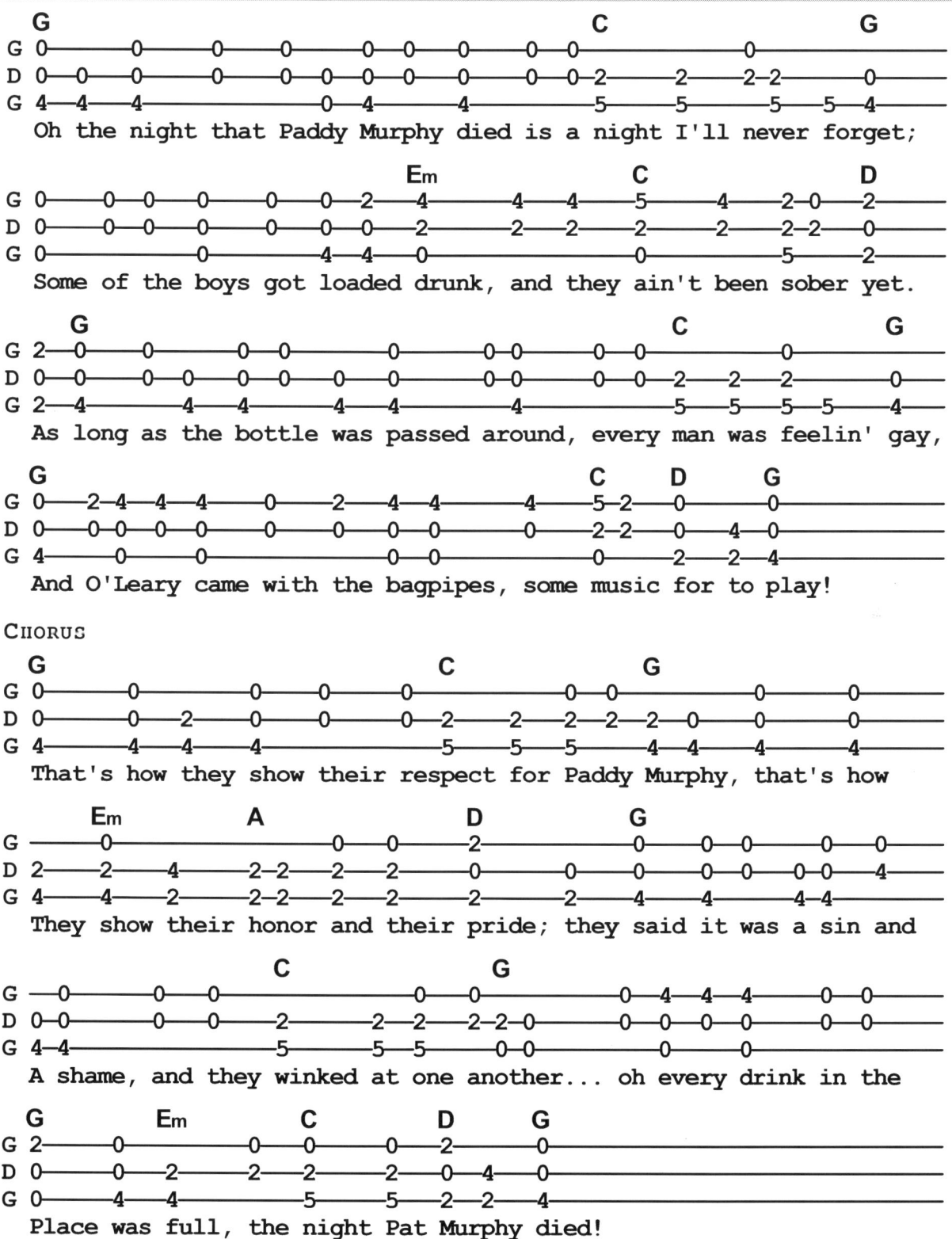

IRISH DRINKING SONG

The Night That Paddy Murphy Died (continued)

Basic Melody

Key of C

```
          C                             F            C
G ─────────────────────────────────────────────────────────
D ─────────────────────────────────────────────────────────
G 5──0──5────5────5─0─5─5────5────5─5─2────2────5─2────2──0─
  Oh the night that Paddy Murphy died is a night I'll never forget;

                         Am           F            G
G ─────────────────────────────────────────────────────────
D ──────────────0──2────2──2────3────2──0────0─────────────
G 5────5─5──5────5──5─────────────────────────────5────────
  Some of the boys got loaded drunk, and they ain't been sober yet.

          C                             F            C
G ─────────────────────────────────────────────────────────
D 0─────────────────────────────────────────────────────────
G ───5────5─0──5─5──0──5────5─5────5─5─2────2──5─2────0─────
  As long as the bottle was passed around, every man was feelin' gay,

          C                             F    G    C
G ─────────────────────────────────────────────────────────
D ──0─2──2──2─────0──2──2─────2────3─0──────────────────────
G 5─────────────5─────────────────────────5────4──5────────
  And O'Leary came with the bagpipes, some music for to play!
```

CHORUS
```
          C                             F            C
G ─────────────────────────────────────────────────────────
D ─────────────────────────────────────────────────────────
G 5────5──2──5────5────5─2──2────5─5──2──0────5────5────────
  That's how they show their respect for Paddy Murphy, that's how

          Am         D         G         C
G ─────────────────────────────────────────────────────────
D ────────────────────────0─────────────────────────────────
G 2────5────4──2─2────5──5────────0──5────5─5────0─5──5─────
  They show their honor and their pride; they said it was a sin and

                                   F              C
G ─────────────────────────────────────────────────────────
D ─────────────────────────────────────────2──2──2──────────
G 0─5────5──5────2────2─5──5─2─0──────5────────────5────5─5─
  A shame, and they winked at one another... oh every drink in the

          C     Am    F    G    C
G ─────────────────────────────────────────────────────────
D 0─────────────────────0───────────────────────────────────
G ────5──2──5────5──5────────4──5───────────────────────────
  Place was full, the night Pat Murphy died!
```

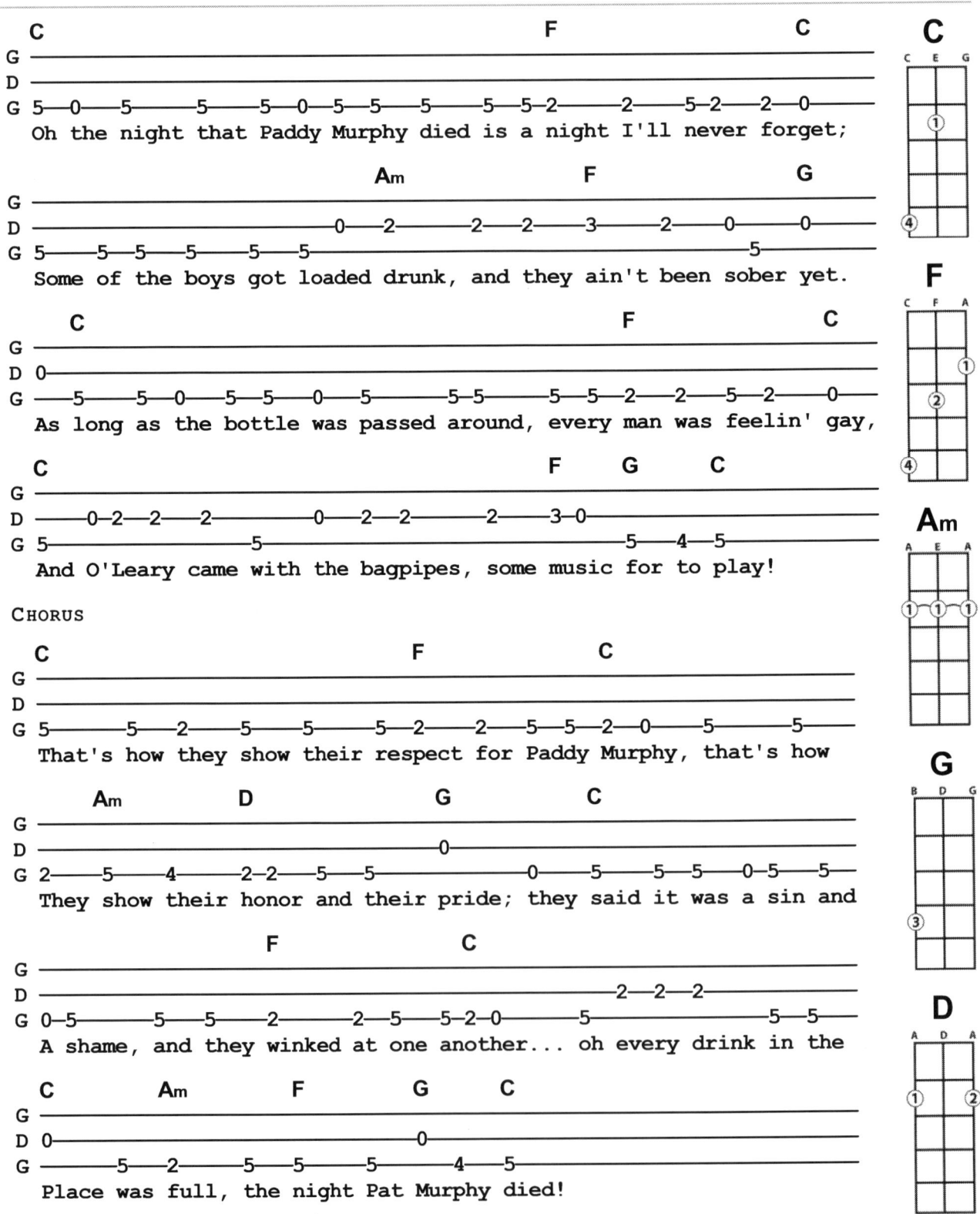

SEA SHANTY / DRINKING SONG

Paddy Doyle's Boots

Basic Melody
Key of G

According to folk history, this was a sea shanty specifically for "bunting" the main sail of the old sailing ships. The rhythm and words were timed to the men's' movements, and the "yah" on each line was where the sailors would have to perform a particularly heavy heave of the bundled sail. Each of the lines below is technically a separate verse.

Words and Music
Traditional

```
       D    G  D    G         C    Em         D         G
G  ————0——2—0-2-4————————5————4———4—4——2———0——2——0——
D  0—0————————————————0————————————————————————————
G  ——————————————————————————————————————————————
   To me way-ay, ay-ay, yah!  We'll pay Paddy Doyle for his boots.

       D    G  D    G         C    Em         D         G
G  ————0——2—0-2-4————————5————4———4—4——2———0——2——0——
D  0—0————————————————0————————————————————————————
G  ——————————————————————————————————————————————
   To me way ay, ay-ay, yah.  We'll all drink whisky and gin.

       D    G  D    G         C    Em         D         G
G  ————0——2—0-2-4————————5————4———4—4——2-0——2——0——
D  0—0————————————————0————————————————————————————
G  ——————————————————————————————————————————————
   To me way ay, ay-ay, yah!  We'll all shave under the chin.

       D    G  D    G         C    Em         D         G
G  ————0——2—0-2-4————————5————4———4—4——2———0——2——0——
D  0—0————————————————0————————————————————————————
G  ——————————————————————————————————————————————
   To me way ay, ay-ay, yah!  We'll all throw muck at the cook.

       D    G  D    G         C       Em         D         G
G  ————0——2—0-2-4————————5——5——4———4—4——2———0——2——0——
D  0—0————————————————0————————————————————————————
G  ——————————————————————————————————————————————
   To me way ay, ay-ay, yah!  For the crusty old man on the poop.

       D    G  D    G         C    Em         D         G
G  ————0——2—0-2-4————————5————4———4—4——2———0——2——0——
D  0—0————————————————0————————————————————————————
G  ——————————————————————————————————————————————
   To me way ay, ay-ay, yah!  We'll pay Paddy Doyle for his boots.
```

Chord Forms

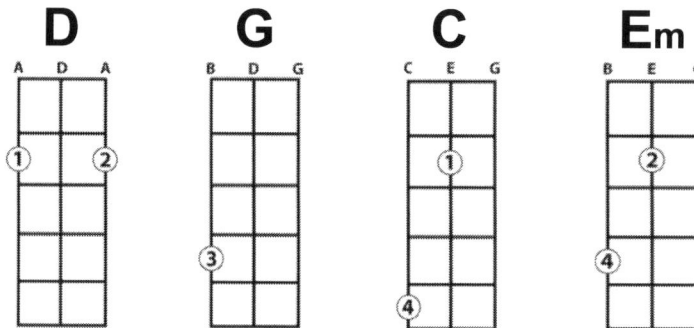

Irish Drinking Songs Cigar Box Guitar Songbook · Copyright 2019 by Hobo Music Works · All Rights Reserved

Paddy Doyle's Boots (continued)

SEA SHANTY/DRINKING SONG

Melody & Chords — Key of G

```
     D    G   D    G        C      Em      D        G
G ———————0———2———0-2-4————5———————4———4———4—2————0———2———0————
D 0———0———0———0———0-0-0—0————2———2———2———2———0————0———0———0————
G 2———2———4———2———————0—0————0———0———0———0———2————2———2———4————
```
To me way-ay, ay-ay, yah! We'll pay Paddy Doyle for his boots.

```
     D    G   D    G        C      Em      D        G
G ———————0———2———0-2-4————5———————4———4———4—2————0———2———0————
D 0———0———0———0———0-0-0—0————2———2———2———2———0————0———0———0————
G 2———2———4———2———————0—0————0———0———0———0———2————2———2———4————
```
To me way ay, ay-ay, yah. We'll all drink whisky and gin.

```
     D    G   D    G        C      Em      D        G
G ———————0———2———0-2-4————5———————4———4———4—2-0————2———0————
D 0———0———0———0———0-0-0—0————2———2———2———2———0-0————0———0————
G 2———2———4———2———————0—0————0———0———0———0———2————2———2———4————
```
To me way ay, ay-ay, yah! We'll all shave under the chin.

```
     D    G   D    G        C      Em      D        G
G ———————0———2———0-2-4————5———————4———4———4—2————0———2———0————
D 0———0———0———0———0-0-0—0————2———2———2———2———0————0———0———0————
G 2———2———4———2———————0—0————0———0———0———0———2————2———2———4————
```
To me way ay, ay-ay, yah! We'll all throw muck at the cook.

```
     D    G   D    G        C      Em      D        G
G ———————0———2———0-2-4————5———5———4———4———4—2————0———2———0————
D 0———0———0———0———0-0-0—0————2———2———2———2———2———0———0———0————
G 2———2———4———2———————0—0————0———0———0———0———0———2———2———2———4————
```
To me way ay, ay-ay, yah! For the crusty old man on the poop.

```
     D    G   D    G        C      Em      D        G
G ———————0———2———0-2-4————5———————4———4———4—2————0———2———0————
D 0———0———0———0———0-0-0—0————2———2———2———2———0————0———0———0————
G 2———2———0———2———2-2-0-0————0———0———0———0———2————2———2———2————
```
To me way ay, ay-ay, yah! We'll pay Paddy Doyle for his boots.

SEA SHANTY/DRINKING SONG

Paddy Doyle's Boots
(continued)

Basic Melody
Key of C

```
    G     C   G      C       F     Am        G         C
G ─────────────────────────────────────────────────────────────
D ───────0───────0─2──────3─────2───2───2─0────────0──────────
G 0──0─5─────5──────0─────────────────────────5─────5─────────
  To me way-ay, ay-ay, yah! We'll pay Paddy Doyle for his boots.

    G     C   G      C       F     Am        G         C
G ─────────────────────────────────────────────────────────────
D ───────0───────0─2──────3─────2───2─────0────────0──────────
G 0──0─5─────5──────0─────────────────────────5─────5─────────
  To me way ay, ay-ay, yah. We'll all drink whisky and gin.

    G     C   G      C       F     Am        G         C
G ─────────────────────────────────────────────────────────────
D ───────0───────0─2──────3─────2───2─────0────────0──────────
G 0──0─5─────5──────0─────────────────────────5─────5─────────
  To me way ay, ay-ay, yah! We'll all shave under the chin.

    G     C   G      C       F     Am        G         C
G ─────────────────────────────────────────────────────────────
D ───────0───────0─2──────3─────2───2─────0────────0──────────
G 0──0─5─────5──────0─────────────────────────5─────5─────────
  To me way ay, ay-ay, yah! We'll all throw muck at the cook.

    G     C   G      C       F       Am          G         C
G ─────────────────────────────────────────────────────────────
D ───────0───────0─2──────3───3───2───2───2─0────────0────────
G 0──0─5─────5──────0─────────────────────────5─────5─────────
  To me way ay, ay-ay, yah! For the crusty old man on the poop.

    G     C   G      C       F     Am        G         C
G ─────────────────────────────────────────────────────────────
D ───────0───────0─2──────3─────2───2─2─0────────0────────────
G 0──0─5─────5──────0─────────────────────────5─────5─────────
  To me way ay, ay-ay, yah! We'll pay Paddy Doyle for his boots.
```

Chord Forms

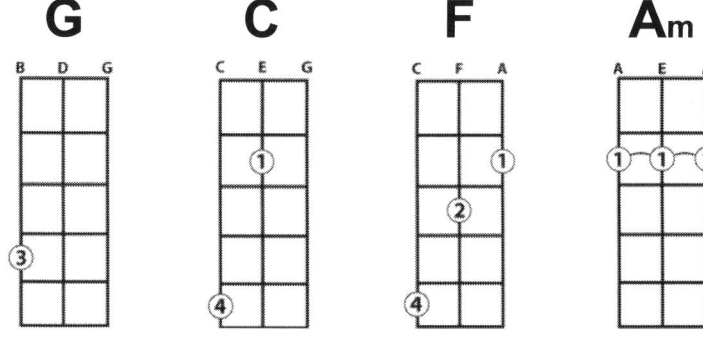

Irish Drinking Songs Cigar Box Guitar Songbook · Copyright 2019 by Hobo Music Works · All Rights Reserved

SCOTTISH BALLAD

The Parting Glass

Basic Melody
Key of Em

Words and Music
Traditional

This beautiful Scottish song first appeared In print in the 1770's, and remains a favorite parting and farewell song at Irish and Scottish parties and sessions. It is often performed acapella. The words below are somewhat modernized from the earlier Scottish versions.

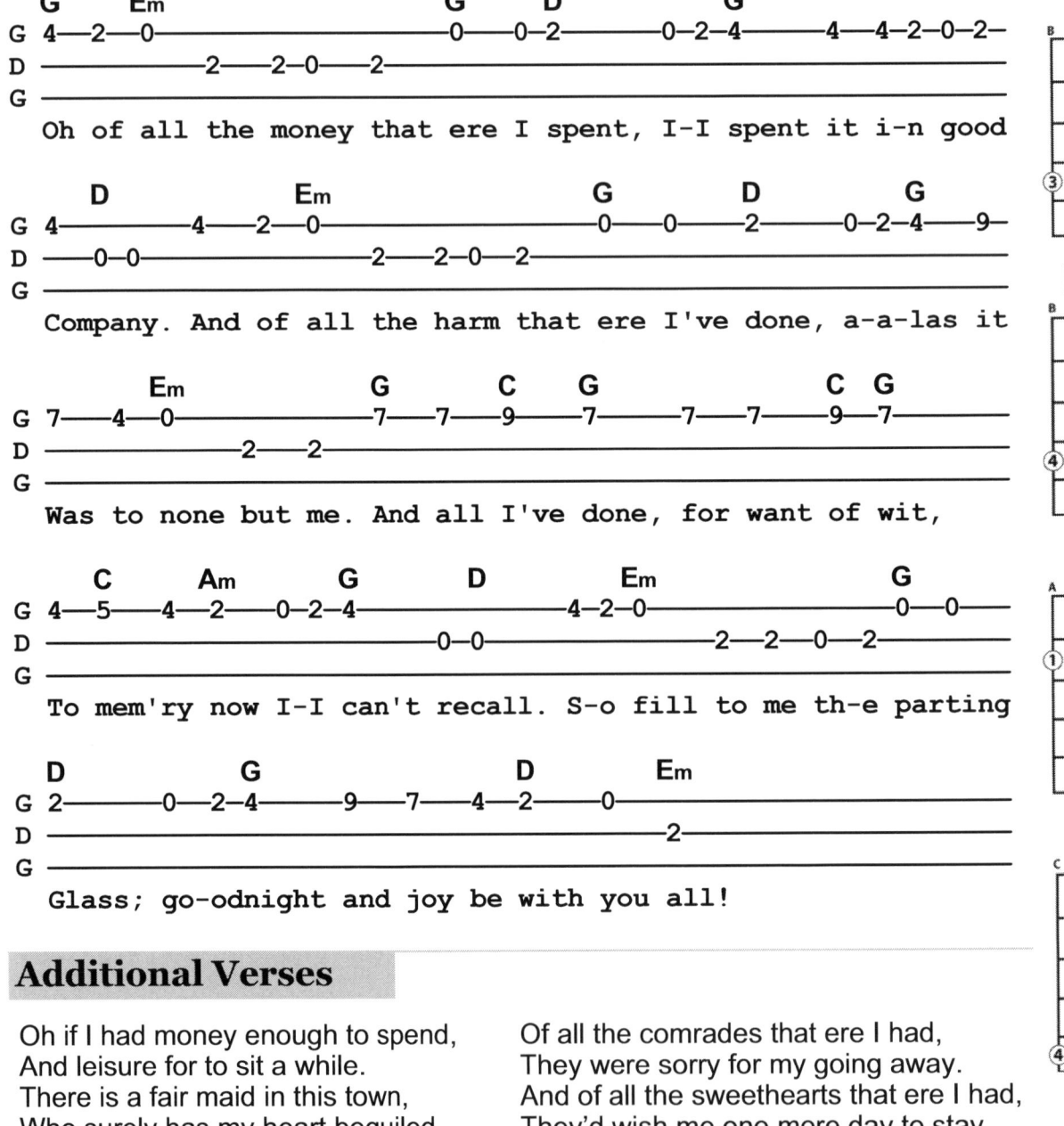

Additional Verses

Oh if I had money enough to spend,
And leisure for to sit a while.
There is a fair maid in this town,
Who surely has my heart beguiled.
Her rosy cheeks, and ruby lips,
Alas she has my heart in thrall;
So fill to me the parting glass,
Goodnight and joy be with you all.

Of all the comrades that ere I had,
They were sorry for my going away.
And of all the sweethearts that ere I had,
They'd wish me one more day to stay.
But since it falls unto my lot,
That I should rise, and you should not,
I'll gently rise, and I'll softly call,
Goodnight and joy be with you all!

The Parting Glass
(continued)

SCOTTISH BALLAD

Melody & Chords

Key of Em

```
       G     Em                      G      D         G
G   4—2—0                  0—0-2       0-2-4     4-4-2-0-2-
D   0—0—0-2    2—2-0—2     0—0-0       0-0-0     0—0-0-0-0-
G   0    4—4   4-4—4       4—4-2       2-2-0     0—0—0—0
    Oh of all the money that ere I spent, I-I spent it i-n good

          D            Em                 G     D         G
G   4           4—2—0                  0—0—2     0-2-4—9—
D   0-0-0—0—0-2    2—2-0-2     0—0         0     0-0-0—10
G   0-2-2—2—2-4    4—4-4-4     4—4         2     2—4
    Company. And of all the harm that ere I've done, a-a-las it

       Em      G        C    G               C  G
G   7—4—0          7—7—9—7        7—7—9—7
D   0   0-2   2—2—0—0—10—0        0—0—10-0
G   0   0-0—4—4—0—0—9—0           0—0—9—0
    Was to none but me. And all I've done, for want of wit,

       C   Am    G       D      Em              G
G   4—5—4—2—0-2-4       4-2-0             0—0
D   0—2—2—2—2-2-0   0-0—0-0-2   2—2-0-2-0-0
G   0—0    5—5-5-0  0-2  2—4    4—4-4—4-4-4
    To mem'ry now I-I can't recall. S-o fill to me th-e parting

       D        G           D      Em
G   2     0-2-4    9—7—4—2  0
D   0     0-0-0   10—0-0-0  0—2
G   2        4     9—0-0—2     4
    Glass; go-odnight and joy be with you all!
```

SCOTTISH BALLAD

The Parting Glass
(continued)

Basic Melody

Key of Am

```
        C   Am                    C       G         C
G  ─────────────────────────────────────────────────────────────
D  2───0─────────────────────0─────────0─2─────2─2─0─────0─
G  ───────5───2───2─0───2─5─────5─────────5─────────────5───
   Oh of all the money that ere I spent, I-I spent it i-n good

        G       Am                C       G         C
G  ─────────────────────────────────────────────────────2─
D  2───────2───0─────────────────────0─────────0─2─────
G  ───0─0─────────5───2───2─0─2───5───5─────5─────────
   Company. And of all the harm that ere I've done, a-a-las it

          Am            C     F   C              F   C
G  0───────────────0───0───2───0───0───0─────2─0
D  ───2─────────────────────────────────────────
G  ─────5───2───2─────────────────────────────
   Was to none but me. And all I've done, for want of wit,

          F   Dm      C         G       Am              C
G  ─────────────────────────────────────────────────────────
D  2───3───2───0─────0─2─────────2─0─────────────────
G  ───────────5─────────0─0─────5───2───2─0───2─5─5
   To mem'ry now I-I can't recall. S-o fill to me th-e parting

          G       C           G       Am
G  ─────────────2───0─────────────────
D  0───────0─2─────────2─0─────────────
G  ───────5─────────────5───2─────────
   Glass; go-odnight and joy be with you all!
```

Chord Forms

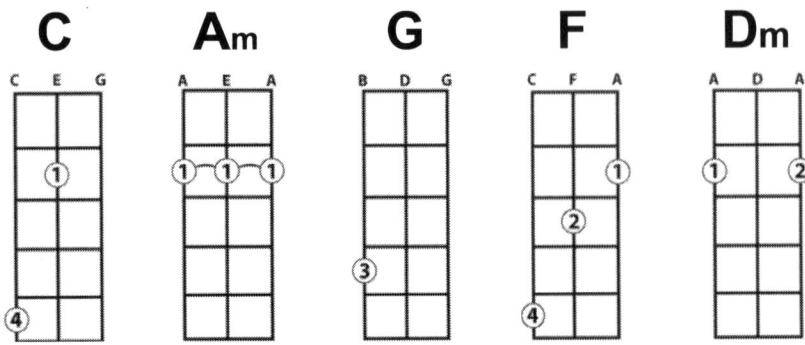

IRISH DRINKING SONG
Poor Old Dicey Reilly

Basic Melody
Key of G

This traditional Irish song tells the tale of an old woman completely given over to drunkenness. Each day she visits the "pop" (slang for a pawn shop) and is then off to begin her drinking. Probably the best known version of this song was recorded by the Dubliners. It is said that the final two verses may have been added by Irish poet Dominic Behan.

Words and Music
Traditional

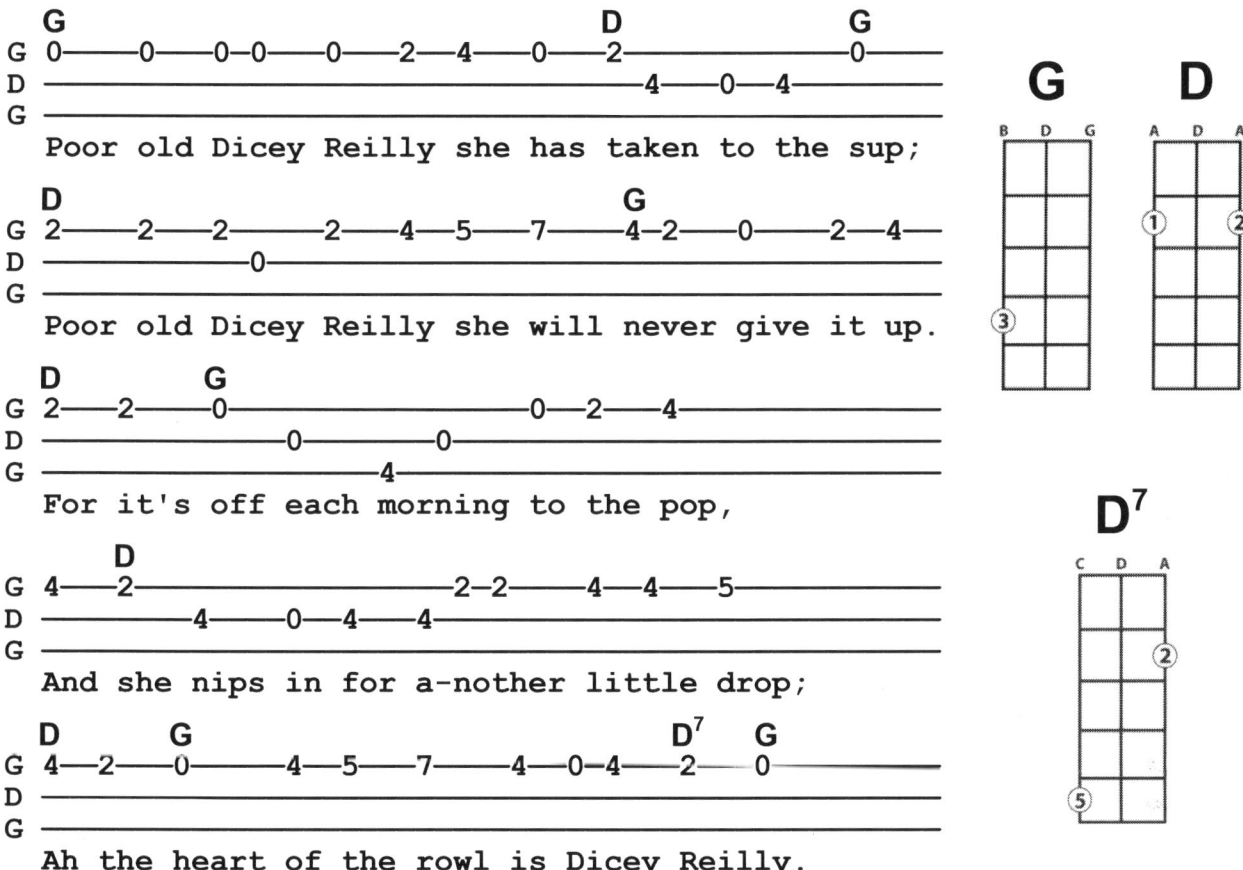

Additional Verses

Oh she walks down Fitzgibbon street with an independent air;
And then it's down by Summerhill and as the people stare...
She says it's nearly half past one, it's time I had another little one...
Oh the heart of the rowl is Dicey Reilly.

She owns a little sweet shop at the corner of the street,
And every evening after school I go to wash her feet;
She leaves me there to mind the shop, while she nips out for another little drop...
Oh the heart of the rowl is Dicey Reilly.

Long years ago when men were men and fancied May Oblong;
Or lovely Becky Cooper or Maggie's Mary Wong...
One woman put them all to shame, only one was worthy of the name...
And the name of that dame was Dicey Reilly.

Oh but time went catching up on her like many pretty whores;
And it's after you along the street before you're out the doors...
The balance weighed and the looks all fade, but out of all that great brigade...
Still the heart of the rowl is Dicey Reilly.

Irish Drinking Songs Cigar Box Guitar Songbook · Copyright 2019 by Hobo Music Works · All Rights Reserved

IRISH DRINKING SONG

Poor Old Dicey Reilly
(continued)

Melody & Chords
Key of G

```
        G                                         D           G
G   0——0——0-0——0——2—4——0—2————————0————
D   0——0——0-0——0——0—0——0—0-4——0—4——0—
G   4————4————4————0————2-2——2-2——4——
    Poor old Dicey Reilly she has taken to the sup;

        D                            G
G   2——2——2——2——4—5——7——4-2——0——2—4—
D   0——0——0-0——0——0——0——0-0——0——0—0—
G   2————2-2——2————7——0————0————0—
    Poor old Dicey Reilly she will never give it up.

        D   G                    
G   2——2——0————0—2—4————————————
D   0——0——0-0——0——0-0——0————————
G   2————4——4——4-4——4—0——0————
    For it's off each morning to the pop,

            D
G   4——2————————2-2——4—4——5————
D   0——0——4——0-4——4-0-0——0——0————
G   0——2——2——2-2——2-2——2——2————
    And she nips in for a-nother little drop;

        D   G                        D⁷  G
G   4——2——0——4—5——7——4—0-4——2——0————
D   0——0——0——0-0——0——0-0-0——0——0————
G   2————4——————0————4——5——4————
    Ah the heart of the rowl is Dicey Reilly.
```

G D

D⁷

[
Here's to a long life and a merry one...
A quick death and an easy one...
A pretty girl and an honest one...
A cold pint -- and another one!

Irish Toast
]

Poor Old Dicey Reilly
(continued)

IRISH DRINKING SONG

Basic Melody
Key of C

```
    C                              G          C
G ─────────────────────────────────────────────────
D ──────────────────────0──2────────0──────────────
G 5───5───5─5───5──────────5──4──0──4──5──
  Poor old Dicey Reilly she has taken to the sup;

    G                          C
G ─────────────────────────0───────────────────
D 0───0───0───0──2──3─────2─0────────0──2──
G ──────────0──────────────────5─────────────
  Poor old Dicey Reilly she will never give it up.

    G      C
G ─────────────────────────────────────
D 0───0──────────────────────0──2──────
G ──────5──5──5──0──5────────────────
  For it's off each morning to the pop,

         G
G ─────────────────────────────────────
D 2──0──────────────0─0──2──2──3──────
G ──────4──0──4──4────────────────────
  And she nips in for a-nother little drop;

    G      C                      G⁷  C
G ─────────────0──────────────────────────
D 2──0────2──3─────2──2──0──────────────
G ──────5──────────────5──────5────────
  Ah the heart of the rowl is Dicey Reilly.
```

Chord Forms

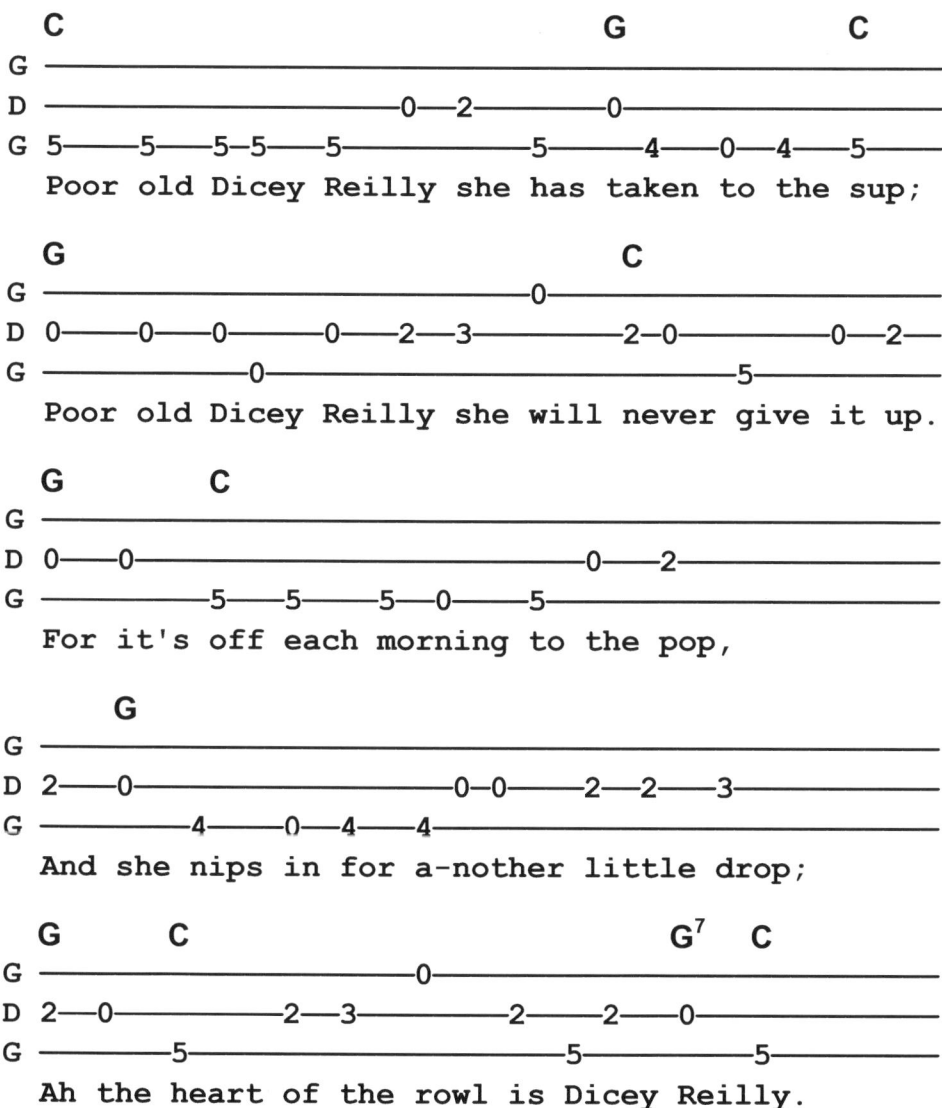

Irish Drinking Songs Cigar Box Guitar Songbook · Copyright 2019 by Hobo Music Works · All Rights Reserved

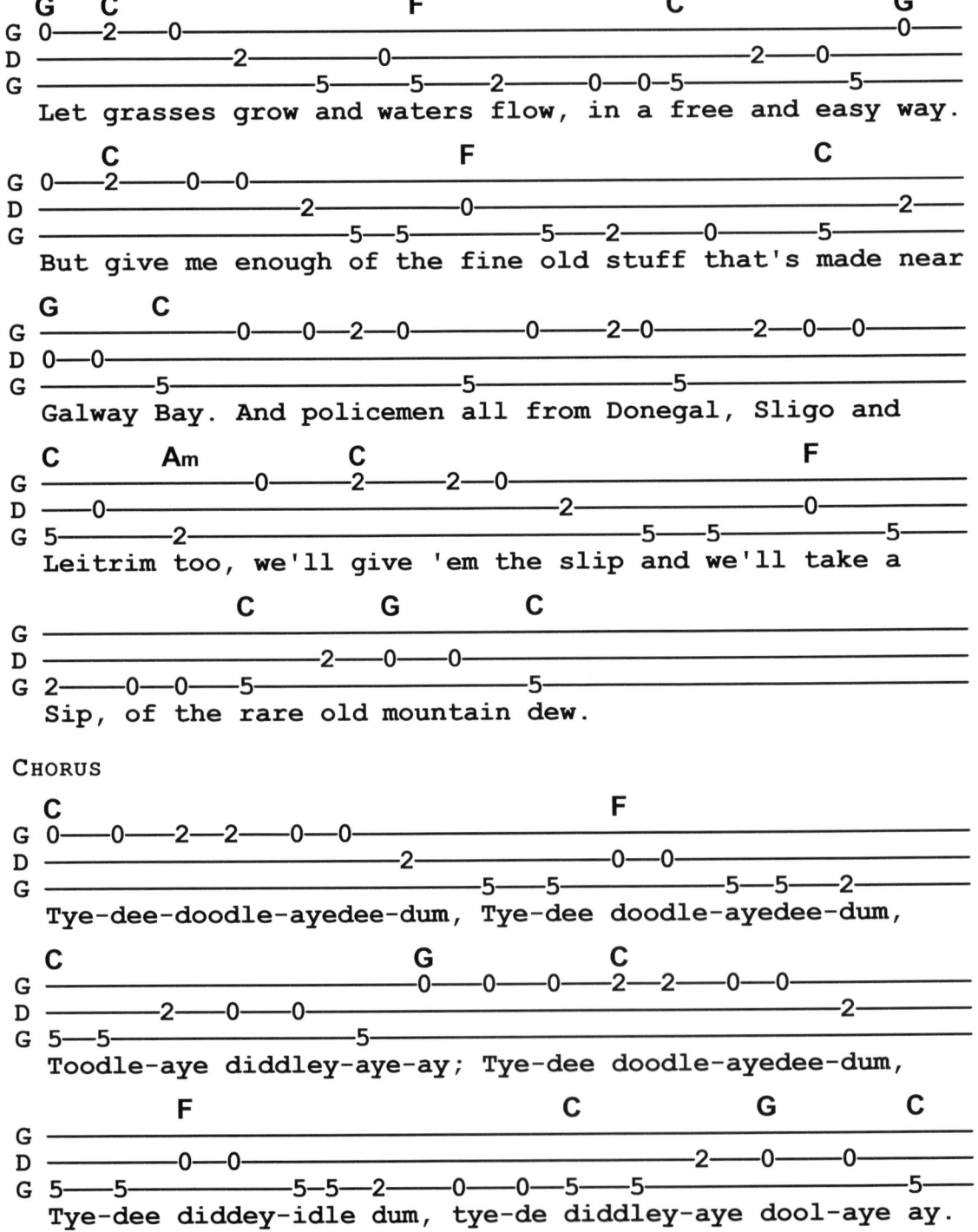

IRISH DRINKING SONG

Rare Old Mountain Dew
(continued)

Chord Forms & Additional Verses
Key of C

Additional Verses

At the foot of the hill there's a neat little still,
Where the smoke curls up to the sky;
By the smoke and the smell, you can plainly tell
That the poteen's brewin' nearby.
Well it fills the air with an odor rare,
And betwixt both me and you,
When home you stroll, you can take a bowl...
Or a bucket of the mountain dew.

Now learn'ed men who use the pen
Have wrote her praises high.
That sweet poteen from Ireland green,
Distilled from wheat and rye.
Put away your pills, it will cure all ills,
Be you pagan, or Christian, or Jew.
Take off your coat and grease your throat
With the rare old mountain dew!

Chord Forms

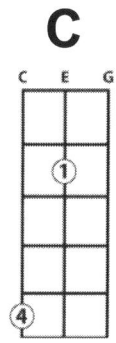
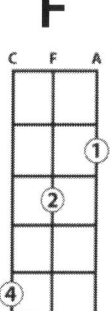
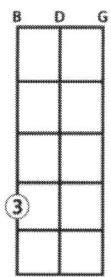
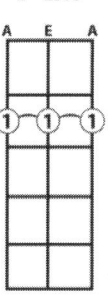

Rare Old Mountain Dew

IRISH DRINKING SONG

Melody & Chords
Key of C

(continued)

```
      G    C                    F               C              G
G  0———2———0———————————————————————————————————————————————————0———
D  0———2———2———2———————————————0———————————————————2———0———————0———
G  4———5———5———5———2-5———2———0—0-5———5———5-5———4———
   Let grasses grow and waters flow, in a free and easy way.
```

```
           C                    F                  C
G  0———2———0—0—————————————————————————————————————————————————
D  0———2———2—2———2———————————0———————————————————————————————2———
G  4———5———5———5—5—5———2———5———2———0———————5———5———
   But give me enough of the fine old stuff that's made near
```

```
      G    C
G  ————————0———0———2———0—————————0———2-0—————2———0—0———
D  0———0———————2———2———2—2———————2———2-2———2———2—2———
G  0———0———5———5———5—————5———5———————5———5—————————
   Galway Bay. And policemen all from Donegal, Sligo and
```

```
   C       Am         C                           F
G  ————————0———————2———2—0—————————————————————————————————
D  ————0———————2———2———2-2———2—————————————————0———————
G  5———2———2———2———5———————5———5———5———2———5———
   Leitrim too, we'll give 'em the slip and we'll take a
```

```
               C       G       C
G  —————————————————————————————————————————————————
D  —————————2———0———0———————————————————————————————
G  2———0—0———5———5———0—0———5———
   Sip, of the rare old mountain dew.
```

CHORUS

```
   C                                 F
G  0———0———2—2———0—0———————————————————————————————
D  2———2———2———2—2———2———2———————0—0———————————————
G  5———5———————5———————5———5—5———2-2———5—5———2———
   Tye-dee-doodle-ayedee-dum, Tye-dee doodle-ayedee-dum,
```

```
   C                        G        C
G  ——————————————————0———0———0———2—2———0—0———
D  ————2———0———0———0—0———0———2—2———2—2———2———
G  5—5———5———0—0———5———4———4———5———5———5———
   Toodle-aye diddley-aye-ay; Tye-dee doodle-ayedee-dum,
```

```
      F                    C          G        C
G  ———————————————————————————————————————————5———
D  ————0—0———————————————————2———0———0———5———
G  5—5———2-2———5-5———2———0———0-5———5———5———0———0———5———
   Tye-dee diddey-idle dum, tye-de diddley-aye dool-aye ay.
```

Rare Old Mountain Dew
(continued)

IRISH DRINKING SONG

Basic Melody

Key of G

```
   D  G              C            G         D
G  7—9—7—0—————————————————0—4—2—0—7
D            9—7—5—2—0—0
G
```
Let grasses grow and waters flow, in a free and easy way.

```
      G              C            G
G  7—9—7—7—0—0——————————————0—4
D            9—7—5—2—0
G
```
But give me enough of the fine old stuff that's made near

```
   D  G
G  2—2—0—7—7—9—7—0—7—9—7—0—9—7—7
D
G
```
Galway Bay. And policemen all from Donegal, Sligo and

```
   G  Em       G              C
G  0—2——7—9—9—7—0—0—2—0
D     2              9
G
```
Leitrim too, we'll give 'em the slip and we'll take a

```
      G     D  G
G  ——0—4—2—2—0
D  2—0—0
G
```
Sip, of the rare old mountain dew.

Chorus

```
   G                           C
G  7—7—9—9—7—7—0—0—2—2—0—0
D                9              2
G
```
Tye-dee-doodle-ayedee-dum, Tye-dee doodle-ayedee-dum,

```
   G           D       G
G  0—0—4—2—2—0—7—7—7—9—9—7—7
D                              9
G
```
Toodle-aye diddley-aye-ay; Tye-dee doodle-ayedee-dum,

```
      C           G       D  G
G  0—0—2—2—0—0—0—0—4—2—2—0
D            2—0—0
G
```
Tye-dee diddey-idle dum, tye-de diddley-aye dool-aye ay.

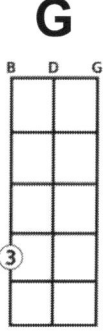
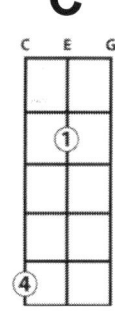
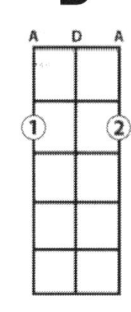
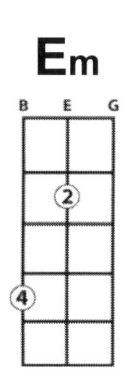

Reilly's Daughter

IRISH BALLAD

Basic Melody
Key of G

Words and Music
Traditional

This humorous and fast-paced song presents the dangers there used to be when marrying a girl without her father's consent. In this case though the new husband is able to send his father-in-law packing. It is meant to be performed energetically, often while pantomiming the story being sung (firing pistols into the air, dunking heads in barrels of water, etc).

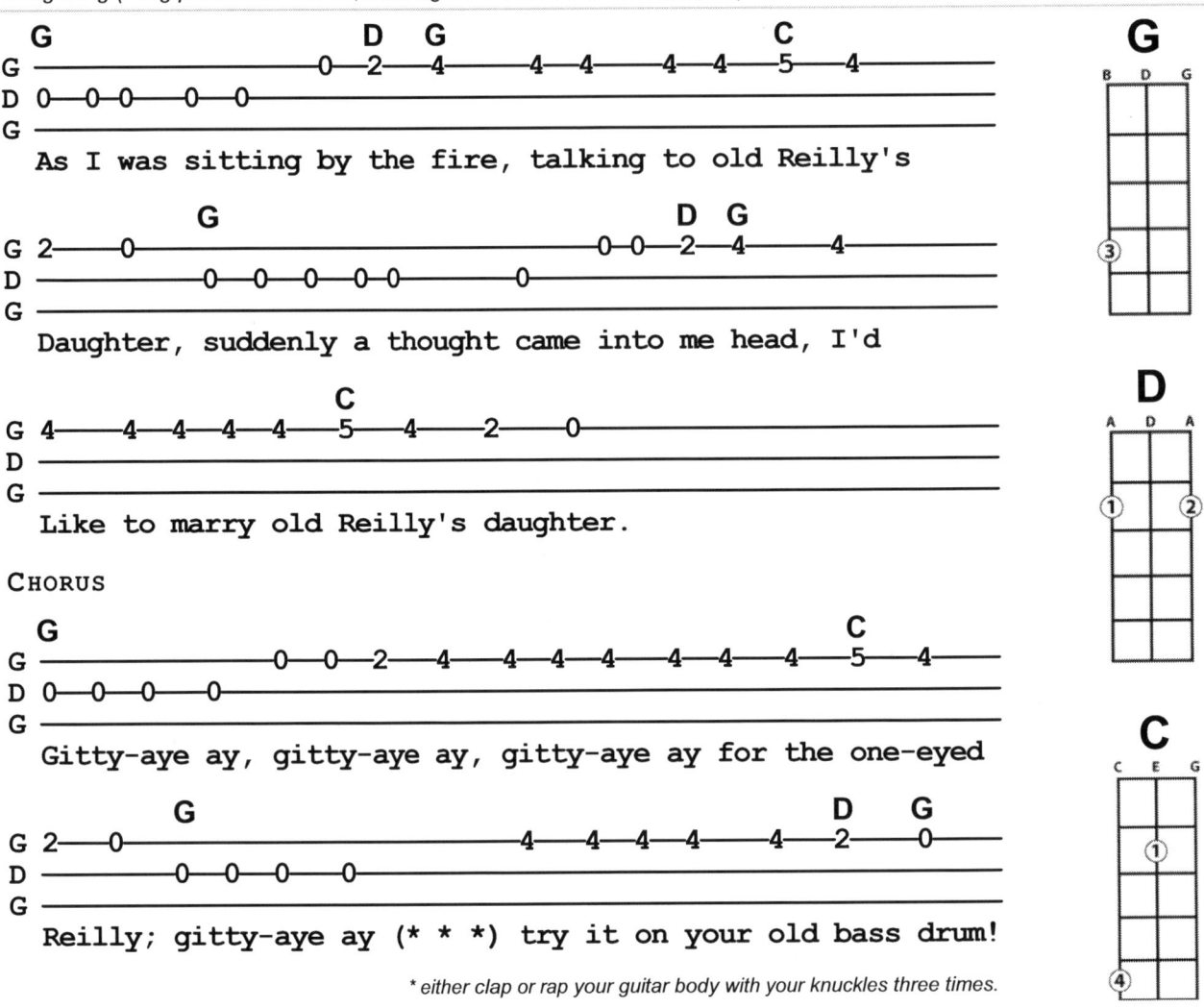

* *either clap or rap your guitar body with your knuckles three times.*

Additional Verses

Reilly played on the big bass drum,
Reilly had a mind for murder and slaughter;
Reilly had a bright red glitterin' eye,
And he kept that eye on his lovely daughter.

Her hair was black and her eyes were blue,
The colonel and the major and the captain sought her,
The sergeant the private and the drum boy too,
Never had a chance with old Reilly's daughter!

I got me a ring and a parson too,
Got me a scratch in the married quarter;

Settled me down for a peaceful life,
Happy as a king with old Reilly's daughter.

Suddenly a footstep on the stair,
Who could it be but Reilly out for slaughter;
With two pistols in his hands,
Looking for the man that had married his daughter.

Well I caught old Reilly by the hair,
Rammed his head in a pail of water;
Fired his pistols into the air,
A damned sight quicker than I married his daughter!

Irish Drinking Songs Cigar Box Guitar Songbook · Copyright 2019 by Hobo Music Works · All Rights Reserved

Reilly's Daughter
(continued)

IRISH BALLAD

Melody & Chords
Key of G

```
       G                  D   G                              C
G  ——————————————0———2———4————4———4———————4———4———5———4——————
D  0———0—0————0——0————0———0——————0———0————0———0———2———2——————
G  0———0—0————0——0————4———2———0——0———0————0———0———0——————————
   As  I  was sitting by  the fire, talking to  old Reilly's
```

```
              G                              D   G
G  2———0——————————————————————————————————0—0———2———4————4——————
D  2———2——0———0———0———0—0—————————0———————0—0———0———0————0——————
G  ——————5——0———0———0———0—0—————————0—————4—4———2———0————0——————
   Daughter, suddenly a  thought came into me  head,  I'd
```

```
                        C
G  4———4—4———4———4———5———4———2———0——————————————————
D  0———0—0———0———0———2———2———2———2——————————————————
G  0———0————0———0———0—————————5———————————————————————
   Like to marry old Reilly's daughter.
```

CHORUS

```
       G                    D                                C
G  ——————————————0———0———2———4———4———4———4———4———4———4———5———4——
D  0———0———0———0—0———0———0———0———0———0———0———0———0———0———2———2——
G  0———0———0———0—4———2———0———0———0———0———0———0———0——————————————
   Gitty-aye ay, gitty-aye ay,  gitty-aye ay for the one-eyed
```

```
              G                                            D   G
G  2———0—————————————————————4———4———4———4—————4———2———0——————
D  2———2——0———0———0———0—————0———0———0———0————0———0———0——————
G  ——————5——0———0———0———0——————0———0———0——————————0———2———4——
   Reilly;  gitty-aye ay (* * *) try it on your old bass drum!
```

> May you have love that never ends,
> lots of money, and lots of friends.
> Health be yours, whatever you do,
> and may God send many blessings to you!
>
> *Irish Wedding Blessing*

IRISH BALLAD

Reilly's Daughter
(continued)

Basic Melody
Key of C

```
       C              G   C                      F
G ----------------------------------------------------------
D ------------------0---2-----2---2-----2---2---3---2------
G 0---0---0---0---0-----5----------------------------------
  As  I  was sitting by the fire, talking to old Reilly's

                   C                           G   C
G ----------------------------------------------------------
D 0---------------------------------------0---2-----2------
G -----5---0---0---0---0---0---------0-----5-5-------------
  Daughter, suddenly a thought came into me head, I'd

                       F
G ----------------------------------------------------------
D 2-----2---2---2---2---3---2-----0------------------------
G ----------------------------------------5----------------
  Like to marry old Reilly's daughter.
```

CHORUS

```
       C              G   C                      F
G ----------------------------------------------------------
D ------------------0---2-----2---2---2---2---2---2---3---2
G 0---0---0---0---5-5---------------------------------------
  Gitty-aye ay, gitty-aye ay, gitty-aye ay for the one-eyed

                   C                                G   C
G ----------------------------------------------------------
D 0-----------------------2---2---2---2-----2---0----------
G -----5---0---0---0---0------------------------------5----
  Reilly; gitty-aye ay (* * *) try it on your old bass drum!
```

Chord Forms

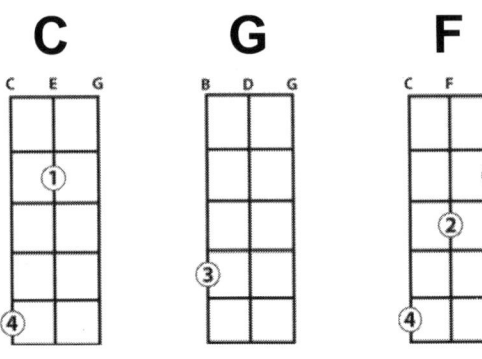

Irish Drinking Songs Cigar Box Guitar Songbook · Copyright 2019 by Hobo Music Works · All Rights Reserved

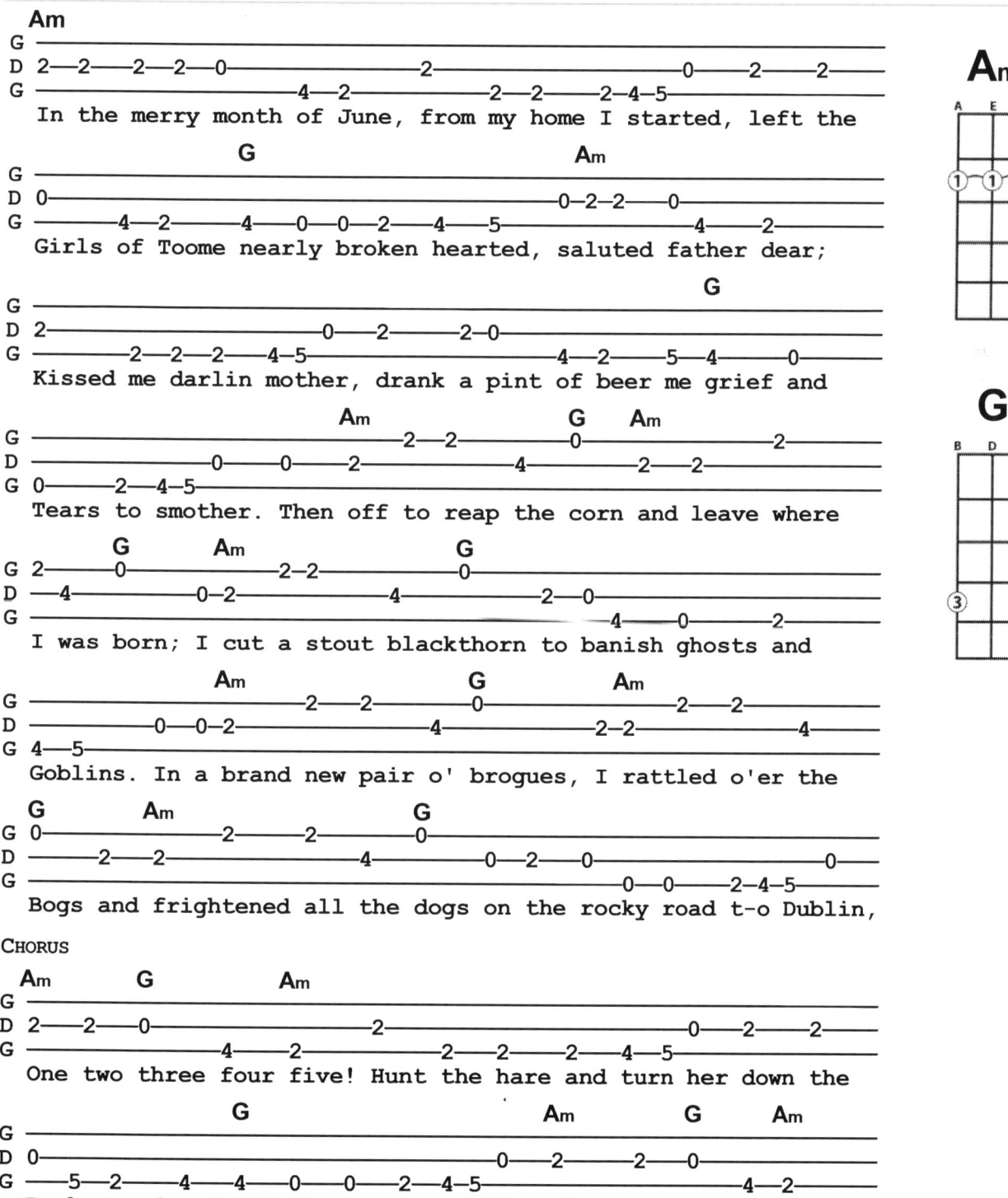

IRISH SLIP JIG

Rocky Road To Dublin
(continued)

Additional Verses

Additional Verses

When in Mullingar that night, I rested limbs so weary,
Started by daylight, me spirits bright an airy,
Took a drop o' the pure, to keep me heart from sinking,
That's the paddy's cure, when e're he's on for drinking;
To see the lassies smile, laughing all the while,
At me curious style, would set your heart to bubbling,
Asked me was I hired, wages I required,
Til I was almost tired on the rocky road to Dublin...

When in Dublin next arrived, I thought it was a pity
To be so soon deprived a view of that fine city,
Then I took a stroll, all among the quality,
Me bundle it was stole, in a neat locality;
Something crossed me mind, when I looked behind,
No bundle could I find upon me stick a wobbling;
Enquiring for the rogue, they said me Connacht brogue
Wasn't much in vogue on the rocky road to Dublin...

Well from there I got away, me spirits never failing,
Landed on the quay, just as the ship was sailing,
Captain at me roared - said that no room had he,
When I jumped aboard a cabin found for Paddy,
Down among the pigs, played some hearty rigs,
Danced some hearty jigs, the water round be bubblin'
When off Holyhead, I wished meself was dead,
Or better far instead on the rocky road to Dublin...

Well the boys of Liverpool, when we safely landed,
Called meself a fool, I could no longer stand it -
Blood began to boil! Temper I was losing,
Poor auld Erin's isle, they began abusing...
Hurrah me soul says I, shillelagh I'll apply,
Some Galway boys were by and saw I was a-hobblin'
Then with a loud hurray, they joined into the affray,
Quickly cleared the way for the rocky road to Dublin...

This song has been recorded by:

- The Dubliners
- The Clancy Brothers & Tommy Makem
- Luke Kelly
- Paddy Reilly
- The Pogues
- The Young Dubliners
- The Chieftains
- The Rolling Stones
- Gaelic Storm
- Christy Moore
- The High Kings
- Dropkick Murphys
- The Tossers
- Celtic Thunder

And many more!

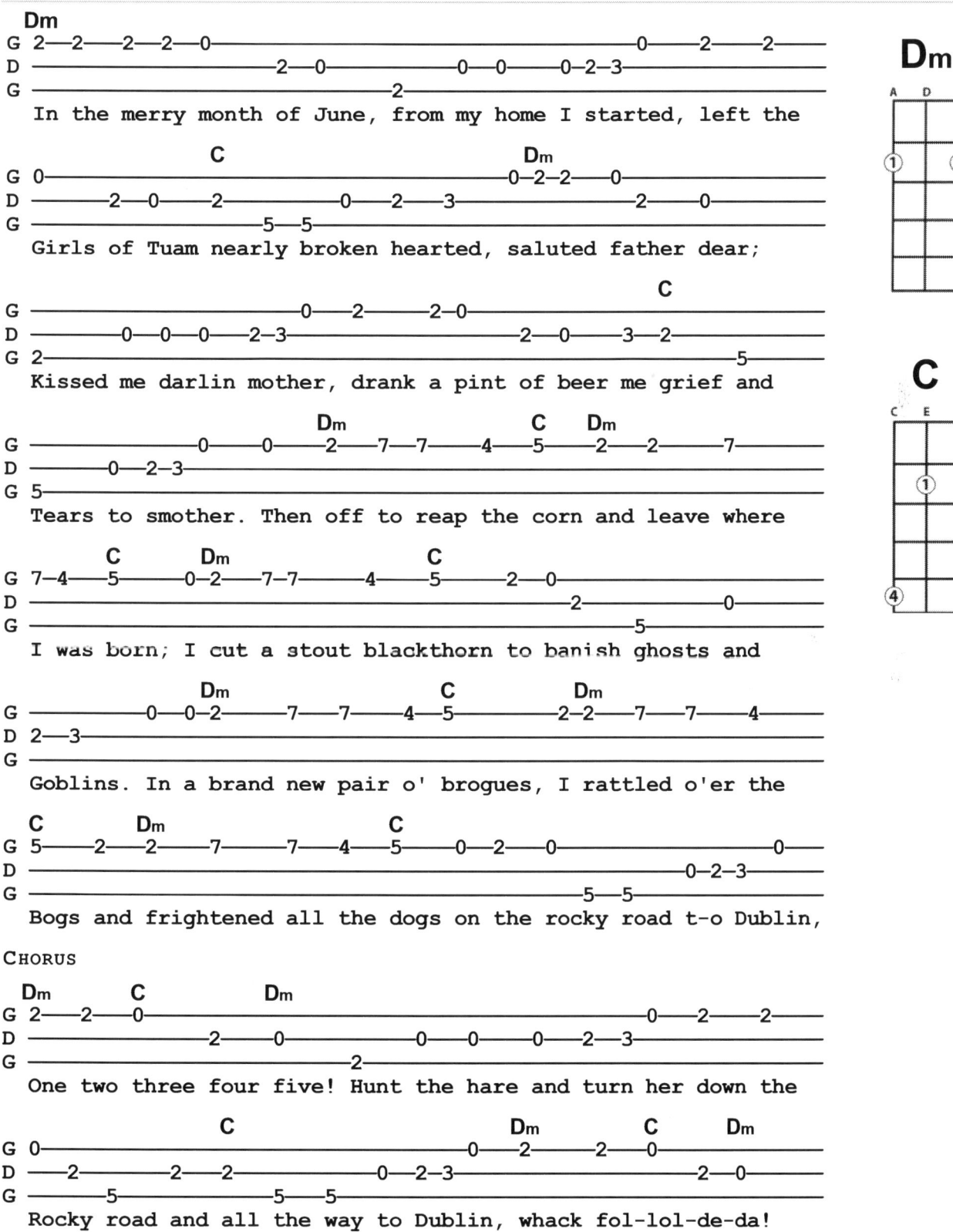

IRISH SLIP JIG

Rocky Road To Dublin
(continued)

Melody & Chords
Key of Dm

```
   Dm
G 2—2—2—2—0————————————————————0——2——2—
D 0—0—0—0—0——2—0———0—0——0-2-3-0——0——0—
G 2———2———2-2——2——2-2——2-2-2-2——2—
  In the merry month of June, from my home I started, left the

         C                           Dm
G 0—————————————————————————0-2-2——0—
D 0——2-0——2———0—2——3——2-0-0——0-2——0—
G 2——2-2——5-5-5-5——5-5——2——2-2——2—
  Girls of Tuam nearly broken hearted, saluted father dear;

                                            C
G ————0——2——2-0—————————————
D ——0-0-0—2-3-0——0———0-0——2-0——3-2—
G 2—2-2—2-2-2——2——2-2——2-2——2-5——5—
  Kissed me darlin mother, drank a pint of beer me grief and

              Dm            C   Dm
G ————0———0——2—7-7——4—5——2——2——7—
D ——0—2-3-2——2——0—7-7——0—5——0——0——7—
G 5—5-5-5-5——5——2——————2-2——
  Tears to smother. Then off to reap the corn and leave where

      C      Dm         C
G 7-4——5———0-2—7-7——4—5——2——0———
D 7-0——5———0-0—7-7——0—5——0-2-2——0—
G ————2—————————5——5—
  I was born; I cut a stout blackthorn to banish ghosts and

              Dm            C   Dm
G ————0——0-2—7-7——4—5——2-2——7-7——4—
D 2—3————2-2-0—7-7——0—5——0-0——7-7——0—
G 5-5——5——2————2-2——
  Goblins. In a brand new pair o' brogues, I rattled o'er the

     C    Dm         C
G 5———2——2—7——7—4—5——0——2——0—————0—
D 5———0——0—7——7—0—5——2——2—2———0-2-3-2—
G ——2——2————5——5-5-5——5-5-5-5—
  Bogs and frightened all the dogs on the rocky road t-o Dublin,

CHORUS

   Dm       C     Dm
G 2——2——0————————————0——2——2—
D 0——0——2——2——0———0——0——0——2-3-0——0——0—
G 2—2—5——5——2——2——2——2——2——2-2-2——2—
  One two three four five! Hunt the hare and turn her down the

        C                    Dm    C   Dm
G 0—————————————0——2——2——0——2—
D 0——2———2——2———0—2-3-2——0——0——2——2——0—
G 2—2—5——0——0——5—5—5-5-5-5——2——2——5——5——2—
  Rocky road and all the way to Dublin, whack fol-lol-de-da!
```

99

IRISH DRINKING BALLAD

Rosin the Bow

Basic Melody
Key of C

Words and Music
Traditional

This old drinking ballad comes down from the British Isles (no one is sure whether from Ireland, England or Scotland) and has been sung with various lyrics over the years. It tells the tale of a man, once young and popular with the ladies, now grown old and preparing for death - but in a darkly humorous way.

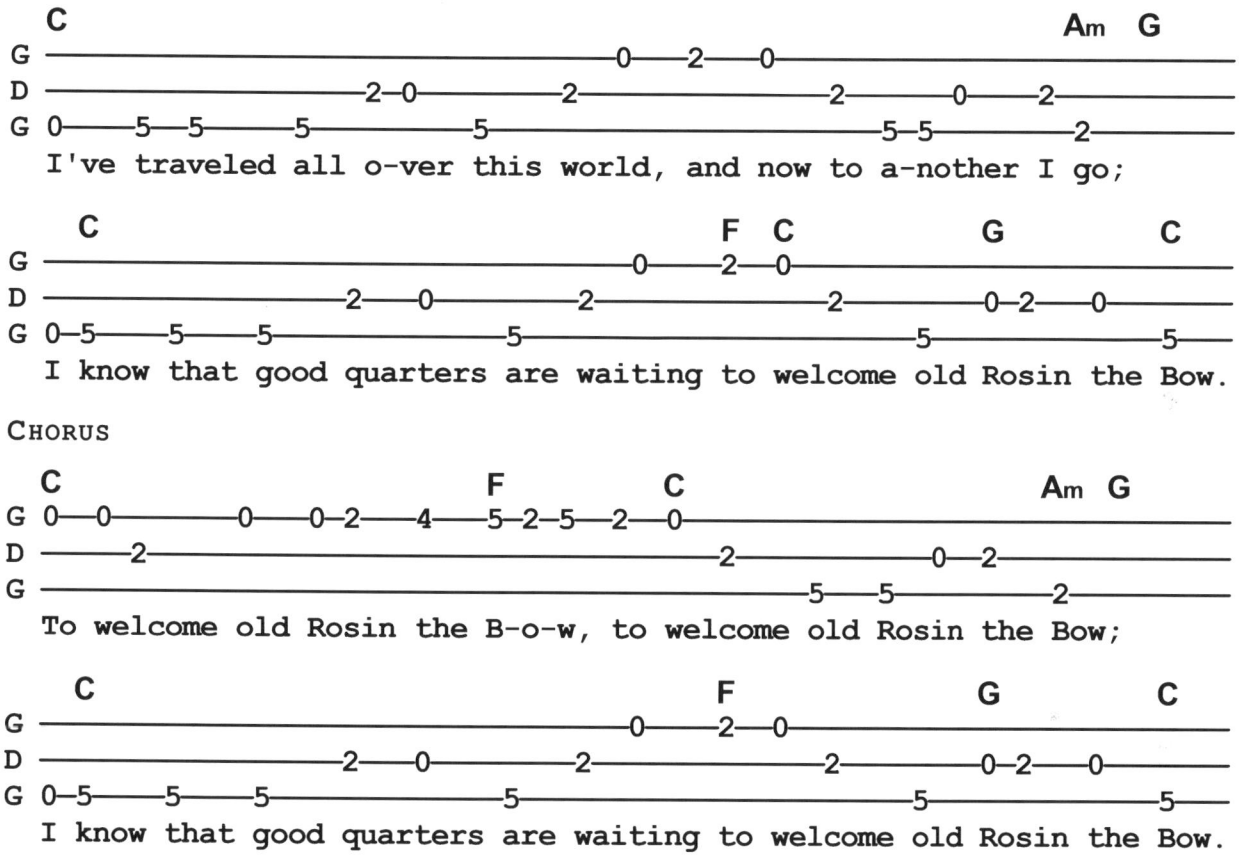

Chord Forms

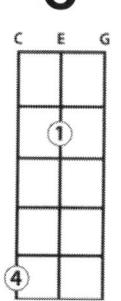
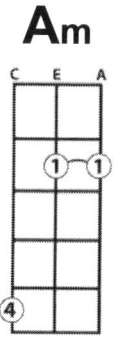
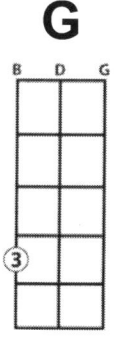
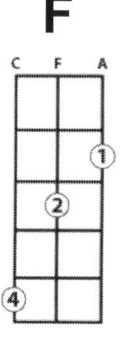

See Additional Verses on Next Page

IRISH DRINKING BALLAD

Rosin the Bow (continued)

Additional Verses

Additional Verses

When I'm dead and laid out on the counter,
A voice you will hear from below;
Saying "Send down a hogshead of whiskey,
To drink with old Rosin the Bow!"
To drink with old Rosin the Bow,
To drink with old Rosin the Bow;
Saying "Send down a hogshead of whiskey,
To drink with old Rosin the Bow!"

Then get a half dozen stout fellows,
And line them all up in a row;
Let them drink out of half gallon bottles,
To the memory of Rosin the Bow.
To the memory of Rosin the Bow,
To the memory of Rosin the Bow;
Let them drink out of half gallon bottles,
To the memory of Rosin the Bow.

Then get this half dozen stout fellows,
And let them all stagger and go...
And dig a great hole in the meadow,
And in it put Rosin the Bow.
And in it put Rosin the Bow,
And in it put Rosin the Bow;
And dig a great hole in the meadow,
And in it put Rosin the Bow.

Then get ye a couple of bottles,
Put one at me head and me toe;
With a diamond ring scratch upon them
The name of old Rosin the Bow.
The name of old Rosin the Bow,
The name of old Rosin the Bow;
With a diamond ring scratch upon them
The name of old Rosin the Bow.

I've only this one consolation,
As out of this world I go;
I know that the next generation
Will resemble old Rosin the Bow.
Will resemble old Rosin the Bow,
Will resemble old Rosin the Bow.
I know that the next generation,
Will resemble old Rosin the Bow.

I fear that old tyrant approaching,
That cruel remorseless old foe;
And I lift up me glass in his honor,
Take a drink with old Rosin the Bow!
Take a drink with old Rosin the Bow,
Take a drink with old Rosin the Bow.
And I lift up me glass in his honor,
Take a drink with old Rosin the Bow!

---

*"Young people don't know what old age is,
and old people forget what youth was."*

"The older the fiddle the sweeter the tune."

"There's nothing so bad that it couldn't be worse."

*"Lose an hour in the morning and
you'll be looking for it all day."*

Old Irish Proverbs & Sayings

Rosin the Bow (continued)

IRISH DRINKING BALLAD

Basic Melody
Key of G

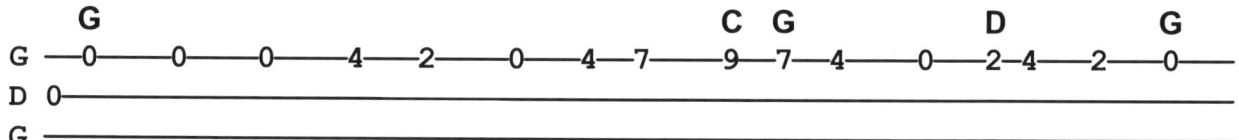

I've traveled all o-ver this world, and now to a-nother I go;

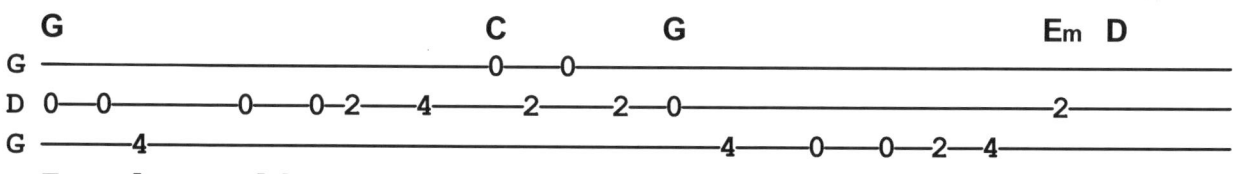

I know that good quarters are waiting to welcome old Rosin the Bow.

CHORUS

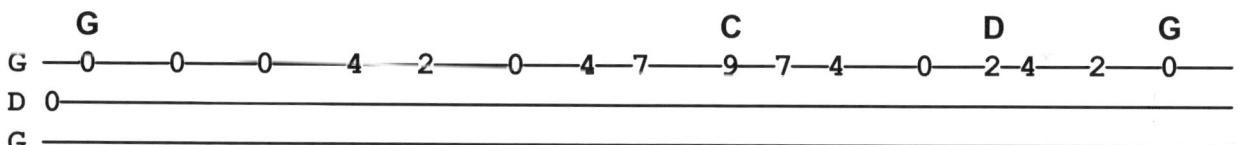

To welcome old Rosin the B-o-w, to welcome old Rosin the Bow;

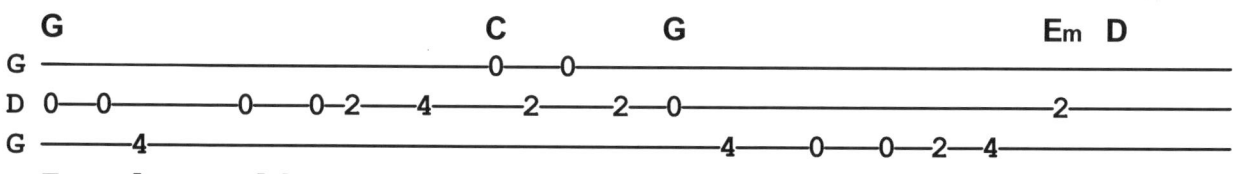

I know that good quarters are waiting to welcome old Rosin the Bow.

Chord Forms

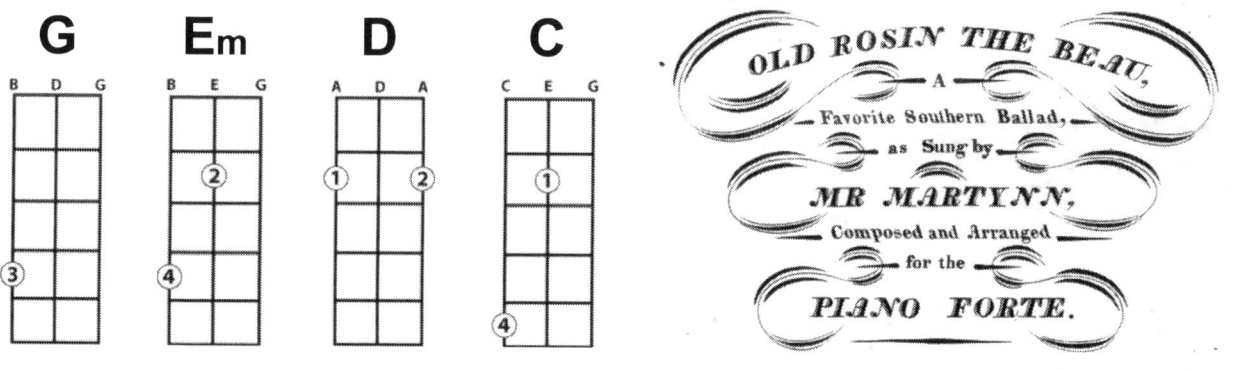

Front-piece from an 1850 publication of sheet music, of the American-ized version of Rosin the Bow.

Rosin the Bow (continued)

IRISH DRINKING BALLAD

Melody & Chords
Key of G

```
         G                                              Em   D
G ——0—0———0—4-2—0—4-7—9-7-4-0-0-2———4——————
D 0———0—0—0—0-0—0—0-0—10-0—0-0-0-0-0—0-2—0——
G 4—4—4—0———————0-0—9-0—0-0—————4-2——
  I've traveled all o-ver this world, and now to a-nother I go;
```

```
  G                                      C  G      D      G
G —0——0——0——4-2—0—4-7—9-7-4—0-2-4—2——0
D 0-0——0——0——0—0——0-0—10-0-0—0-0-0—0—0
G 0-4———4——0———0-0—9-0———0-2——0—4
  I know that good quarters are waiting to welcome old Rosin the Bow.
```

CHORUS

```
  G           C       G               Em   D
G ——————————0—0——————————————————
D 0—0———0—0-2—4—2-2-2—2—0———————2—0
G 4—4-4——4—4-4—4—5-5-5—5—4-4——0—0-2-4—4-2
  To welcome old Rosin the B-o-w, to welcome old Rosin the Bow;
```

```
  G                                 C      D      G
G —0——0——0—4-2—0—4-7—9-7-4—0-2-4—2——0
D 0-0——0——0—0——0—0-0—10-0-0—0-0-0—0—0
G 0-4———4——0———0-0—9-0———0-2——0—4
  I know that good quarters are waiting to welcome old Rosin the Bow.
```

Chord Forms

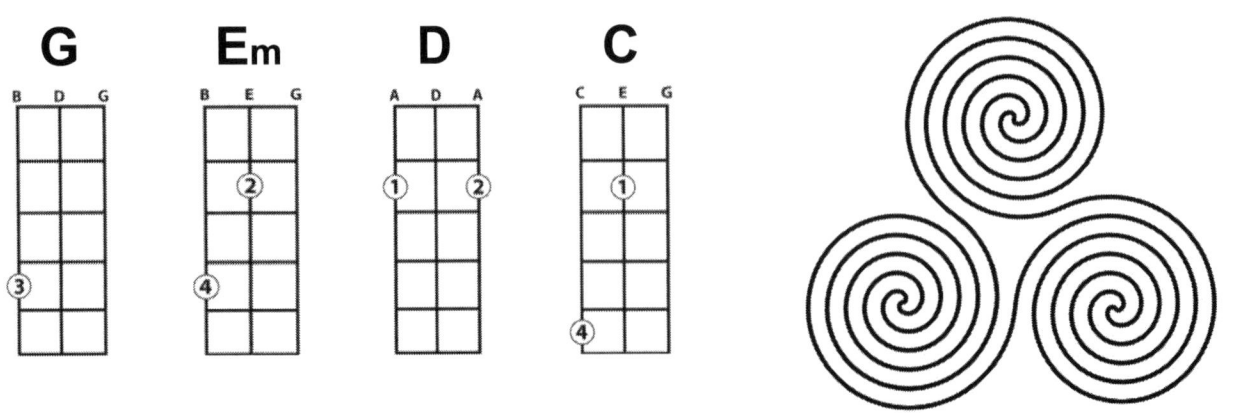

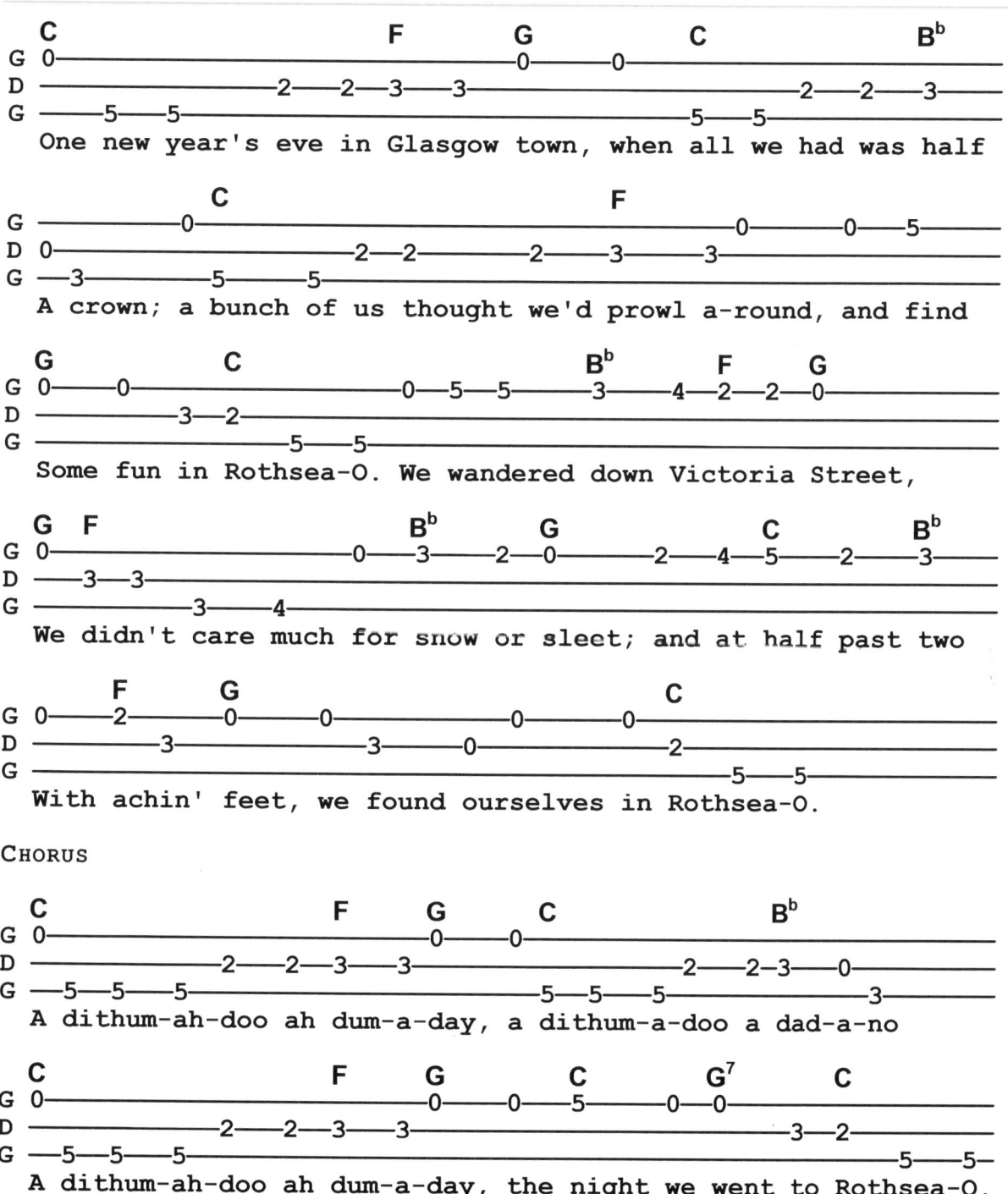

SCOTTISH BALLAD

Rothsea-O (continued)

Additional Verses & Chord Forms

Key of C

Additional Verses

Pat Boyle here, he's a bit of a lout,
Said he'd treat us all to a pint of stout;
So as quick as we could we all set out,
For a public house in Rothsea-O.
Said he "My lads I'd like to sing,"
Says I "You'll do no such a thing."
He said, "Clear the room and we'll make a ring,
And I'll fight ye all in Rothsea-O."

We had to find a place to sleep,
We were all too drunk to even creep;
We found a place that was really cheap,
In a boarding house in Rothsea-O.
We all laid down to take our ease,
When somebody happened for to sneeze;
And he wakened half a million fleas,
In a single room in Rothsea-O!

There were several different kinds of pests,
They ran and they jumped inside our vests;
They got in our hair and they built their nests,
And they cried "Hurrah for Rothsea-O!"
Says I "I think I'll head for home,"
And we swore we never more would roam;
And we're scratching still as we sing this song,
Of the night we went to Rothsea-O.

Chord Forms

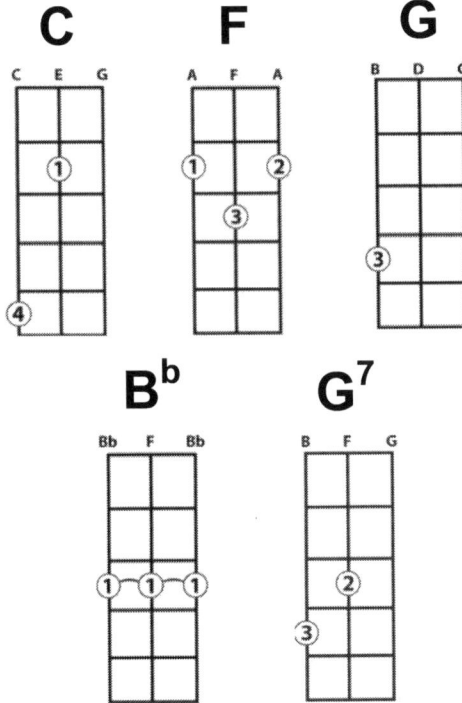

A street scene in Edinburgh, Scotland.

Rothsea-O (continued)

SCOTTISH BALLAD

Melody & Chords
Key of C

```
     C              F   G         C           Bb
G  0----------------------0----0-------------------------
D  2---------------2--2--3--3--0--0--------2--2--3-------
G  5--5--5---5--5--5--5--5--4--4--5--5--5--5--5--3-------
   One new year's eve in Glasgow town, when all we had was half

            C                    F
G  -----------0---------------------------0---0--5-------
D  0---2------2--2---2--2----2--3--3-5----0---3----------
G  3--3-------5--5--5--5-----5--5--5-5----------2--------
   A crown; a bunch of us thought we'd prowl a-round, and find

     G      C              Bb     F  G
G  0-----0---------0--5--5--3--4--2--2--0-----------------
D  3--3--3--2-----2--2--2--3--3--3--3--0-----------------
G  4--4--4--5--5--5--5--0-----------5-----0--------------
   Some fun in Rothsea-O. We wandered down Victoria Street,

     G  F           Bb     G         C        Bb
G  0-----------0---3--2--0--2--4--5--2---3----------------
D  0--3--3----3--3--3--0--0--0--2--2--5------------------
G  ----5--5--3--4---------0--------0---------------------
   We didn't care much for snow or sleet; and at half past two

        F   G                       C
G  0----2--0-----0-----0-----0--------------------------
D  0----3--3--0--0--3--0--0--3--2-----------------------
G  ----5--5--4--4--4--4--4--4--5--5--5------------------
   With achin' feet, we found ourselves in Rothsea-O.
```

CHORUS

```
     C              F   G      C           Bb
G  0----------------------0----0-------------------------
D  2---------------2--2--3--3-0--0--------2--2--3--0-----
G  5--5--5---5--5--5--5--5--4--5--5--5--5--5--3--3--3----
   A dithum-ah-doo ah dum-a-day, a dithum-a-doo a dad-a-no

     C              F   G      C       G7        C
G  0----------------------0----0--5----0--0-----------5--
D  2---------------2--2--3--3-0--0--2--2--0--3--2-----5--
G  5--5--5---5--5--5--5--5--4--0-------4--4--5--5--5-----
   A dithum-ah-doo ah dum-a-day, the night we went to Rothsea-O.
```

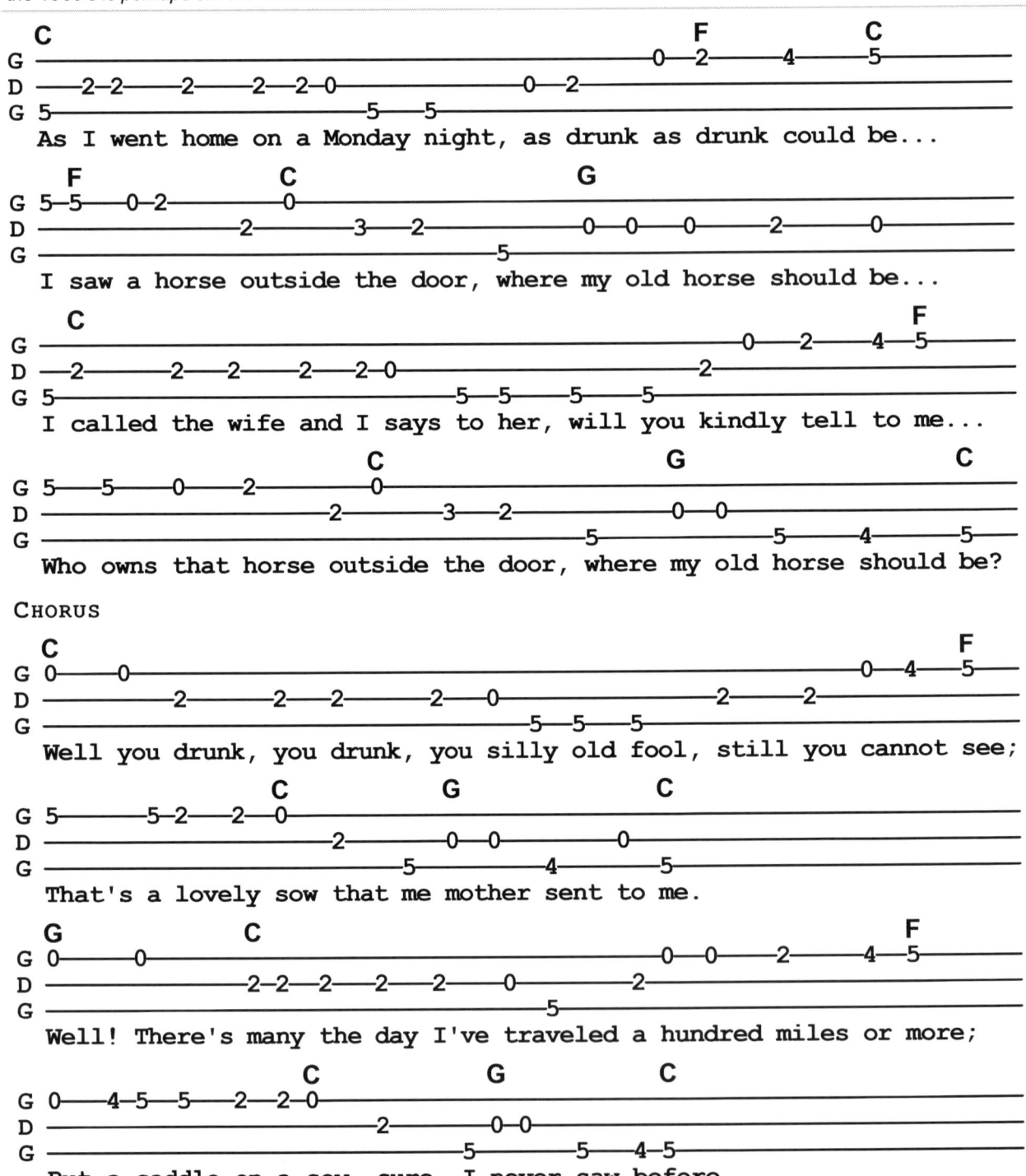

Seven Drunken Nights
(continued)

IRISH DRINKING SONG

Chords & Additional Verses

Key of C

Additional Verses

And as I went home on Tuesday night, as drunk as drunk could be,
I saw a coat behind the door, where my old coat should be.
Well, I called me wife and I said to her,
"Will you kindly tell to me, who owns that coat behind the door,
Where my old coat should be?"

Ay, you're drunk you're drunk you silly old fool, still you cannot see;
That's a woolen blanket that me mother sent to me.
Well, it's many a day I've traveled, a hundred miles or more,
But buttons on a blanket, sure, I never saw before.

And as I went home on Wednesday night, as drunk as drunk could be,
I saw a pipe upon the chair, where my old pipe should be;
Well, I called my wife and I said to her,
"Will you kindly tell to me, who owns that pipe upon the chair,
Where my old pipe should be?"

Ay, you're drunk you're drunk you silly old fool, still you cannot see!
That's a lovely tin-whistle, that me mother sent to me.
Well, it's many a day I've traveled, a hundred miles or more,
But tobacco in a tin-whistle, sure, I never saw before!

And I went home on Thursday night, as drunk as drunk could be,
I saw two boots beneath the bed, where my old boots should be;
Well, I called me wife and I said to her,
"Will you kindly tell to me, who owns them boots beneath the bed,
Where my old boots should be?"

Ay, you're drunk you're drunk you silly old fool, still you cannot see,
They're two lovely geranium pots me mother sent to me.
Well, it's many a day I've traveled, a hundred miles or more,
But laces in geranium pots I never saw before!

And as I came home on Friday night, as drunk as drunk could be,
I saw a head upon the bed where my old head should be;
Well, I called my wife and I said to her,
"Will you kindly tell to me, who owns that head upon the bed,
Where my old head should be?"

Ay, you're drunk you're drunk you silly old fool still you cannot see,
That's a baby boy that me mother sent to me.
Well, it's many a day I've traveled, a hundred miles or more,
But a baby boy with his whiskers on, sure I never saw before!

There are various versions of two additional very bawdy verses that are sometimes sung to this song, though not in polite company. Look them up on Wikipedia if you would like to learn them.

Chord Forms

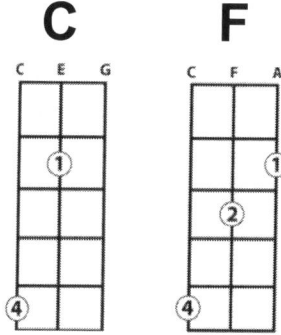

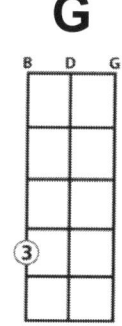

IRISH DRINKING SONG

Seven Drunken Nights
(continued)

Melody & Chords
Key of C

```
        C                                              F        C
G ─────────────────────────────────────────0──2────4────5─────
D ──2─2─────2─────2─2─0──────────────0──2──2──3────3────2─────
G  5─5─5────5─────5─5─4─5────5──────0──5──5──5─────────0─────
  As I went home on a Monday night, as drunk as drunk could be...

     F        C            G
G  5─5───0─2──────0───────────────────────────────────────────
D  2─3───3─3──────2──2──3──2─────────0──0──0─────2────0──────
G  0─2───────2──5─────5──5────5──4──4───4────4──────0────────
  I saw a horse outside the door, where my old horse should be...

        C                                                 F
G ──────────────────────────────────────────────0──2──4──5────
D ──2───────2─────2─────2─2─0──────────────2──2─2──2──3───────
G  5─5──────5─────5─────5─5─4──5──5──5──5──5──5─────────2─────
  I called the wife and I says to her, will you kindly tell to me...

                        C             G              C
G  5────5───0──2────────0─────────────────────────────────────
D  3────3───3──3────────2──2──3──2────0──0───────────────────
G  2────2───────2──5────5──5─────5──4─4──5───4───5───────────
  Who owns that horse outside the door, where my old horse should be?
```

CHORUS

```
        C                                                  F
G  0────0─────────────────────────────────────────0──4──5────
D  2────2─────2─────2─────2─────2──0──────────2────2──2──3───
G  5────5─────5─────5─────5─────5──5──5──5──5──5──5─────2────
  Well you drunk, you drunk, you silly old fool, still you cannot see;

                  C        G         C
G  5─────5─2──2──0────────────────────────────────────────
D  3─────3─3──3──2──2─────0──0──────0──────────────────────
G  2───────2────5──5──5──4──4──4────0──5──────────────────
  That's a lovely sow that me mother sent to me.

     G        C                                             F
G  0────0────────────────────────────0──0──2──4──5──────────
D  0────0──────2─2─2─2─2──0──────2─2─2──2──2──3────────────
G  4────4──────5─5─5─5─5──4──5──5─5──────────2────────────
  Well! There's many the day I've traveled a hundred miles or more;

                     C         G          C
G  0──4─5─5───2─2─0─────────────────5──────────────────────
D  2──2─3─3───3─3─2──2───0──0───────2──────────────────────
G  ───2────2──5────5──5─4─4──5──4─5──────────────────────
  But a saddle on a sow, sure, I never saw before.
```

SEAFARING SONG

South Australia

Basic Melody
Key of C

Words and Music
Traditional

While not technically a drinking song, in that it doesn't actually mention drinking, this great old seafaring song is perfect for belting out over a few pints in your favorite pub. Patrick Boyle has been performing this one for many years at sessions and Irish parties in and around Dover, New Hampshire.

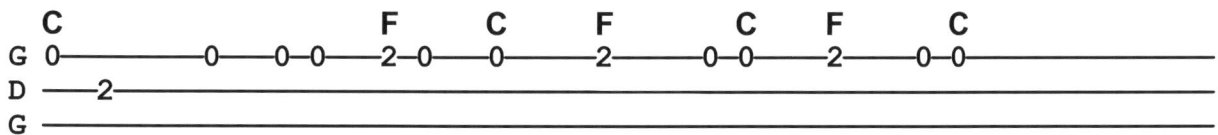
In South Australia I was born, heave a-way, haul a-way;

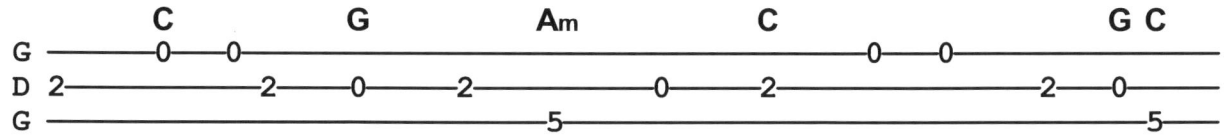
South Australia 'round Cape Horn, we're bound for South Australia!

CHORUS

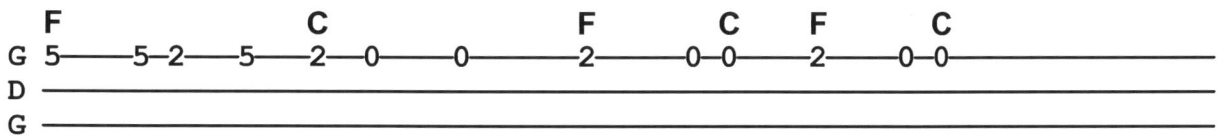
Haul a-way you rolling kings, heave a-way, haul a-way;

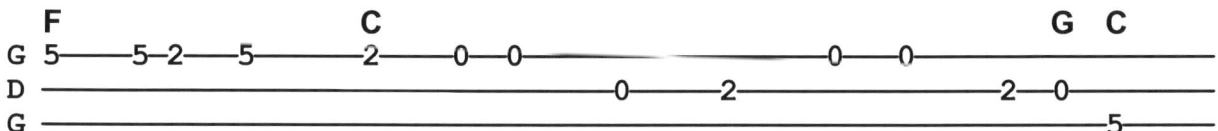
Haul a-way you'll hear me sing, we're bound for South Australia!

Additional Verses

As I walked out one morning fair,
Heave away, haul away;
It's there I met Miss Nancy Blair,
We're bound for South Australia.

I shook her up, I shook her down,
Heave away, haul away;
I shook her 'round and 'round the town,
We're bound for South Australia.

There is just one thing grieves me mind,
Heave away, haul away;
To leave Miss Nancy Blair behind,
We're bound for South Australia.

And as we wallop around Cape Horn,
Heave away, haul away;
You'll wish to Christ you'd never been born,
We're bound for South Australia.

Chord Forms

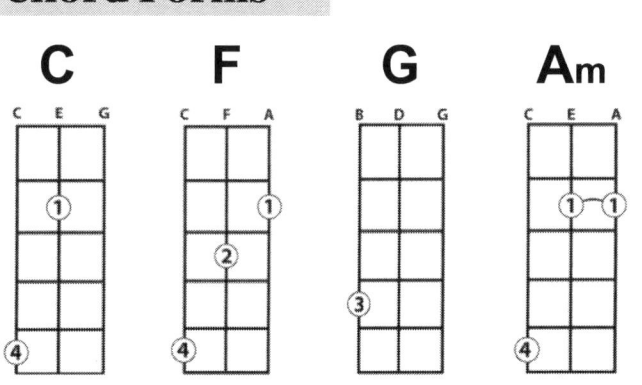

Irish Drinking Songs Cigar Box Guitar Songbook · Copyright 2019 by Hobo Music Works · All Rights Reserved

South Australia (continued)

SEAFARING SONG

Melody & Chords
Key of C

```
     C                F    C    F    C    F    C
G  0--------0--0------2-0------0------2--0-0------2------0-0
D  2---2------2--2-2--3-2------2------3--2-2------3------2-2
G  5---5------5-------5-------5-------5--5--------5------5
   In South Australia I was born, heave a-way, haul a-way;

        C       G    Am       C                    G  C
G  --------0--0----------2-------------0--0-------------
D  2---2---2--2-2--0----2---2--0---2---2--2----2---2--0
G  5---5---5----4----4----5---2---5---5--5-----5---4--5
   South Australia 'round Cape Horn, we're bound for South Australia!
```

CHORUS

```
   F             C          F    C    F    C
G  5----5-2--5---2-0--0-----2-------0-0------2------0-0
D  3----3-3--3---2-2--2-----3-------2-2------3------2-2
G  2------------5------5----5--5-------5-----5------5
   Haul a-way you rolling kings, heave a-way, haul a-way;

   F             C                           G  C
G  5----5-2--5---2-0--0--------------0---0----------5
D  3----3-3--3---2--2-2---0----2-----2---2----2--0--5
G  2------------5------5--0--5-------5--------5--4--5
   Haul a-way you'll hear me sing, we're bound for South Australia!
```

Victorian era British sailors.

South Australia (continued)

SEAFARING SONG
Basic Melody
Key of G

```
         G              C  G   C       G  C      G
G ─────────────────────────────────────────────────────
D 0────────0──0─0──2─0───0────2───0─0──2───0─0──
G ──4─────────────────────────────────────────────────
  In South Australia I was born, heave a-way, haul a-way;

         G       D     Em       G               D G
G ─────────────────────────────────────────────────────
D ────0──0─────────────────────────0──0────────────────
G 4─────4────2───4───0───2────4───────────4──2─0──
  South Australia 'round Cape Horn, we're bound for South Australia!
```

CHORUS

```
  C          G         C     G    C      G
G 0──0──0──────────────────────────────────────
D ────2────2─0────0────2───0─0───2────0─0──
G ─────────────────────────────────────────────
  Haul a-way you rolling kings, heave a-way, haul a-way;

  C          G                          D   G
G 0──0──0──────────────────────────────────────
D ────2────2─0─0────────────────0──0───────────
G ──────────────2───4───────────4─2─0───
  Haul a-way you'll hear me sing, we're bound for South Australia!
```

Chord Forms

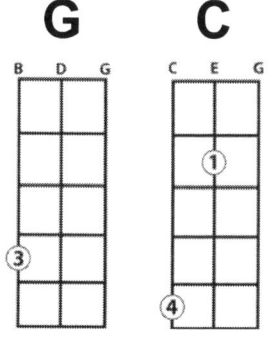
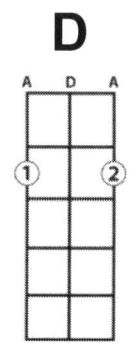
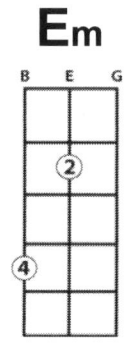

Patrick and Charlie Boyle at the Greenhouse, St. Patrick's Day 2017.

SEA SHANTY

What Do We Do With A Drunken Sailor

Basic Melody

Key of Am

Words and Music

Traditional

This is one of the quintessential sailing songs, or sea shanties, known throughout the English-speaking world. It asks the question of what the crew is to do with one of their inebriated fellows, and proposes some more or less humorous courses of action. Quite a few other verses have been penned over the years, some of them quite bawdy. We have only included a few of the tamer ones here.

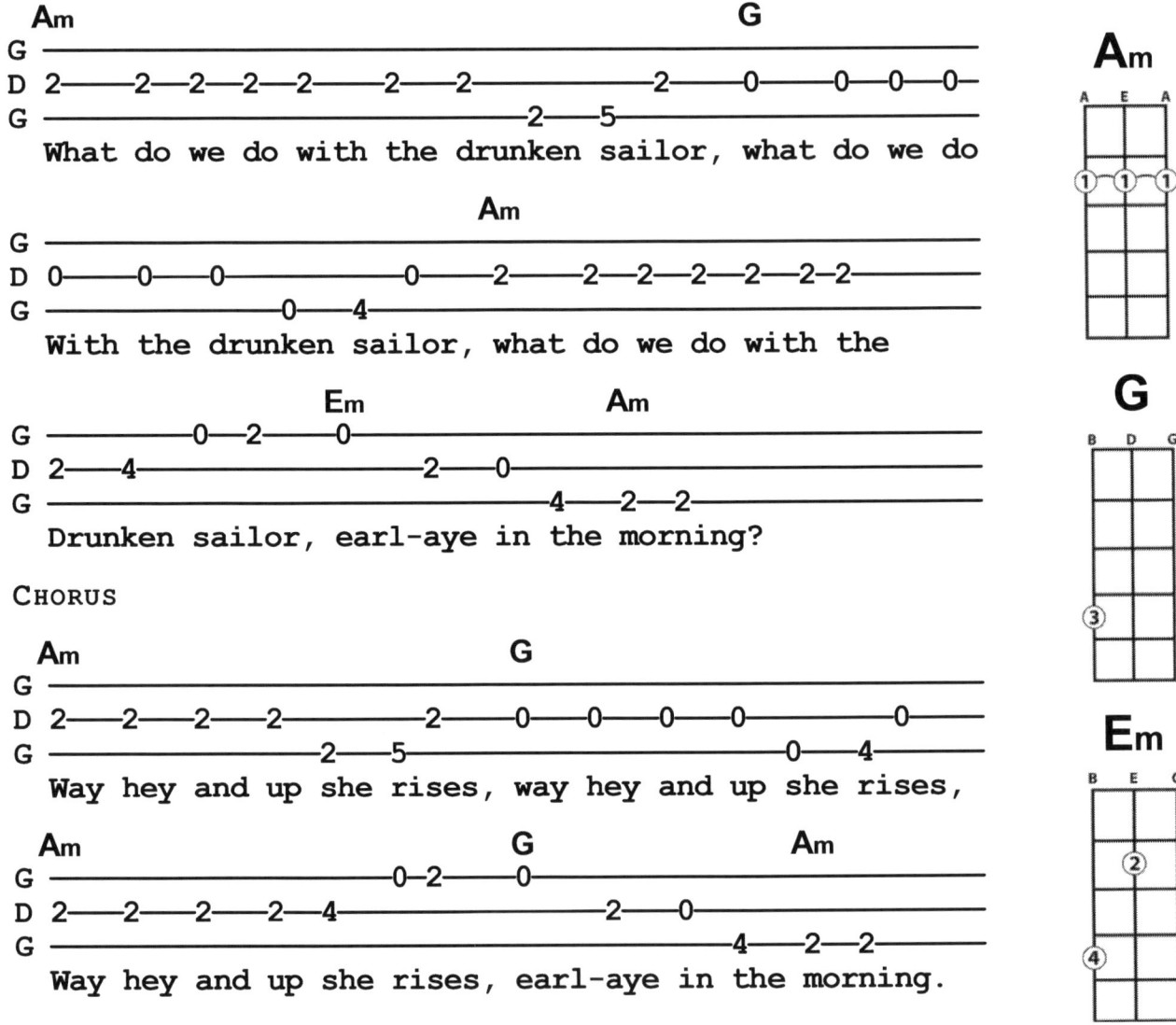

CHORUS

Additional Verses

Put him in a longboat, throw the tarp over... (3x)
Earl-aye in the morning!

Put him in the guardroom till he's sober... (3x)
Earl-aye in the morning!

Shave his belly with a rusty razor... (3x)
Earl-aye in the morning!

Put him in the scuppers with a hosepipe on him...(3x)
Earl-aye in the morning!

Pull out the plug and wet him all over... (3x)
Earl-aye in the morning!

Give 'im a hair of the dog that bit him... (3x)
Earl-aye in the morning!

Irish Drinking Songs Cigar Box Guitar Songbook · Copyright 2019 by Hobo Music Works · All Rights Reserved

SEA SHANTY

What Do We Do With A Drunken Sailor (continued)

Basic Melody

Key of Em

```
   Em                                    D
G  4—4—4—4—4—4—4—————0—4—2———2—2—2—
D  ———————————————2—————————————————
G  —————————————————————————————————
```
What do we do with the drunken sailor, what do we do

```
                              Em
G  2———2———2———————2———4—4—4—4—4—4—
D  ——————————0———4——————————————————
G  —————————————————————————————————
```
With the drunken sailor, what do we do with the

```
                Bm              Em
G  4—4—6—9———7—4—2—————————————————
D  ————————————————————4—2—2————————
G  —————————————————————————————————
```
Drunken sailor, earl-aye in the morning?

CHORUS

```
   Em                  D
G  4—4—4—4———0—4—2—2—2—2—————————2—
D  ——————————2————————————————0—4——
G  —————————————————————————————————
```
Way hey and up she rises, way hey and up she rises,

```
   Em                        D         Em
G  4—4—4—4—6———7—9———7—4—2—————————————
D  ————————————————————————4—2—2————————
G  —————————————————————————————————————
```
Way hey and up she rises, earl-aye in the morning.

Chord Forms

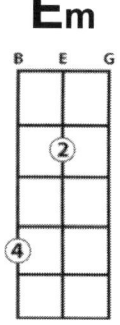
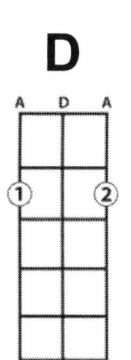
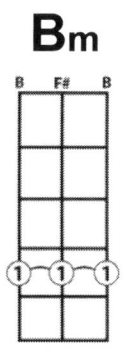

Irish Drinking Songs Cigar Box Guitar Songbook · Copyright 2019 by Hobo Music Works · All Rights Reserved

SEA SHANTY

What Do We Do With A Drunken Sailor (continued)

Melody & Chords

Key of Em

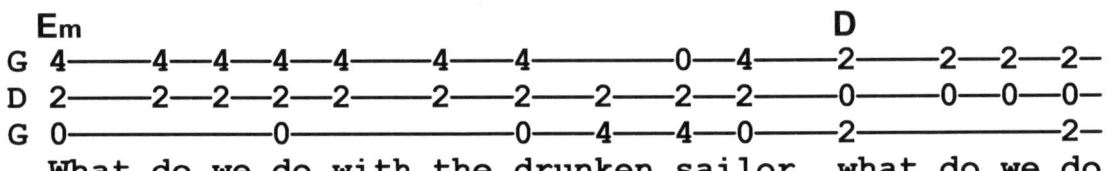
```
   Em                                            D
G  4——4—4—4—4——4——4———0-4——2——2—2—2-
D  2——2—2—2—2——2——2—————2—2——0——0—0—0-
G  0————————0—————————0—4—4—0——2————2-
   What do we do with the drunken sailor, what do we do
```

```
                                 Em
G  2———2——2———————2——4——4—4—4—4——4
D  0——0—0—0—0—4—0——2——2—2—2—2——2
G  ————2—2—2—2—0——————0
   With the drunken sailor, what do we do with the
```

```
                   Bm             Em
G  4——4——6—9——7——4——2————————————
D  2——2——6—6——4——4—4—4——2—2————————
G  0————————————————2—4—4———————
   Drunken sailor, earl-aye in the morning?
```

CHORUS

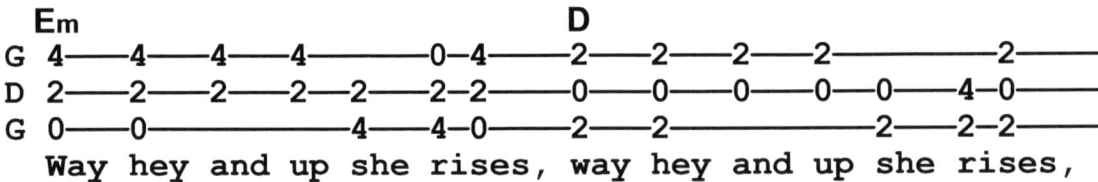
```
   Em                           D
G  4——4——4——4——0-4——2——2—2—2————2
D  2——2——2——2—2-2——0——0—0—0—0——4-0
G  0—0————4—4-0——2——2————2—2-2
   Way hey and up she rises, way hey and up she rises,
```

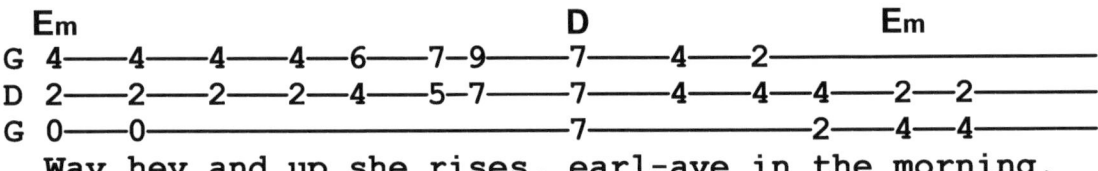
```
   Em                          D             Em
G  4——4——4——4—6——7-9——7——4——2
D  2——2——2——2—4——5-7——7——4—4—4——2—2
G  0—0————————————7————2—4—4
   Way hey and up she rises, earl-aye in the morning.
```

Chord Forms

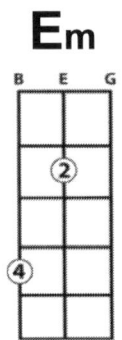
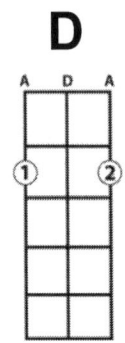
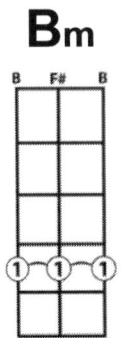

Irish Drinking Songs Cigar Box Guitar Songbook · Copyright 2019 by Hobo Music Works · All Rights Reserved

IRISH BALLAD

Whiskey In the Jar

Basic Melody
Key of C

Words and Music
Traditional

This well-known Irish song is set in the mountains of Ireland and tells the story of a highwayman who runs afoul of the law. It has been recorded by a wide range of performers over the years, from Burl Ives to Thin Lizzy, The Grateful Dead to Metallica. There are a number of variations on the lyrics and verses, but the tune seems to have remained unchanged over the years.

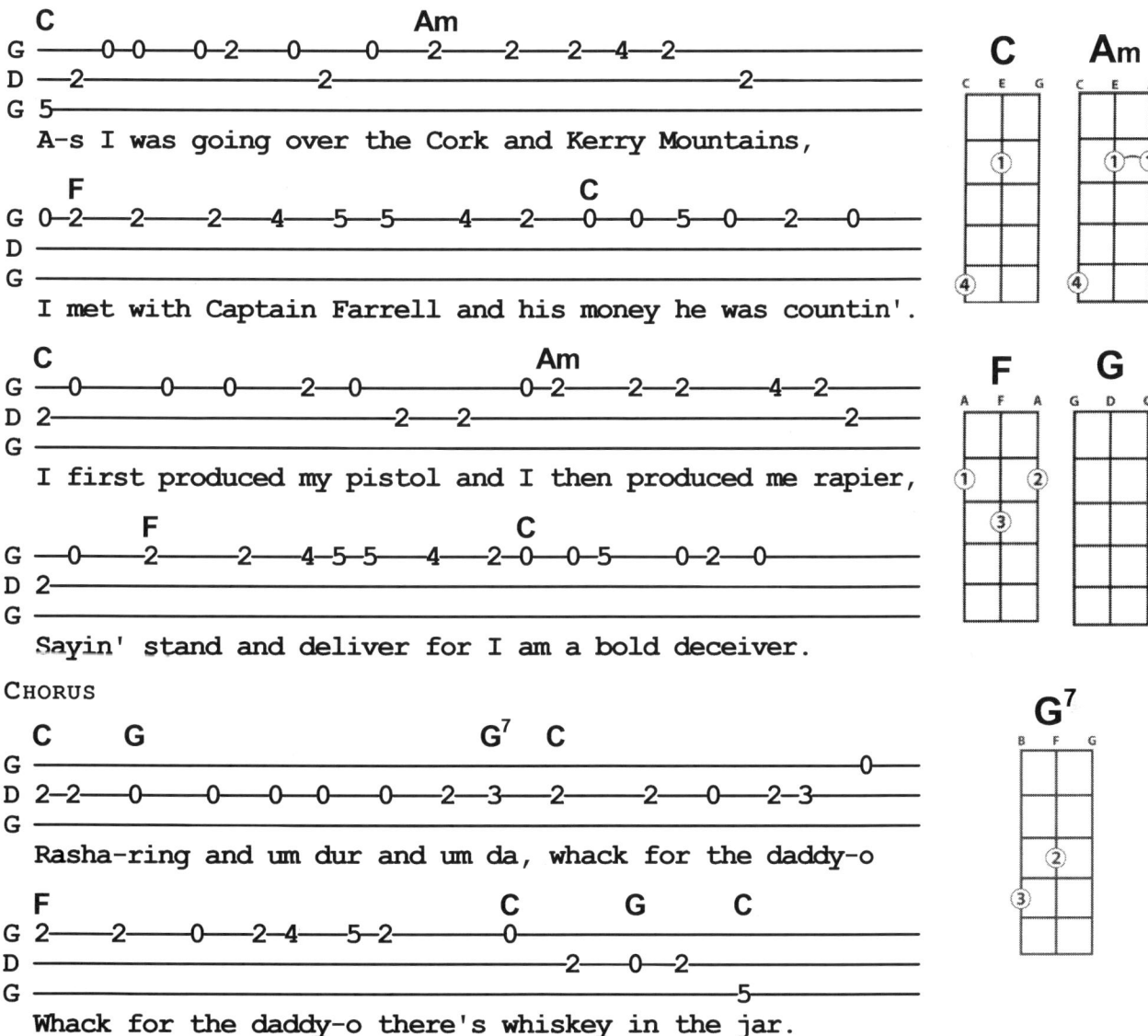

Additional Verses

I counted out his money and it made a pretty penny,
I put it in me pockets and I took it home to Jenny.
She sighed and she swore that she never would betray me;
But the Devil take the women for they never can be easy.

I went unto me chamber, all for to take a slumber.
I dreamt of gold and jewels, and sure it was no wonder.
But Jenny took me charges and she filled them up with water,
And sent for Captain Farrell to be ready for the slaughter.

It was early in the morning just before I rose to travel,
Up stepped a band of footmen, and likewise Captain Farrell.

I first produced me pistols for she'd stolen away me rapier,
But I couldn't shoot the water so a pris'ner I was taken.

If anyone can aid me, 'tis me brother in the army,
If I can find his station, in Cork or in Killarney.
And if he'll go with me, we'll go rollin' in Kilkenny;
And I'm sure he'll treat me better than me old miss sportin' Jenny.

Now there's some take delight in the carriages a-rollin',
And others take delight in the hurlin' and the bowlin'.
But I take delight in the juice of the barley,
And courtin' pretty fair maids in the mornin' bright and early!

Irish Drinking Songs Cigar Box Guitar Songbook · Copyright 2019 by Hobo Music Works · All Rights Reserved

IRISH BALLAD

Whiskey In the Jar
(continued)

Melody & Chords
Key of C

```
        C                              Am
G ———0—0———0—2———0———0———2———2———2—4—2——————
D ——2—2—2———2—2———2—2———2———2———2—2—2———2———
G  5—5—5———————5———5—5———2———2———2——————————
   A-s   I was going over the Cork and Kerry Mountains,

         F                        C
G  0—2———2———2—4—5—5———4———2—0—0—5——0—2—0——
D  2—3———3———3—3—3—3———3———3—2—2—2——2—2—2——
G  ——5———5———5———2—2———————5—5—————0—5——————
   I met with Captain Farrell and his money he was countin'.

        C                              Am
G ———0———0—0———2—0———————0—2———2—2———4—2———
D  2—2———2———2———2—2———2———2—2———2—2———2—2—2
G  5—5———5———————————5—5———2———2—2———————2—2
   I first produced my pistol and I then produced me rapier,

         F                        C
G ——0———2———2—4—5—5———4———2—0—0—5———0—2—0——
D  2—2———3———3—3—3—3———3———3—2—2—2———2—2—2——
G  2—————5———5———2—————————5———0———5———5——
   Sayin' stand and deliver for I am a bold deceiver.
```

CHORUS

```
   C    G                    G⁷   C
G ——————————————————————————————————————————0———
D  2—2———0———0———0———0———0———2—3———2———2———0—2—3———2
G  5—5———0———0———0———4———4———4—4———5———5———0———5—5———5
   Rasha-ring and um dur and um da, whack for the daddy-o

    F                  C      G      C
G  2———2———0—2—4—5—2———0—————————————5———
D  3———3———3—3—3—3—3———2———2———0—2———5———
G  5———5———————2———————5———5———0—0———5———
   Whack for the daddy-o there's whiskey in the jar.
```

Irish Drinking Songs Cigar Box Guitar Songbook · Copyright 2019 by Hobo Music Works · All Rights Reserved

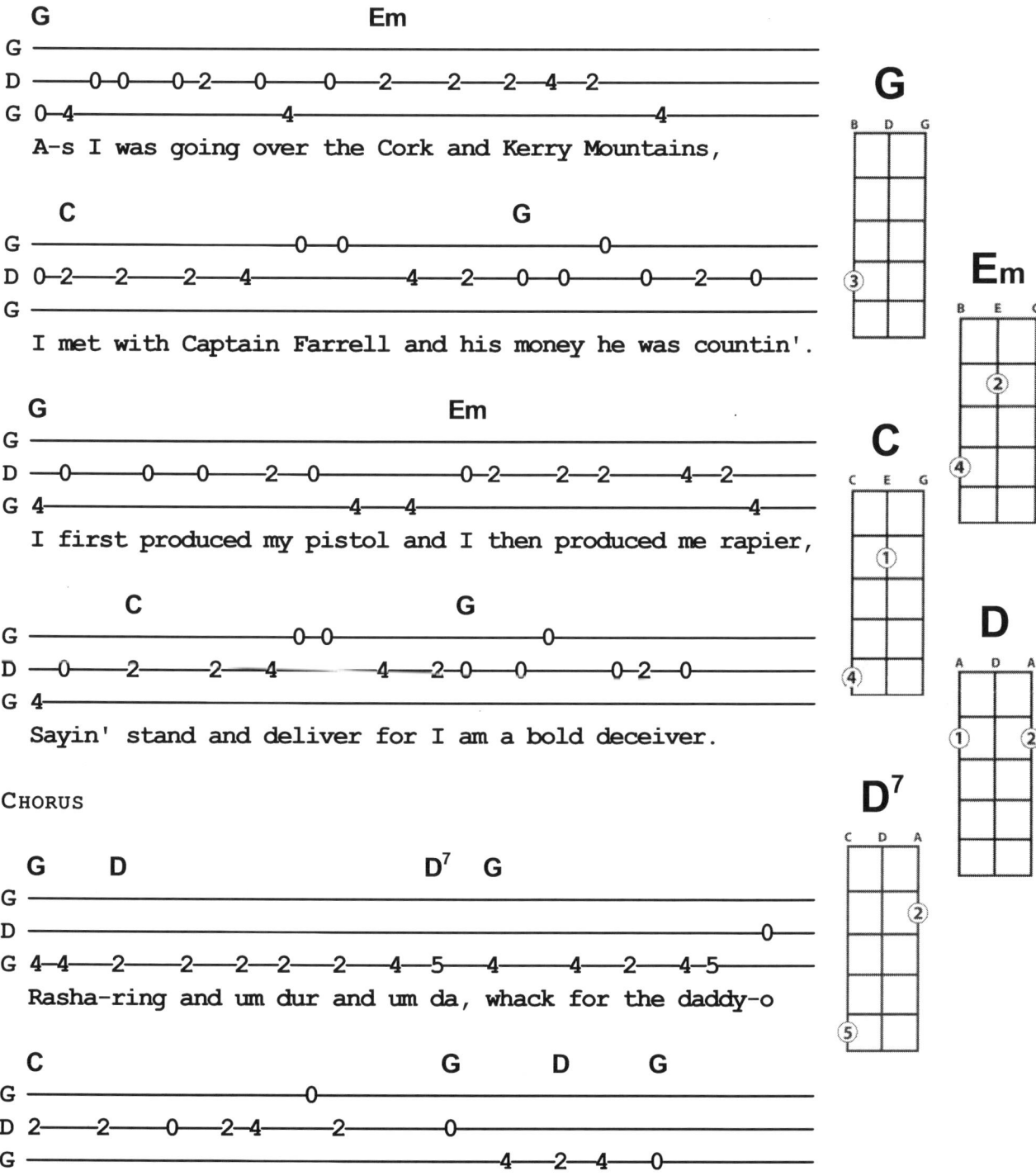

IRISH DRINKING SONG

Whiskey You're the Devil

Basic Melody
Key of G

This is another great old drinking song that the Clancy Brothers and Tommy Makem set the standard for. It is meant to be performed at a brisk pace and quite energetically. Search YouTube for the recording on the "Come Fill Your Glass With Us" album.

Words and Music
Traditional

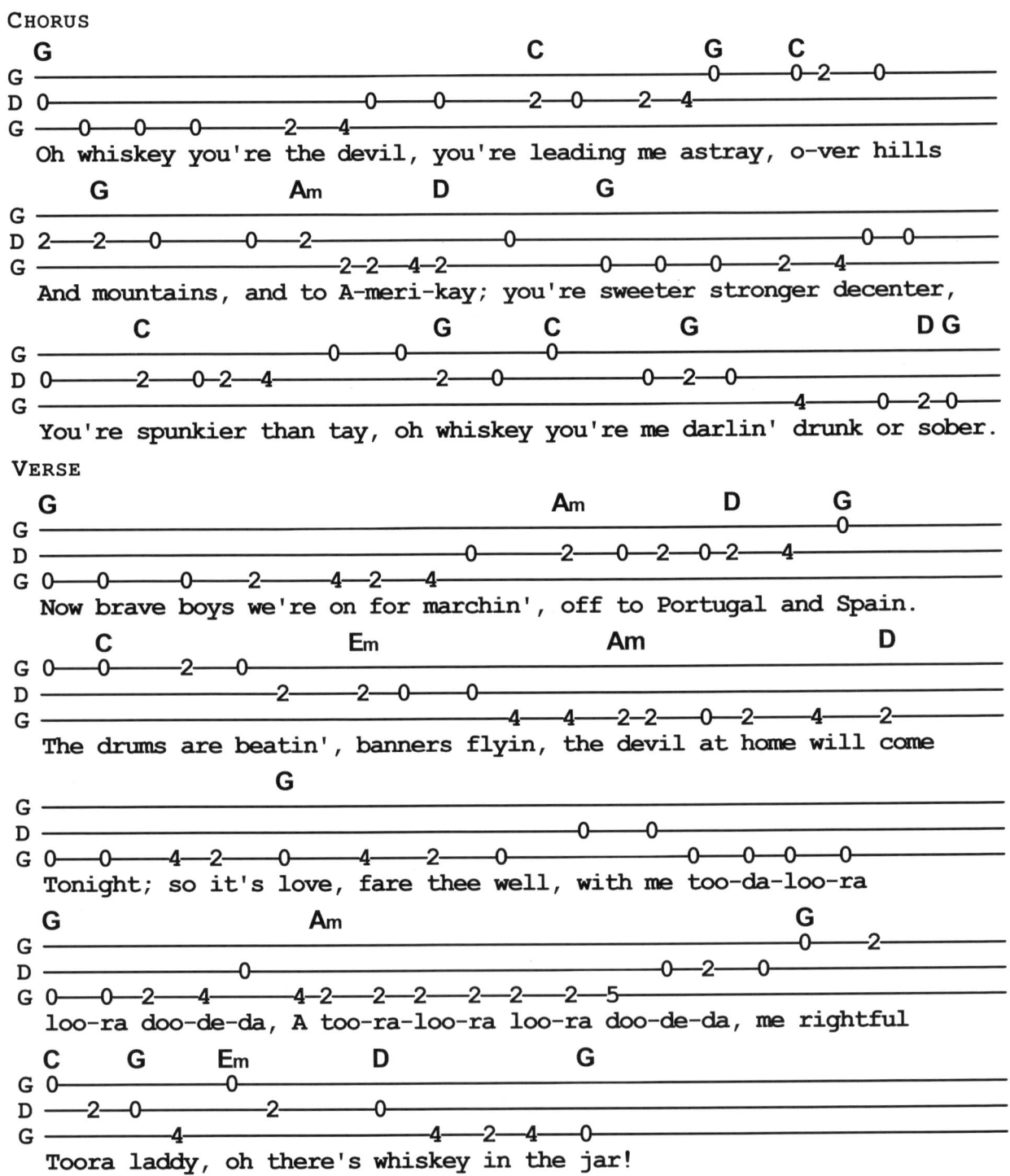

See Chord Forms and Additional Verses on Next Page

Irish Drinking Songs Cigar Box Guitar Songbook · Copyright 2019 by Hobo Music Works · All Rights Reserved

IRISH DRINKING SONG

Whiskey You're the Devil
(continued)

Additional Verses & Chord Forms

Key of G

Additional Verses

The French are fighting boldly, men are dying hot and coldly,
Give every man his flask of powder, his firelock on his shoulder;
And its love, fare thee well with me too da loo ra loo ra doo de da,
A too ra loo ra loo ra doo de, me rightful toora laddie-o,
There's whisky in the jar!

Says the old one do not wrong me, don't take me daughter from me,
For if you do I will torment you, and when I'm dead my ghost will haunt you;
So its love, fare thee well with me too da loo ra loo ra doo de da,
A too ra loo ra loo ra doo de, me rightful toora laddie-o,
There's whisky in the jar!

Chord Forms (Key of G, previous page)

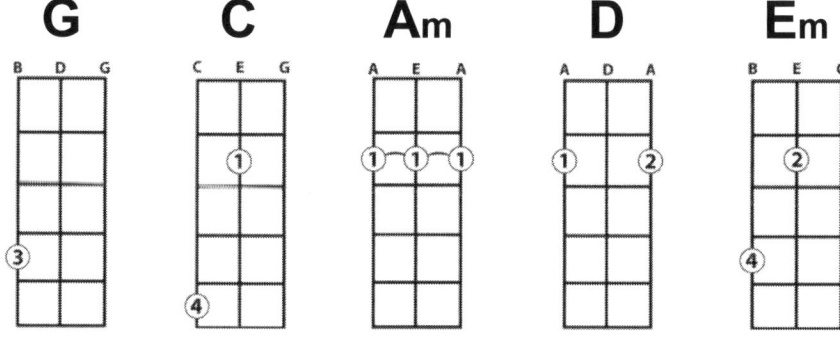

Chord Forms (Key of C, next page)

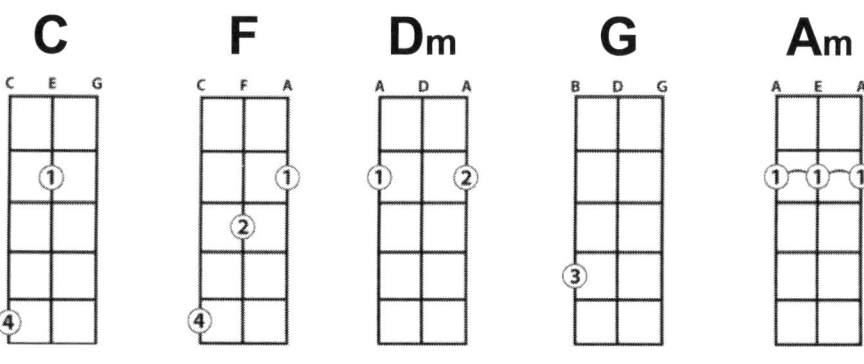

Irish Drinking Songs Cigar Box Guitar Songbook · Copyright 2019 by Hobo Music Works · All Rights Reserved

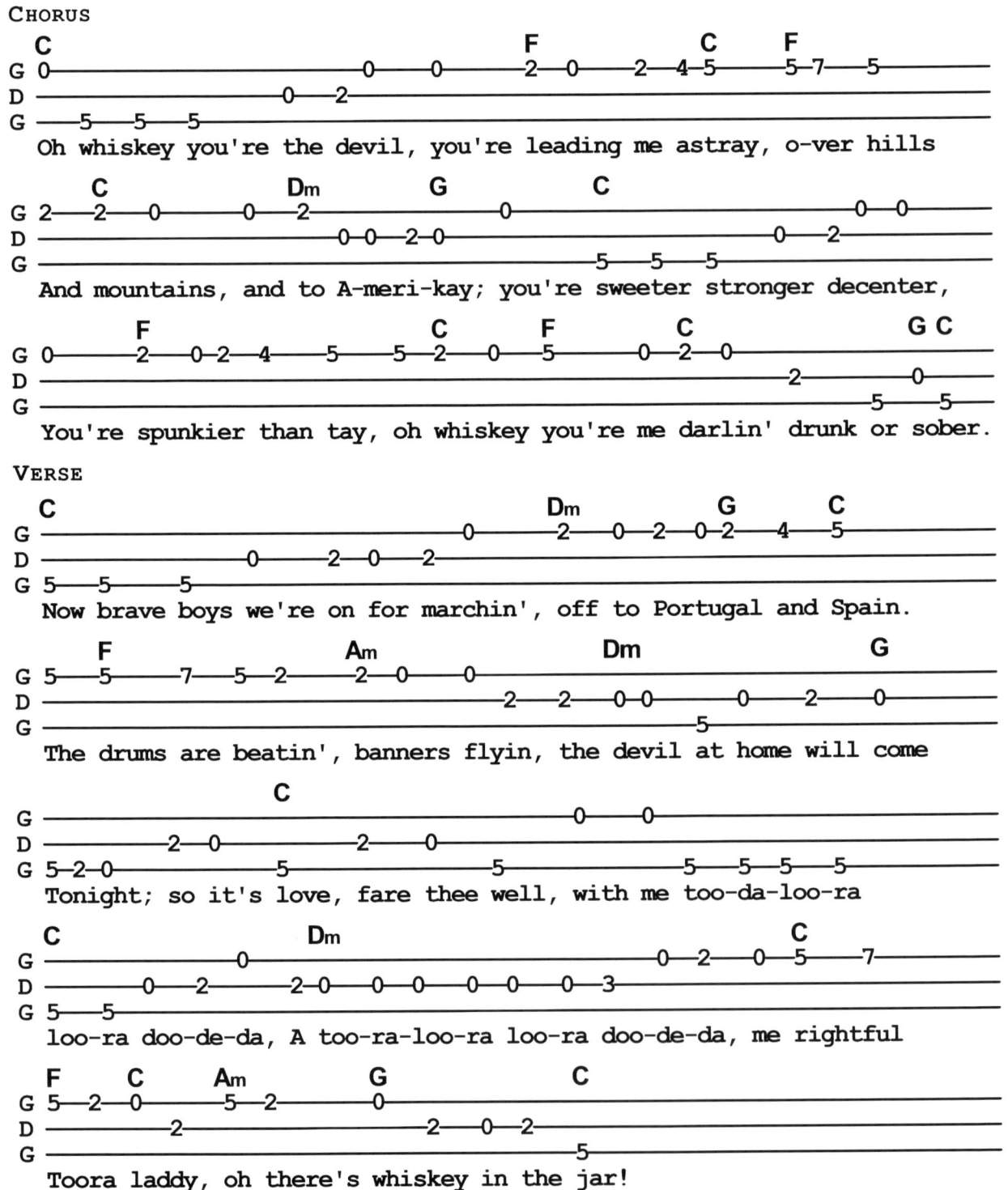

IRISH DRINKING SONG

Whiskey You're the Devil
(continued)

Melody & Chords
Key of C

CHORUS

```
        C                                    F         C     F
G  0---------------------0---0---------2-0---2-4-5-----5-7---5
D  2-----------0---2-2-------2---------3-3---3-3-2-----3-5---3
G  5-5-5-5-----5---5-5-5-----5---------5-----5-0---2---------2
   Oh whiskey you're the devil, you're leading me astray, o-ver hills

        C         Dm        G           C
G  2---2-0-----0--2---------0-----------------------0-0
D  3---2-2-----2----0-0-0-2-0---0-------------0-2-2-2
G  ----5-5---------2-2-2-2---4---4---5-5-5-0-5-----5
   And mountains, and to A-meri-kay; you're sweeter stronger decenter,

        F           C       F       C             G C
G  0----2--0-2-4---5-5-2-0--5-------0-2-0---------
D  2----3--2-3-3---3-3-2----2---3---0-2-2---2-----0
G  5----5----------2--2-5-----------5-------5-4-5
   You're spunkier than tay, oh whiskey you're me darlin' drunk or sober.
```

VERSE

```
        C                           Dm        G       C
G  ----------------------------------0------2-0-2-0-2-4---5
D  ----------0-----2-0-2-2-----------3-0-0-0-0-0-0---0-----2
G  5-5---5-0---5-0-5-5---------------2-2---2-0-------0
   Now brave boys we're on for marchin', off to Portugal and Spain.

        F           Am              Dm              G
G  5---5---7-5-2---2-0---0-----------------------------
D  2-3---5-3-3-----2-2---2-2---2-0-0---0-----2-0-------
G  ----2-----------2-----2-2---2-2-5---2-----2-0-------
   The drums are beatin', banners flyin, the devil at home will come

                  C
G  ------------------------------0---0
D  -------2-0--------2---0-------2---2
G  5-2-0-4-4---5-----5-0-5-------5-5-5-5
   Tonight; so it's love, fare thee well, with me too-da-loo-ra

        C             Dm                      C
G  ------0-------------------------0-2-0-5---7
D  --0-2-2-2-0-0-0-0-0-0-0-3-0-0-0-2---------5
G  5-5-0-0-5-2-2-2-2-2-2-2-2-2-----0
   loo-ra doo-de-da, A too-ra-loo-ra loo-ra doo-de-da, me rightful

        F   C   Am      G           C
G  5-2-0---5-2---0---------------5
D  3-3-2-2---2-2---0-2---0-2-----5
G  2---5-5---2-----4---4-4-4-----5
   Toora laddy, oh there's whiskey in the jar!
```

See Chord Forms and Additional Verses on Previous Page

IRISH BALLAD

The Wild Colonial Boy

Basic Melody
Key of C

This old Irish song tells the story of Jack Duggan, who left Ireland to travel to Australia where he became a Robin Hood-style highwayman. He eventually met his fate at the hands of some British soldiers. Traditionally this was sung in a slower, more mournful manner, but the Clancy Brothers and Tommy Makem sped it up to make it a rousing song, and that is the way it is usually performed today.

Words and Music

Traditional

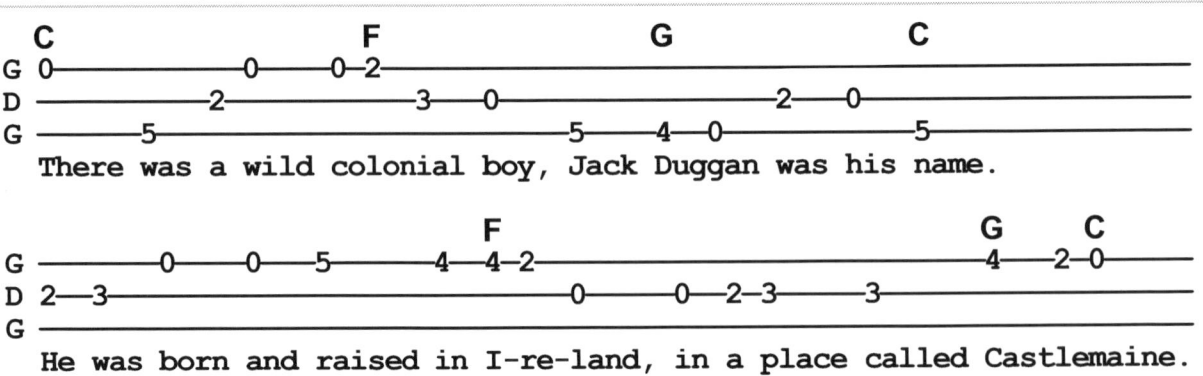

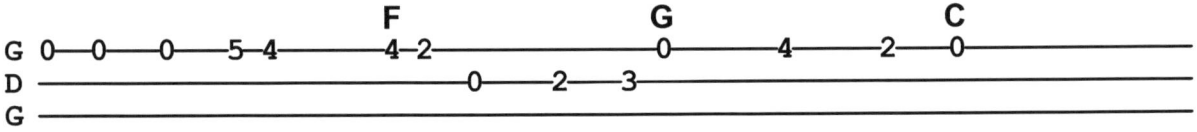

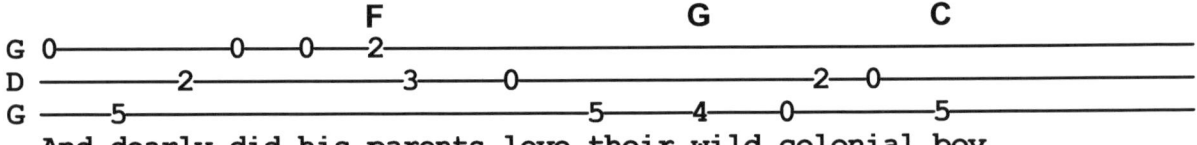

Additional Verses

At the early age of sixteen years, he left his native home;
And to Australia's sunny shore he was inclined to roam.
He robbed the rich, he helped the poor, he shot James McAvoy;
A terror to Australia was the wild colonial boy.

One morning on the prairie as Jack he rode along,
A-listening to the mockingbird a singing a cheerful song;
Out stepped a band of troopers, Kelly, Davis and Fitzroy;
They'd all set out to capture him, the wild colonial boy.

"Surrender now Jack Duggan for you see we're three to one.
Surrender in the Queen's high name for you are a plundering son"
Jack drew two pistols from his belt and proudly waved them high;
"I'll fight, but not surrender!" said the wild colonial boy.

He fired a shot at Kelly, which brought him to the ground;
And turning 'round to Davis, he received a fatal wound.
A bullet pierced his proud young heart from the pistol of Fitzroy,
And that was how they captured him, the wild colonial boy.

Chord Forms

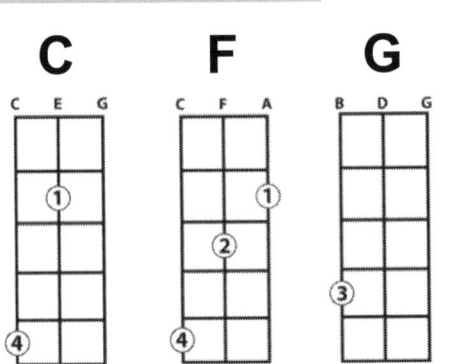

Irish Drinking Songs Cigar Box Guitar Songbook · Copyright 2019 by Hobo Music Works · All Rights Reserved

The Wild Colonial Boy
(continued)

Irish Ballad

Melody & Chords
Key of C

```
    C                F              G             C
G   0------0---0-2------------------------------------------
D   2--------2-2---2-3-3---0----------2---0---2------------
G   5--5--5-5----5---2---2-----5---4-0---4---4---5---------
    There was a wild colonial boy, Jack Duggan was his name.
```

```
                         F                          G   C
G   ----0---0---5----4-4-2----------------------4----2-0-----
D   2-3---2---2---2----2-3-3-0----0-2-3----3------0---0-2----
G   5-5-5-------0--------2---2-2-2----2------0----5----------
    He was born and raised in I-re-land, in a place called Castlemaine.
```

```
                    F            G           C
G   0-0-0-5-4----4-2---------0-----4---2-0---------------
D   2-2-2-2-2----3-3-0---2-3-0---0---0---2---------------
G   5-5-----0------2---2-2-0---0---5-----------------
    He was his father's only son, his mother's pride and joy;
```

```
                F            G          C
G   0-------0-0-2------------------5---------------------
D   2-----2-2-2---3-3---0---------2-0-2------------------
G   5-5-5-5-----2---2---5----4---0-4-4-5-----------------
    And dearly did his parents love their wild colonial boy.
```

IRISH DRINKING SONG

The Wild Rover

Basic Melody
Key of G

This is one of the best-known of the Irish pub/drinking songs, and is definitely a Saint Patrick's Day favorite. It is said to date back to the 1500's. The chorus is often accompanied by audience participation via clapping: four claps after the first "no nay never", two claps after "no nay never no more", and then a single clap after the final "no never, no more."

Words and Music
Traditional

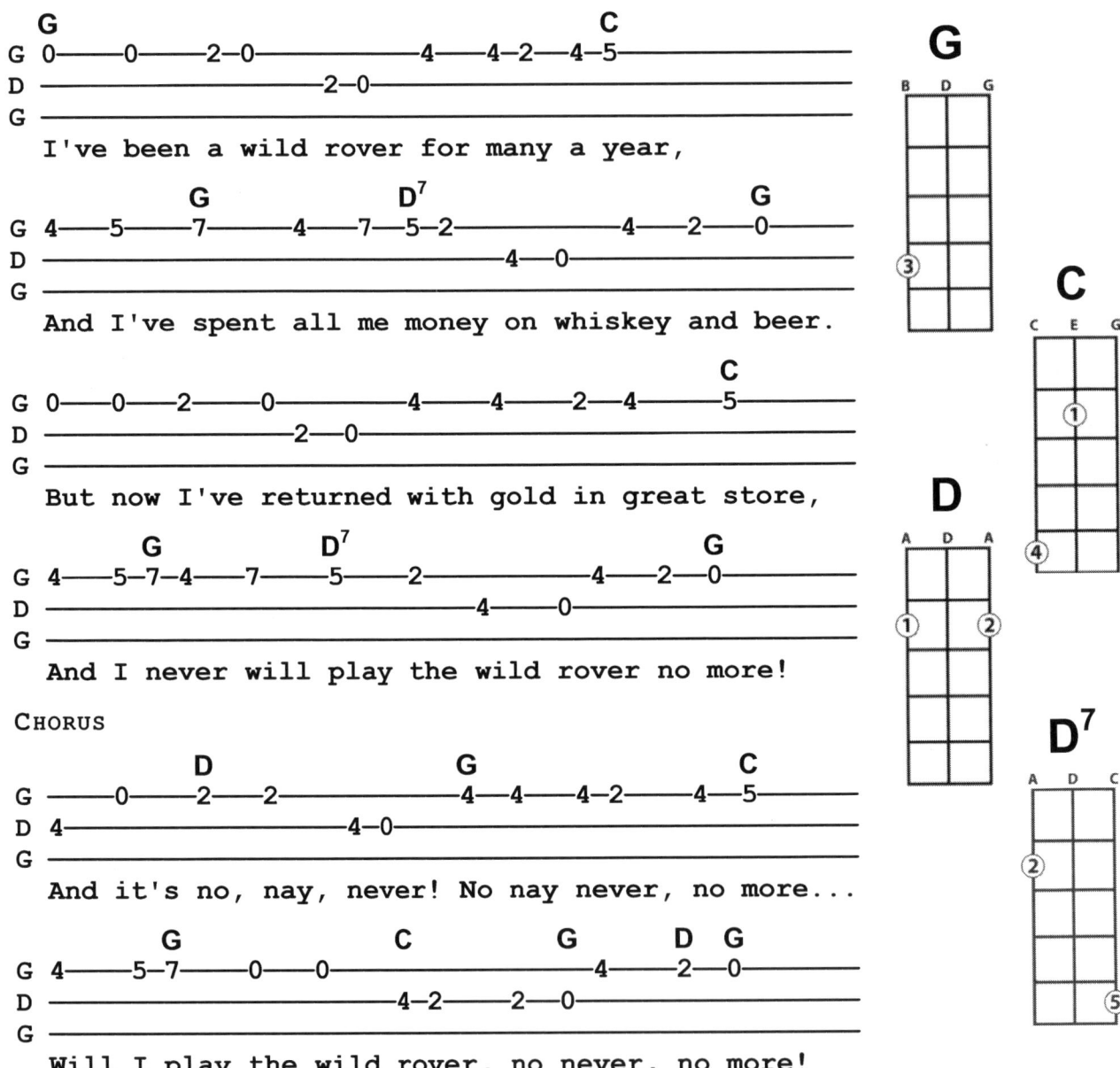

Additional Verses

I went into an alehouse I used to frequent,
And I told the landlady me money was spent.
I asked her for credit, she answered me nay...
Such a custom as yours I can have any day.

Then out of me pockets I took sovereigns bright,
And the landlady's eyes opened wide with delight.

She said I have whiskey, and wines of the best...
And the words that I spoke you were only in jest.

I'll go back to my parents, confess what I've done.
And I'll ask them to pardon their prodigal son.
And if they caress me as oft times before,
Then I never will play the wild rover no more!

Irish Drinking Songs Cigar Box Guitar Songbook · Copyright 2019 by Hobo Music Works · All Rights Reserved

IRISH DRINKING SONG

The Wild Rover (continued)

Melody & Chords
Key of G

```
     G                              C
G  0——0——2—0————4——4-2—4-5————
D  0——0——0-0——2-0—0——0-0—0-2————
G  4——4————0-0—0——0————0————
   I've been a wild rover for many a year,

        G           D⁷              G
G  4——5——7——4——7—5-2————4——2—0————
D  2——2——0——0——0—0-0——4—0——0—0—0——
G  ————0————2————2—2—2—2—4————
   And I've spent all me money on whiskey and beer.

     G                              C
G  0——0——2——0————4——4—2-4——5————
D  0——0——0——0-2—0——0——0-0—0——2————
G  4——4————0-0—0——0——————0————
   But now I've returned with gold in great store,

        G            D⁷             G
G  4——5-7-4——7——5——2————4——2—0————
D  2——2-0-0——0——0——0——4—0-0——0——
G  0————0——0—2————2—2-2—2—4————
   And I never will play the wild rover no more!
```

CHORUS

```
        D       G              C
G  ——0——2—2————4—4——4-2——4—5————
D  4——0——0-0——4-0——0-0——0-0——0—2————
G  2————2-2——2-2——0-0——0————0————
   And it's no, nay, never! No nay never, no more...

        G           C       G    D  G
G  4——5-7——0—0————————4——2—0————
D  2——2-0——0—0——4-2——2—0-0——0—0——
G  ————0————5-5——5-4-0——2—4————
   Will I play the wild rover, no never, no more!
```

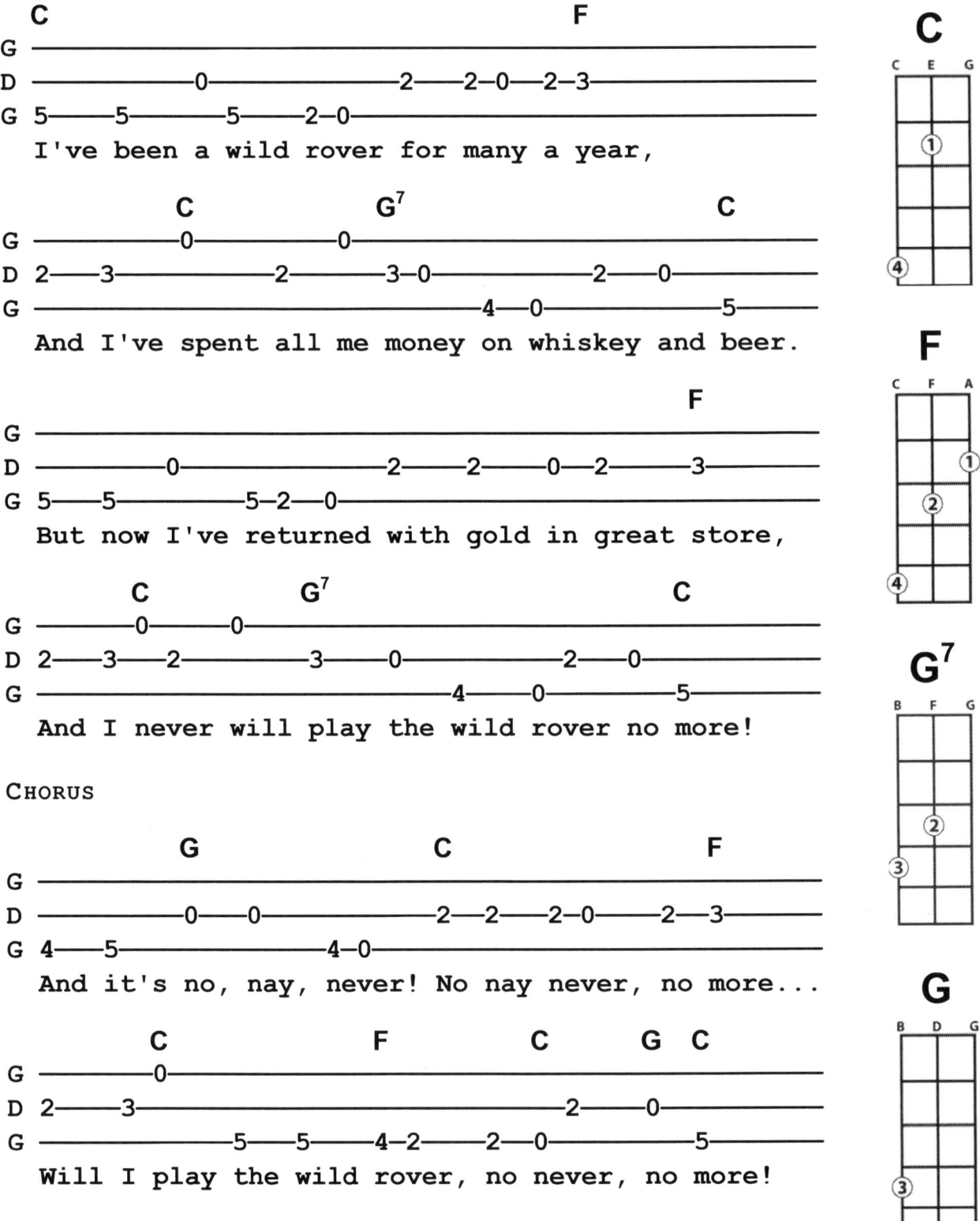

IRISH DRINKING SONG

The Work Of the Weavers

Basic Melody
Key of G

Words and Music
Traditional

This old song extols the virtues of those who weave wool into cloth, and tells how badly off the world would be without them. This is a favorite song of the descendants of Irish immigrants who came over to work in the woolen mills around northern New England, and you can often hear The Dover Rovers singing it in and around Dover, New Hampshire.

```
         G                              C         G
G ————————————————————————————————————0———0—————————————
D 0————————0——————0—0—0——————0————2——————————————0——————
G ——————4——————————————————————————————————————4———5————
  We're all here together, to sit and to craic, with our

                    Em          C             D
G ——————————————————————0———0———5———5—4——————4———2——————
D 0————0——2———0————0—————————————————————————————————————
G ————————————————————————————————————————————————————————
  Glasses in our hands, and our work u-pon our backs;

              G                              C         G
G ——————————————————————————————————————————0———0———————
D 0————————————0—0——————0—0——————0—0————0——2—————————0——
G ————4———————————————————————————————————————————————————
  There's nay a trade among 'em that can mend or can mack;

                     Em        D  G
G ——————————————————————0———4——2——0——————————————————————
D ——————0——————0—0—2——————0————————————————————————————————
G 4———5———————————————————————————————————————————————————
  If it wasn't-a for the work of the weavers!
```

Chorus

```
  G              D          C          D
G 0—2—4——4—4—4——4—2—2——————0——————0——————0—————————————
D ——————————————————————————————————————————————4——————
G ————————————————————————————————————————————————————————
  If it wasn't-a for the weavers, what would you do?

  C             G                C     D
G ——————0———0————————0———0——————5——4—2————————————————
D 4—2——————2—2—————0——————————————————————————————————
G ————————————————————————————————————————————————————
  Ye wouldn't-a hae the clothes that are made of wool;

              G                              C     G
G ——————————————————————————————————————————0———0——————
D 0————————————0——————0——————0——————0—————2————————0———
G ————4————4————4—————————————————————————————————————
  Ye wouldn't-a hae the coat of the black or the blue,

                     Em        D  G
G ——————————————————————0———4——2——0——————————————————————
D ——————0——————0—0—2——————2————0——————————————————————————
G 4———5———————————————————————————————————————————————————
  If it wasn't-a for the work of the weavers!
```

See Chord Forms and Additional Verses on Next Page

IRISH DRINKING SONG

The Work of the Weavers
(continued)

Additional Verses & Chord Forms

Key of G

Additional Verses

There's soldiers and there's sailors and glaziers and all;
There's doctors and there's ministers and them that live the law.
And our friends in South America, though them we never saw,
But we hear they wear the work of the weavers.

Now weavin' is a trade that never can fail,
As long as we need clothes for to keep another hale;
So let us all be merry and drinkers of good ale,
And we'll drink to the health of the weavers!

Chord Forms

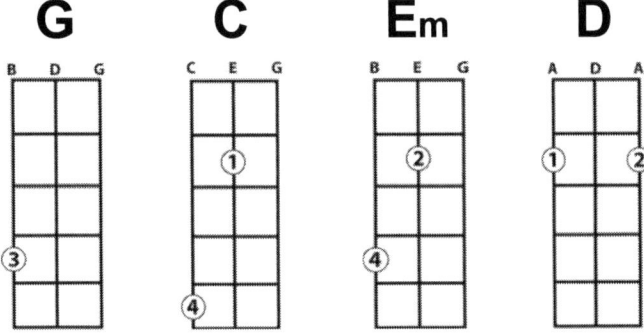

A photo from the 1890's of weaving room workers at the woolen mill in Gonic, New Hampshire, which now is the home of C. B. Gitty Crafter Supply.

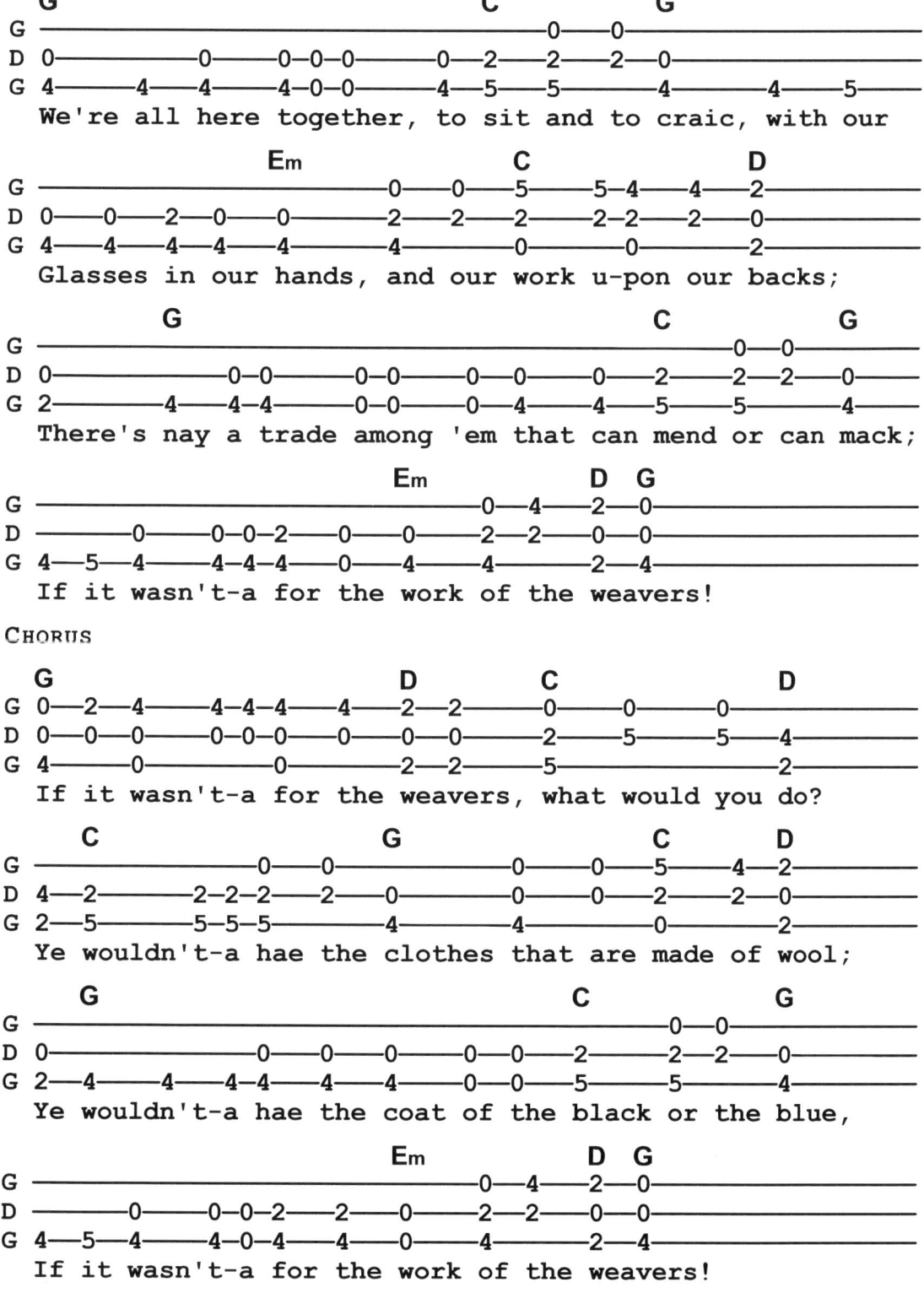

INSTRUCTIONAL

MORE RESOURCES

www.CigarBoxGuitar.com - There is a growing library of free cigar box guitar tablature available on this site. Just click the "Cigar Box Guitar Tablature" link in the right-hand menu to access it. Selections include some more modern songs, with pieces by The Beatles, the Violent Femmes, Bob Dylan, Elvis, Willy Nelson, Johnny Cash and more, in addition to some of the traditional public domain songs contained in this songbook. There are also resources and video links on how to build and play the cigar box guitars - all for free!

www.CigarBoxNation.com - Cigar Box Nation is the home base and nerve center of the worldwide homemade/handmade instruments movement. In addition to information about cigar box guitars, you can find a vast collection of photos, videos, forum posts and more related to canjos, washtub basses and all sorts of other handmade instruments.

Your Own Experimenting - As you become more familiar with playing your cigar box guitar, don't be afraid to noodle around and try to pick out tunes on your own. If a song occurs to you, hum it to yourself. Then try to find the starting note on the cigar box guitar neck. Here is a hint: As you can see from the songs in this book, most songs in the keys of G or C will start on one of the following notes:
- Open (0 / unfretted) on the top or bottom string (G)
- Open (0 / unfretted) on the middle string (D)
- Fourth fret on the top or bottom string (B)
- Fifth fret on the top or bottom string (C)

Decide whether the second note goes up or down from the first one, when humming… and then start moving your finger in that direction to find it. Then proceed to the third note and beyond. You'll probably surprise yourself with how easy it is to pick out simple tunes!

EDUCATIONAL OUTREACH

We have worked with many teachers all around the United States and internationally to help them get instrument building projects added to their school's curriculum. Building handmade instruments fits nicely into most STEAM (Science, Technology, Engineering, Arts & Math) programs!

We have created a number of kits and packages specifically for teachers, from basic one-string canjos (tin can banjos) through more advanced electric guitars. Teachers from grades 3 through 12 have used our kits and parts to teach everything from art and basic music theory and performance through advanced placement high school science courses studying the physics of electrical waves and sound.

If you know of a school or teacher that might be interested in this idea, let them know about us! We also work with summer camps, church groups, Boy Scout troops, community centers, senior centers, and folks wanting to host a local workshop.

E-mail us at **support@cbgitty.com** to get the ball rolling!

INSTRUCTIONAL
Blank Tablature Sheets

Cigar box guitars are inherently a DIY (do-it-yourself) sort of thing. From building them to playing them, everyone is encouraged to get in there and "try things themselves". In keeping with that, the next few pages are blank tablature sheets that you can use when "tabbing out" songs yourself.

It really isn't as hard as you might think! Here are some basic guidelines:

First, it helps to start with a song that you are very familiar with, one you know by heart.

Start by grabbing your cigar box guitar and strumming an open G chord. Now try humming your song and try to find the first note that would sound right with the G chord you are strumming. Finding the starting note can be the trickiest part of the whole endeavor.

Here is a hint: As you can see from the songs in this book, most songs in the keys of G or C will start on one of the following notes:

- Open (0 / unfretted) on the top or bottom string (G note)
- Open (0 / unfretted) on the middle string (D note)
- Fourth fret on the top or bottom string (B note)
- Fifth fret on the top or bottom string (C note)
- Second fret on the middle string (E note)

Once you are pretty sure you have that first note, decide whether the second note goes up or down (in pitch) from the first one, when humming… and then start playing notes upward or downward (in pitch) on the cigar box guitar to find it. Check out the tablature of the keys of G and C scales below to help figure out where to "look" for the notes, moving up or down. The notes in parentheses are the "blues" notes in each scale.

Then proceed to the third note and beyond. You'll probably surprise yourself with how easy it is to pick out simple tunes!

Key of G Scale

```
G ——————————————————0—2—4—5—7—9—(10)—11—12—14—16—17—
D ———————————0—2—(3)—4——————————————————————————————
G —0—2—4—5——————————————————————————————————————————
```

Key of C Scale

```
G ——————————————————0—2—(3)—4—5—7—9—10—12—14—(15)—16—17—
D ———————————0—2—3——————————————————————————————————————
G 0—2—(3)—4—5———————————————————————————————————————————
```

```
G _____
D _____
G _____


G _____
D _____
G _____


G _____
D _____
G _____


G _____
D _____
G _____


G _____
D _____
G _____


G _____
D _____
G _____
```

```
G ────────────────────────────────
D ────────────────────────────────
G ────────────────────────────────


G ────────────────────────────────
D ────────────────────────────────
G ────────────────────────────────


G ────────────────────────────────
D ────────────────────────────────
G ────────────────────────────────


G ────────────────────────────────
D ────────────────────────────────
G ────────────────────────────────


G ────────────────────────────────
D ────────────────────────────────
G ────────────────────────────────


G ────────────────────────────────
D ────────────────────────────────
G ────────────────────────────────
```

```
G ────────────────────────────────────────────
D ────────────────────────────────────────────
G ────────────────────────────────────────────


G ────────────────────────────────────────────
D ────────────────────────────────────────────
G ────────────────────────────────────────────


G ────────────────────────────────────────────
D ────────────────────────────────────────────
G ────────────────────────────────────────────


G ────────────────────────────────────────────
D ────────────────────────────────────────────
G ────────────────────────────────────────────


G ────────────────────────────────────────────
D ────────────────────────────────────────────
G ────────────────────────────────────────────


G ────────────────────────────────────────────
D ────────────────────────────────────────────
G ────────────────────────────────────────────
```

```
G ─────────────────────────────────────────────
D ─────────────────────────────────────────────
G ─────────────────────────────────────────────


G ─────────────────────────────────────────────
D ─────────────────────────────────────────────
G ─────────────────────────────────────────────


G ─────────────────────────────────────────────
D ─────────────────────────────────────────────
G ─────────────────────────────────────────────


G ─────────────────────────────────────────────
D ─────────────────────────────────────────────
G ─────────────────────────────────────────────


G ─────────────────────────────────────────────
D ─────────────────────────────────────────────
G ─────────────────────────────────────────────


G ─────────────────────────────────────────────
D ─────────────────────────────────────────────
G ─────────────────────────────────────────────
```

DIY Musical Instrument Kits
by C. B. Gitty

$79.99

PURE & SIMPLE CIGAR BOX GUITAR KIT - UNFRETTED
Our flagship UNFRETTED (SLIDE) cigar box guitar kit. Includes everything you need, and only requires a screwdriver to assemble. Goes together in under an hour, and sounds great.. Ages 14+.

$99.99

PURE & SIMPLE CIGAR BOX GUITAR KIT - FRETTED
Our flagship FRETTED cigar box guitar kit. Includes everything you need, and only requires a screwdriver to assemble. Goes together in under an hour, and sounds great! Ages 14+.

$79.99

CIGAR BOX UKULELE KIT

Build a classic cigar box ukulele... just like the ones the Hawaiian masters experimented with 100+ years ago, when designing the first ukuleles! Ages 16+.

$59.99

GITTYLELE DIY UKULELE KIT

These ukuleles have a distinctive design and a great sound... and they are fun and easy to build! Ages 14+.

$24.99

CIGAR BOX DIDDLEY BOW KIT

Diddley bows helped create the Blues! Inspired by classic instruments from the Mississippi Delta, this is one of our easiest kits. Ages 14+.

$29.99

AMERICAN CANJO KIT

What's more fun than a simple one-string tin can banjo. Perfect for both young and young-at-heart pickers. Ages 12+.

$54.99

2X4 LAP STEEL GUITAR KIT

You supply the 2x4, we supply the parts and how-to! Yields a six-string lap steel slide guitar, perfect for country & western or Hawaiian-style playing. Ages 14+.

$49.99

CIGAR BOX AMPLIFIER KIT
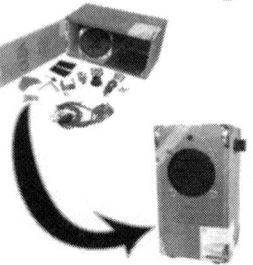
Create a rocking amplifier to go with your cigar box guitar or electric guitar! Some soldering required. Ages 14+.

$19.99

TIN CAN MICROPHONE KIT

Build a mic that captures that vintage AM radio sound! No soldering required. Ages 14+

Order Now! www.CBGitty.com/Kits

Printed in Great Britain
by Amazon